The Which? Guide to
Changing Careers

About the author

Sue Bennett has made several successful career changes, both into different jobs and between industries during a working life of over 25 years. She has been a secretary/PA, junior researcher, book designer, buyer, project manager, management trainer and writer, in fields such as university research, academic publishing and training and development.

Following redundancy in 1991, she started her own training consultancy, in which context she advises individuals and groups on all aspects of job search and career development. She specialises in outplacement and redundancy counselling following organisational restructures.

The Which? Guide to Changing Careers

Sue Bennett

 CONSUMERS' ASSOCIATION

Which? Books are commissioned and researched by
Consumers' Association and published by
Which? Ltd, 2 Marylebone Road, London NW1 4DF
Email address: books@which.net

Distributed by The Penguin Group:
Penguin Books Ltd, 27 Wrights Lane, London W8 5TZ

First edition March 1998
Reprinted December 1999
Second edition March 2001

British Library Cataloguing-in-Publication Data
A catalogue record for this book is available from the British Library

ISBN 0 85202 850 4

For a full list of *Which?* books, please write to Which? Books, Castlemead, Gascoyne Way,
Hertford X, SG14 1LH or access our web site at www.which.net

Acknowledgements: The author and publishers are indebted to Jonquil Lowe and Anthony
Bailey for their help with the sections on pensions and tax

Cover and text design by Kysen Creative Consultants
Cover photograph by Pictor International

Typeset by Saxon Graphics Ltd, Derby
Printed and bound in Great Britain by Clays Ltd, Bungay, Suffolk

Contents

★An asterisk next to the name of an organisation in the text indicates that the address can be found in this section

Introduction

When the first edition of this book was published in 1998, there were many industry sectors where too many people were chasing too few jobs. Now, in a more optimistic economic climate, the picture is somewhat different. In some areas – especially customer service, IT and general management – employers are struggling to find suitable candidates and retain their experienced staff. According to the Autumn 2000 Recruitment Confidence Index, 22 per cent of organisations surveyed had experienced problems in recruitment. A buoyant job market also means that people are more inclined to, for example, move to a new organisation, take a chance on an e-commerce job, or try freelance work.

Fundamental changes in employment have come about in recent years, reflecting general trends. National and international economic pressures and swift technological advances are radically altering the global workplace. Organisational structures are becoming flatter with fewer layers of management. Many organisations have a mixed workforce – a core of salaried workers plus contractors and temporary workers – each with different sorts of contract with their employer. The 'job for life' is now a distant memory.

In today's employment market, we need to demonstrate not only our competence – having the skills to do the job – but, increasingly, our motivation and compatibility with an organisation. Motivation is about showing enthusiasm, initiative and self-reliance – having the 'get up and go' to ask for the support which might have been provided automatically by an old-style, more hierarchical structure. And fitting well into an organisation's culture has become more important because flatter-structured systems rely more on effective teamwork for their stability and success.

What do these changes mean for the jobseeker and career changer?

- You can expect employers to want what are called 'generic' skills. These are skills that are needed in any work situation, and can be seen as a minimum requirement for employability.

- As organisations now employ fewer 'core' workers, redundancy and early retirement are more commonplace than, say, a generation ago. Although it has been suggested that early retirement is now becoming outmoded, it is still a popular 'rationalisation' mechanism for many employers.
- Multi-functional teams and reduced layers of management mean that the value placed on flexibility is high, and traditional career progression almost an alien concept in some industries. Rather than ascend linearly, you might take jobs in different, but related, roles to maximise your employability.
- You will need the personal resilience to cope with a more ambiguous working environment.

The implications of this new world of work for the career changer are threefold. Firstly, you must reckon on managing your own career, because nobody else can or will. Secondly, you need to become *au fait* with how recruitment has changed, and the possibilities offered by the Internet in relation to your search for work. A high proportion of employers now use this medium for recruitment, and it is a powerful resource for the jobseeker. Thirdly, you may need to alter your idea of what constitutes a 'good career'. It could mean, for example, taking jobs with different functions in different industries, rather than staying in one sector for most of your working life; or spending some time as a salaried employee and some as a contractor or supplier.

This book is mainly intended for three sorts of people who are wanting to change careers: those who have been or are about to be made redundant, voluntarily or otherwise; those who are returning to work following a career break; and those who simply want to make more of their potential. Whatever your situation, you will need to make well-informed, careful decisions on the options available to you, and on how to go about realising your goals.

Changing direction is never straightforward or easy. Though you may be dissatisfied with your present circumstances, you may yet decide to stay with the security of the known rather than take a chance on something new. This book will help you reach the right decision for you at this time in your life. It provides a wealth of useful information, pointers to further resources, an insight into the current job market, and illustrates the importance of determination and enthusiasm with real-life examples. If you do decide to take the plunge, it will arm you with the confidence to make your career change.

Chapter 1

Changes in the workplace

- Changing patterns of work mean that more people are likely to work part-time, be self-employed, work on contracts, or work away from their office base or for a variety of employers.
- Some industry sectors will experience a boom as others decline.
- Technical skills are no longer sufficient – good 'generic skills' are needed too.
- Having a portfolio of jobs to provide equivalent income to that of a full-time salary may eventually become the norm for many of us.

Whereas many people entering employment in earlier decades could have assumed that they would have a life-long career in their chosen field – perhaps in a single organisation – the 'job for life' has disappeared forever. The reasons for this include the rate of technological change, the communications revolution, increased global competition and changes in practices, patterns, and expectations of what we mean by the term 'work'. Some jobs may be more or less affected by the changes we discuss later in this book – depending on the type of work, the level of seniority, whether it is in the public or private sector, and so on – but everyone will be affected to some degree. Few of us can expect job security. Instead, employees operate within an environment in which there may be no clearly defined career path; contract work and flexible hours come with the territory, and survival in the job market may well mean they have to be multi-skilled and highly adaptable.

Employees must now be prepared to change jobs, not just within their field, but perhaps to an entirely different one. Such a change may be imposed, through redundancy or the closure of a company. It could also be voluntary: changing career may be an entirely positive step, forming part of a strategy to make more of your potential.

Changing your career is never straightforward or easy. Although you may not be entirely happy with the job you do now, which may or may not be secure, you might well prefer to stay with it, if you can, rather than take a chance on something different, particularly in the light of the changes which took place in employment practice during the 1990s. This chapter summarises the main developments, discusses how they will affect you if you are about to change your career, whatever the reason, and provides an overview of employment prospects in various industries and occupations. It also looks at changes in patterns of work.

Changes in the job market

Among employers, the buzzword to beat all other buzzwords has been, since the mid-1980s, 'change'. It is expected to retain its prime position for the foreseeable future. Meanwhile, we are all supposed to cope with it and manage it well. Some job advertisements ask for 'people who are good agents for [or managers of] change'. Many people find change difficult, especially when it is forced upon them.

Being able to manage change means being prepared to:

- be flexible – willing and able to adapt to different sorts of people, approaches, practices and ideas
- take the initiative, rather than waiting for change to be imposed upon you or sitting back and hoping that things will improve of their own accord
- be positive, in a personal sense as well as in the context of the job
- set up good working practices and systems
- put time into researching new possibilities
- prioritise – decide what to discard and what to retain.

It also requires focus – clarity about what our aims and objectives are, and the ability to communicate this to others.

These qualities are encapsulated by the acronym PAPOF, invented by Daryl Conner (see Bibliography), and stands for 'proactive, adaptable, positive, organised and focused'.

Flatter structures/fewer staff

During the 1980s and 1990s many organisations, for reasons which included growing international competition and technological advances, were forced to take a long, hard look at their existing structures and to question many of the assumptions on which their business was based, which may have gone unchallenged for many years.

This 'long, hard look' brought about a revolution in the way organisations, in both the public and the private sectors, do what they do – resulting in, among other things, what is known in corporate jargon as business process re-engineering, and down-sizing or right-sizing. For example, because the total cost of having an employee on-site can be 50 per cent (or even more) of his or her salary, many companies are out-sourcing functions which have traditionally been performed in-house, such as payroll, IT, catering, legal services, facilities management and asset leasing. According to the spring 1997 Labour Force Survey, 70 per cent of large firms in the UK contract out non-core operations. In addition, organisations are employing more fixed-term contract and freelance staff, who have the advantage of being excluded from headcount figures and the flexibility to be 'turned off' when there is a downturn in business activity.

Organisations have also looked at the cost of office space and how key employees use it. For example, sales people and engineers do not spend 100 per cent of their time at a desk: indeed, they would be failing to do their job properly if they were not out spending time with existing and prospective customers and clients. The same applies to many other types of employee, as a result of which many businesses have experimented with 'hot-desking' – the sharing of desks and associated facilities such as telephones, PCs, fax machines, secretarial time and meeting space by people who do not need to occupy desk space for much of their working time. To make this change in working practices effective, staff are provided with suitable electronic equipment (portable PCs with modems, email, voice mail, pagers, mobile telephones) and encouraged to work wherever they happen to be – at home, in hotels, in their car and so on, perhaps coming into the office only for the purpose of collecting papers and post and having meetings with colleagues and customers. For example, Unisys, the US-owned computer company, has set up 'business centres' where its engineers can book a desk, and/or a meeting room, collect their mail, and see their colleagues and customers.

Another consequence of organisations examining and changing the way they work is fewer management and supervisory levels, which has affected management jobs at all levels. Many businesses in both the public and the private sectors have gone from seven or eight layers of management down to only three or four. There has also been a move away from functional groups towards multi-functional and sometimes self-managing teams, in which people acquire skills such as how to resolve conflict, make decisions, set clear objectives and communicate clearly.

Since the 1980s many organisations striving to control their overheads have enforced a strict capping of employee numbers. These measures have been successful, with the result that many organisations now employ fewer people to do the same or more work than before.

Consequences for you

What do these changes mean for you? The consequences of flatter structures and fewer staff for anyone changing career are that the chances of getting a 'traditional' job in which you are employed to do your work at your employer's premises are decreasing. Also, you may no longer have any reasonable expectation of career progression with promotions every few years, because organisations have become less hierarchical. The term 'career progression' may come to refer simply to a series of jobs in different functions in different parts of the business: you may find yourself weaving your way through the organisation rather than ascending a ladder.

A 1994 report by the Confederation of British Industry (CBI) suggested that a distinction is sometimes made between employees who are seen as 'core' (i.e. essential to the organisation) and 'non-core' (peripheral workers often regarded as the flexible workforce). It found that even core workers are not necessarily full-time or permanent, and often include part-time and temporary professional staff. A good analogy is that of a bicycle wheel with the core staff in the centre as the hub and the non-core workers as the spokes of the wheel. You may choose to become a contract worker or freelance working around the core. This is an increasingly popular idea, particularly for smaller businesses, which in the UK substantially outnumber large ones. (Over 99 per cent of UK businesses employ fewer than 50 people and only 0.1 per cent employ more than 500 people. Household names such as Sainsbury's and the John Lewis Partnership, which employ 130,000 and 43,000 people respectively, are very much the exception.)

As you cannot expect to stay in the same or similar work or industry sector throughout your working life, you need to be able to adapt the skills you have, and acquire new ones. See 'Skills needed', below, for details of the kinds of skills you need to be able to respond to changing demands in the labour market.

Advances in technology

The speed of technological change in recent decades has been extraordinary. For example, in the mid-1990s you could get pairs of socks which had a microchip in them and played a jolly tune: they contained more computing power than existed anywhere in the world before 1950. In 1969 when we first put men on the moon, we did so with less computing power than today's standard office PC offers. Computers are used by most of us in some or all aspects of our home and work lives. We send emails and digital pictures, research holidays, shop for airline tickets, send our CVs to prospective employers, track documents, compile and link databases, and research organisations on the Net. Business life without computers would now be impossible.

Changes in information technology have affected the work we do and how we do it. Some kinds of work which were once done by lots of people are now done by few people and many machines. For example, the big clearing banks once employed thousands of people to process their paperwork. With new technology, the number needed to do this work has been reduced significantly.

The communications revolution which has brought us the Internet and email has made a huge difference to many jobs. We can work with people on the other side of the world almost as easily as with someone in the same building: collaborating on research, jointly writing documents and publishing them on the Net – all without meeting up or perhaps even speaking.

Some tasks that were once considered specialised are no longer thought to be so. When only secretaries and clerk/typists had a typewriter on their desks, everyone else was dependent on these skilled workers to produce presentable documents. Technological change means that most people now have access to computing power on their desks. Some people who might once have thought it below them to be able to type would now be devastated if their PC were removed. We have all been turned into editors as we write, re-write and edit our documents.

Consequences for you

How will these technological advances affect people changing their career? If you are not already PC-literate, it is time to become so. The 1997 Labour Force Survey confirms computing as one of the key 'generic skills' (see 'Skills needed, below). The 2000 report from the National Skills Task Force is more emphatic: 'Most jobs now require some basic level of skill in Information Technology (IT). Such skills are now a minimum requirement for "employability" and for this reason can be regarded as "generic".' The range of software available is very wide, and the variety of jobs which require some degree of computer literacy is increasing all the time. Training is available using workbooks, computer-based training (CBT) and in various classes. Some courses have enticing names such as 'Computing for the terrified' to encourage beginners to face up to the challenge.

What you cannot do is to ignore the problem, or to assume that companies will be prepared to train you to use a computer from scratch: you have to make the effort to acquire some degree of competence to be employable.

Globalisation

Changes in technology and the lowering of trade barriers mean that many more organisations than before compete in a global market-place. This is especially true in all aspects of communication with instant data exchange and phenomenally powerful telecommunications systems. Some companies in the West now operate in effect round the clock, because their data processing is done overnight on the other side of the world.

As individuals we also compete in a global job market. Many companies have their help desks and manufacturing units outside the UK. For example, when you telephone Dell Computers you are in fact speaking to a help desk in Dublin. If you call the British Airways 24-hour booking and information service during the night in the UK, your call is routed to the USA, yet it still costs you the price of a local call. Physical distance is not as important as it used to be.

Moreover, because long-distance travel has become quicker, easier and more convenient, people can travel far greater distances and think of it as part of their working day. For instance, some people now commute on a daily or weekly basis to Edinburgh or Glasgow from, say, London or Birmingham. Improved connections with mainland Europe also mean that they can now extend their commute and consider working in cities such as Brussels and Paris. Similarly, those in Belgium or France have ready access to the UK job market. Indeed, many French companies are setting up bases in Kent because it is cheaper and easier for their employees in northern France to commute to Kent than to travel to and from Paris. National barriers are now less significant than they used to be.

Consequences for you

Globalisation is both a threat and an opportunity to career changers. The threat is that some jobs such as the traditional back-office functions – customer service, help desks and reservations – can be handled anywhere in the world. The cheaper labour and large potential workforce in less developed countries, for example, mean that as an employee in the UK you cannot be complacent about your skills levels: there may be someone halfway across the world who could do the same job as well as you for far less money. Again, see 'Skills needed', below.

The major advantage of globalisation is that you now have access to a far larger job market than you did before. You could take a job in Brussels and commute weekly – but you will need to make sure you have the skills, especially in computing and languages, and a good understanding of cross-cultural differences, to work in a global job market.

Discrimination against older workers

Age discrimination occurs when, according to the Industrial Society, employers 'make decisions affecting procedures for advertising, recruitment, selection, promotion, training and development on the basis of individuals' age rather than their skills, abilities, qualifications and potential'. At present, however, it is not illegal. There is some indication that this could change: in July 2000 the government published its voluntary Code of Practice on Age Diversity for employers – details are available from the Department for Education and Employment (DfEE) web site.★ At the time of writing, the European Union (EU) has a draft directive on discrimination in employment, including age, which may become law during 2001.

Although unemployment among the over-50s is at its lowest level since the government began to collect figures by age in 1983, age discrimination is still prevalent. A 1993 study of 4,000 job advertisements by the Industrial Relations Services, a research and publishing organisation, found that over 30 per cent of them specified that applicants should be aged 45 years or under. Some adverts specified 35 years or under. (See also Chapter 4.) However, the changing profile of the UK's population poses a challenge to this attitude. By 2009 it is expected that 62 per cent of the working age population will be 35 years or over – compared with 52 per cent in 1979.

The slowdown in the economy in the early 1990s meant that many organisations had to cut down the number of staff they had. Generally, people eligible for early retirement were targeted and older workers were made redundant ahead of younger ones, for a variety of reasons: they probably have fewer family commitments, so they may be less reliant on their salaries or wages than younger employees; they are often assumed to be keen to retire early; they are easy to identify as a group; and they are perceived to be less easy to mould into new cultures and working methods.

Two reasons are generally proffered for discrimination on the basis of age:

- **cost**. Older staff, having accumulated years of service and perhaps seniority in the company hierarchy, may be more expensive;

younger workers are usually cheaper to employ than older people because they are nearer the bottom of the pay scale and have not acquired seniority. Older workers are thought to cost employers more in terms of benefits such as sick leave

- **perceptions**. Younger staff are seen to be more flexible with regard to changes in business practices, have greater aptitude for coping with changes in technology, and be more inclined to work long hours in the hope of rapid promotion – for them, sacrificing some quality of life now for possible future rewards is a risk worth taking.

Consequences for you

Gradually, organisations are realising that there is a downside to age discrimination. They are finding that when their older staff leave some fundamental and valuable things are lost: their knowledge about the company, job function and industry; skills built up over many years; and their breadth and depth of experience. When companies which had made their older workers redundant found their fortunes improving as the recession of the early-to-mid 1990s eased, they recruited younger staff to replace the older workers. However, they were then faced with a skills vacuum as no experienced staff were left to coach and train the newcomers. They also found themselves with little or no 'corporate history', i.e. few people with an acquired knowledge of the customers, suppliers and products, often stretching back many years. These problems sometimes led to a hiatus, a period of low productivity as the organisation struggled to become efficient and effective as quickly as possible without that bank of skills, knowledge and experience.

Moreover, companies in the service sector, including retail, banking and insurance, found that some of their older customers, clients and suppliers prefer to deal with older staff. Many organisations are now reaching the conclusion that it is to their advantage to have workers of different ages.

Groups such as the Employers Forum on Age (EFA),* a network for employers, are campaigning for mixed-age workforces. The EFA operates in conjunction with Age Concern,* and the founder members include the Industrial Society, HSBC, Sainsbury's and Manpower Employment. It holds regular seminars for people working in human resources (HR), providing advice and guidance on how to implement a mixed-age workforce policy.

The following case study from HSBC highlights the positive approach to older workers advocated by all EFA members. Andrew had over 20 years' experience teaching in higher education, and decided he wanted a complete change of career, so he took a one-year MSc in Computer Science. The MSc allowed him to re-train and also to consider what type of organisation and industry sector he wanted to work for. He joined HSBC as an assistant programmer in the company's Retail Banking IT section in January 2000. 'There have been no difficulties, everyone has been friendly, professional and helpful. Put simply, the bank's policy on and approach to age-related issues is right for its staff and right for its business.'

The use of older staff as interim managers has been growing in the UK since the mid-1980s, and a number of well-established recruitment agencies now specialise in this market, hiring experienced managers who go into companies and take the reins for a while (see also Chapter 4). Examples are commonplace of short-term assignments becoming longer; one interim manager took on an ostensibly short-term job of three months which lasted three years. One agency's research in 1997 suggests that about 10,000 senior managers are employed as 'interims' on a regular basis. Of these, 60 per cent are aged 45 to 55. Two-fifths of them took up interim management after being made redundant. If interim management interests you, contact the Association of Temporary and Interim Executive Services.*

The ageing of the workforce (mirroring the population) means that a shortage of labour is likely to affect the UK till about 2010. This prediction prompted the DIY retailer B&Q in the late 1980s to explore alternative sources of labour – women returners, the long-term unemployed, older workers and the disabled. At the time, its staff was predominantly young, and an in-house analysis found that staff turnover was highest among the younger employees. To tackle both the issues, in 1989 B&Q opened a store in Macclesfield staffed entirely by people over 50, and in 1990 opened another in Exmouth.

The view held by senior management at B&Q was that older people are more likely to be home owners and to have done DIY themselves and that therefore their knowledge and interest in DIY and DIY products is likely to be higher than in younger age groups. Moreover, mature employees are also likely to have a different perspective of what constitutes good customer service, so they are likely to spend more time with customers helping them with their DIY queries.

The Macclesfield and Exmouth experiments led to rapid cultural change within the company as store managers acknowledged their success and began to actively encourage mature applicants for jobs at their own stores. All branches now have staff of different ages, experience and backgrounds. B&Q abolished compulsory retirement in 1989, and in 1999 the company did away with retirement age altogether. Managers believe that a balance of age and experience creates a positive atmosphere in their stores.

Other large employers, including Asda, Sainsbury's and McDonalds, are also recognising the benefits of having a mixed workforce. For example, McDonalds has found that in its front-of-house operations older workers help create a family atmosphere.

The service culture

The UK was once notorious for its surly and unco-operative staff, and for shops, banks and public facilities being shut when everyone wanted to use them. In today's far more consumer-oriented and customer-focused society, heavily influenced by trends in the USA, we are far more likely to come across bright, charming service workers, whose customer-interaction skills are being constantly evaluated by their employers, in businesses which may well be open seven days a week. Some businesses, including supermarkets, are employing shiftworkers to provide 24-hour opening, implying a 'we never close' ethos, dedicated to customer services.

Many organisations have 'mission statements' or slogans to reflect this new service culture, and are working to ensure that the whole workforce, not only the staff who are in regular face-to-face or telephone contact with customers, is aware of them. In many service industries, such as retail, insurance, banking, catering and tourism, better customer service may be the one weapon remaining with which to increase market share, and as a result these sectors have experienced a job boom. This has become known as Customer Relationship Management (CRM). According to the Industrial Society, CRM is 'a customer-focused strategy designed to maximise revenue, profitability and customer satisfaction through systems that monitor and support customer relations'. Technology such as Internet communication and sophisticated back-office systems make this new approach workable.

Many organisations are using improved technology to cut the number of people engaged in traditional processes and procedures. Some of these newly released employees are being deployed in jobs which bring them into more direct contact with customers. The high-street banks are a prime example of this trend. Staff who would have been behind the scenes processing bits of paper are now dealing with customer queries face-to-face on the banking floor. Moreover, the bank staff who have been freed up by the increased use by customers of automated teller machines are now able to have direct contact with other customers who need more personal attention.

Consequences for you

If you are changing your career, you should be aware of these trends in the types of employee required. If you enjoy dealing with customers and clients face-to-face, the service industries, where the numbers of jobs available are increasing, could be a fruitful area in which to seek work. You may even decide to set up your own service business, or take on a franchise (see Chapter 6).

New skills are required to adapt to the trend. Customer service jobs place a premium on interpersonal skills: in this context, this means the ability to communicate with clients and solve problems related to those clients' needs. Moving away from the front line – the people who are in what are called 'customer-facing' roles – is the broader arena of meeting the demand for better, larger and more sophisticated products and services. All employees will need problem-solving, communication and social skills. See 'Skills needed', below.

Employment by industry sectors

The DfEE commissioned research during 1997–98 to forecast which employment sectors would experience an increase, and which a decline, in the decade 1998–2009. It also examined changes in skills demanded by employers and what types of jobs would be required. Six broad industry sectors – primary and utilities; manufacturing; construction; distribution, transport etc.; business and miscellaneous services; and non-marketed services – were looked at. According to this research:

- female employment is expected to grow by 1.5 million over the period to 2009, while male employment will increase by 0.8 million. Full-time jobs, mostly held by men, will be lost from the primary and manufacturing sectors. The growth of jobs in the service sector has created more opportunities for women, particularly those wanting to work part-time
- the level of unemployment is expected to remain stable
- declining sectors are primary and utilities, and manufacturing
- sectors where employment will rise are: distribution, transport etc.; business and miscellaneous services; and non-marketed services
- employment rates in construction will stay at current levels.

Over the decade, 2.3 million new jobs will be created, the majority of these in service industries. Because of falls elsewhere (see overleaf) the overall rise in employment numbers in the three groups below will be 3 million. The increases will be as follows:

Sector	No. of jobs (million)		% change
	1998	2009	
Distribution, hotel, catering, transport, communications.	7.60	8.33	+9.7
Business and miscellaneous services (inc. financial)	6.46	8.32	+29
Non-marketed services (public administration, defence, education, health)	6.12	6.53	+6.8

There will be a decrease of 800,000 jobs over the same ten-year period in the following sectors:

Sector	No. of jobs (million)		% change
	1998	2009	
Primary and utilities (inc. agriculture, mining, electricity, gas)	0.76	0.66	−13%
Manufacturing	4.42	3.75	−15%
Construction	1.76	1.73	−1.7%

The DfEE also looked at changes in employment by occupation. Overall, manual and other low-skill jobs continue to decline, with professional, managerial and technical jobs on the increase.

The decade will see growth for:

- **managers and administrators**: 365,000 jobs; growth is expected to be particularly good for corporate administrators, notably specialist managers in private commercial organisations
- **professionals**: 883,000 jobs; all sub-groups are expected to increase, but the highest growth is expected for business and public-service professionals, especially financial specialists
- **associate professionals and technicians**: 768,000 jobs; most sub-groups can expect strong growth, with especially strong growth for associate professionals working in computing, and those in business and finance
- **personal and protective services workers**: 649,000 jobs; women will be the main beneficiaries of the gains in this group, which are focused on caring, personal services occupations, particularly healthcare and childcare
- **sales occupations**: 181,000; this group also includes customer service jobs.

The decade will see a decline in employment in:

- **craft and related occupations**: 356,000 jobs; almost all the sub-groups expect a decline, with the largest job losses in skilled metal and electrical trades
- **other (low-skill) occupations**: 180,000 jobs; job reduction is most severe for those unskilled jobs which are linked to the primary and manufacturing sectors

- **plant and machine operatives**: 55,000 jobs; the largest losses are expected for plant and machine operatives who work in factories and on construction sites
- **secretarial and administrative**: 11,000 jobs.

However, even in declining industries the news is not all bad. Occupations in which the number of jobs is expected to fall will still need people with suitable skills. This is because the numbers lost from a particular occupation owing to retirement and moves to other occupations may be greater than the numbers lost to changes in practices within an occupation.

Skills needed

The National Skills Task Force (STF), set up in November 1997 by the DfEE, worked during 1998–99 and published its final report in 2000. A key aim was to identify areas in which there was a mismatch between skill supply and demand, and to use this information to set priorities for future spending on education and training.

In broad terms the research shows that employers want a more skilled and flexible workforce, no matter which industry sector they are in or what level of job they are trying to fill. Manual jobs are in decline, and are being replaced by professional, managerial and technical posts. Of course, you must remember that the skills required by individual organisations, job functions and industries vary immensely and are constantly changing. See also Chapter 4 for details on skills.

The STF looked at skills under five headings:

1. Basic skills
2. Generic skills
3. Management skills
4. Professional skills
5. Intermediate-level skills.

1. Basic skills
Evidence gathered by the STF suggested that as many as 7 million adults (one in five) are functionally illiterate, and one in four adults have very low levels of numeracy.

2. Generic skills
Generic skills are those that are transferable across different occupations. It is now generally recognised that individuals need a

platform of generic skills on which to build a range of more technical and job-specific skills. Six skills have been identified as underlying good performance at work:

- communication
- numeracy
- IT
- working with others/team working
- improving own learning and performance
- problem-solving.

Three of these – communication, team working and problem-solving – are the skills that employers say they need most.

3. Management skills

Changes in the job market and economy have increased the demand for, and proficient delivery of, management skills. More informal, relaxed and less hierarchical organisational cultures mean that the demand for traditional management-type skills (such as work organisation and decision-making) is pushed to lower levels in the organisation, and that managers need to rely more heavily on persuasion and influencing, and much less on directing and controlling. The skills required of senior managers now include:

- organisational skills and technical know-how to manage operations, monitor performance and develop the business
- conceptual and cognitive skills to think strategically, analyse information, solve problems and make decisions
- people skills – to manage relationships with staff, colleagues and customers – and personal effectiveness skills.

4. Professional skills

The number of jobs in professional occupations has been growing rapidly, especially in business services, health and engineering. The STF found concern among employers that professional skills may be out of date, and in some cases need to be supplemented by generic skills. For example, a financial adviser needs technical and financial skills to do his or her job well, but he or she also needs the generic skill of good communication with his or her clients.

5. Intermediate-level skills

Employers are demanding an upgrading of traditional craft or blue-collar skills to what the STF identifies as 'higher intermediate skills'. For example, chambermaids used to just clean hotel rooms and make beds. They are now expected to interact with the guests as well, with 'customer-facing' skills. Because manufacturing wants a multi-skilled and flexible workforce, people with traditional craft skills have had to upgrade and broaden their skills to remain employable.

Consequences for you

The message is clear: as a career changer, be sure you have the necessary generic (transferable) and vocational skills to prove you are flexible and able to transfer between jobs and industries. Particularly if you have been with one organisation for some time, you must emphasise these skills and set your achievements and experience in a wider context, rather than a company-specific one. Chapter 5 gives you more guidance on this.

Another implication of the changes in the kinds of skills needed by organisations is that employees are now expected to be 'life-long learners' – i.e. to acquire new skills and to stretch themselves and develop. You could achieve this by attending courses or learning on the job.

Changes in patterns of work

It is not just what work people do that has changed over the last few years, the way in which it is done is also quite different now. We have seen that technological advances, increased globalisation and the emergence of the service culture have brought about substantial change; different methods in working practices are needed to adapt to them. Being at the place of work for eight hours a day, five days a week – which was once, for most people in desk-based jobs, the only alternative to unemployment – is now just one of many types of work pattern. (For example, a job advertisement in September 2000 asked for 'overnight translators' to work from home from 3am to 8am, Monday to Friday, to provide English summaries of European press articles.) More people are moving to and between flexible, part-time and temporary jobs or becoming self-employed.

Max Comfort, in his book *Portfolio People,* identifies a growing trend of the 'portfolio approach' – having a number of jobs which together generate equivalent income to a full-time salary. But it is not only changes in the job market that are making people move away from the traditional work pattern: many of us are now more likely to re-examine our priorities in life, and our quality of life, and to ask ourselves whether we are working to live or living to work.

Part-time working

The number of people who work part-time (generally defined as fewer than 30 hours a week) has increased in recent years. According to the DfEE *Labour Market and Skill Trends 2000* report, over 25 per cent of employees worked part-time in 1999, up from 21 per cent in 1984. This trend is expected to continue.

Factors such as the need to increase competitiveness and to reduce costs (including staff costs), and the effects of both global competition and technological change have led many employers to offer more part-time working because this gives them greater flexibility in, for example, opening hours and improved service delivery. Generally, the benefits are cost-effectiveness, efficiency and a better response to customer demands.

As for part-time employees, their rights are improving all the time. The European Court of Justice (ECJ), the Employment Protection (Part-time Employees) Regulations 1995, the Part-time Workers Regulations 2000 (effective from July 2000) and the European Union Part-time Work Directive (97/81/EC) have all dramatically changed the rights of part-time workers for the better with respect to a broad range of employment issues: unfair dismissal, redundancy payments, time off for public duties or trade union duties, minimum statutory notice, time off with pay for antenatal care, maternity leave, same (pro rata) pay rates as full-timers, access to pensions, and the right to overtime at same (pro rata) rate as full-timers.

People with caring responsibilities have always needed the option of working part-time, but prior to these initiatives they had fewer legal rights and were more disadvantaged than their full-time colleagues. The changes outlined above mean that part-time working is now a more viable option for people who wish to balance the advantages of work (the need to work for the money, the companionship and the satisfaction) with caring for others, pursuing their leisure interests or taking up education as a part-timer. This deliberate balancing of home and work is a growing trend.

About a quarter of employees in the UK work part-time, according to research by the Institute of Employment Research/ Cambridge Econometrics in 2000. Significantly, 90 per cent of part-timers work in the service sector. The largest numbers are in retail distribution, where businesses tend to stay open for longer hours from Monday to Saturday and also on Sundays. Education, medical and health services, hotels and catering, and banking, finance and insurance also employ large numbers of part-time workers.

Self-employment

The number of people who are self-employed, according to the DFEE *Labour Market and Skill Trends 2000* report, was relatively stable throughout the 1990s, after doubling between 1979 and 1990. In spring 1999, there were just under 3.2 million self-employed in the UK, corresponding to around 12 per cent of total employment.

According to DfEE research (see 'Employment by industry sectors' on page 20), two sectors in which general employment prospects look good (business and miscellaneous services, including financial) will also see considerable increases in self-employment. Self-employment in the construction industry is likely to decline. Distribution, hotel catering, transport and communications will see an increase in general employment, and some parts of this sector, such as catering and transport, could go to the self-employed.

The Institute of Employment Research has found that health, engineering, business and finance, and education are the main sources of self-employment for professionals, a category which includes scientists, engineers, teachers, doctors, lawyers and chartered accountants.

An area in which self-employment has grown and continues to grow is in managing contracted-out services for larger organisations. The types of function that are typically contracted out include payroll, IT, building services, facilities management, catering and training. Within certain industries, some jobs which were contracted out because of the drive to cut overheads in the 1980s have remained contracted out. For example, in-house copy-editors and proofreaders were once commonly employed by book and journal publishers, but this work is now generally done by freelance workers. Companies which once had advertising departments are now more likely to use agencies; marketing, sales and distribution are other functions which can be handled by external companies.

If you are thinking about self-employment as a career-changing option, consider carefully whether the service or product you are offering is in an industry sector which is in decline or on the up. You will need to research every aspect of being self-employed before you launch yourself into it. Chapter 6 looks at the main issues involved in setting up your own business.

Flexible working

An increase in part-time working, and even self-employment, can be regarded as part of a wider trend towards more and more flexibility in employment. Only some 75 per cent of the working population in spring 2000 was in full-time employment (DfEE, 2000). All other workers were working in other, more flexible, ways. These work patterns cover ways which can benefit both employee and employer, and include flexitime, annualised hours, working full-time hours over four days, flexible shifts, term-time working and job-sharing; taking breaks in employment such as career breaks, sabbaticals and secondments; and flexibility in the location, including homeworking and teleworking (which can include working from home but is specifically reliant on IT).

Such work patterns can benefit:

- those with families, particularly single parents
- the estimated 5.7 million people in the UK with other responsibilities, such as caring for an elderly or disabled relative
- people who want to combine work with other activities such as being a volunteer, enrolling for an academic, vocational or other self-improvement course, or pursuing leisure interests.

Temporary work

As with part-time work and self-employment, temporary work has also been increasing. Until 1993 the use of temporary workers had remained fairly constant for a number of years, at around 5 per cent of all employees. By 1999 this had increased by roughly a third (DfEE, 2000). The 1997 Labour Force Survey mentioned earlier found that temps are not being used to displace part of the permanent workforce but to cover employee absence, cope with general or seasonal fluctuations in the work or carry out one-off projects. It appears that flexible and temporary contracts have grown faster among large and medium-sized companies.

The next chapter discusses in detail the practical side of coping with redundancy or early retirement and what help you can access during this time of change.

Chapter 2

Redundancy and early retirement

- In addition to a minimum notice period and a redundancy payment, many employers offer practical help to employees who have the relevant length of service and have been made redundant.
- Practical financial planning – of income and expenditure, mortgage payments and rent, pensions and state benefits – will help you to gain control.
- Many schemes are available through Jobcentres to help people find jobs and improve their prospects through training.

From time to time organisations are prompted to look at their overhead costs for a number of reasons, which could include:

- profits being lower than forecast
- a downturn in business caused by external factors (for example, recession or increased competition)
- other external changes (for example, the introduction of competitive tendering)
- a financial situation so dire that the company is in danger of folding
- a major re-structure with cost-cutting and job losses across the organisation
- acquisition by another organisation, and the consequent rationalisation of certain functions.

As employees' salaries are an easily identifiable category of expenditure and usually represent a large percentage of overheads, organisations often make savings by cutting back on staff. Redundancies and early retirements are the inevitable result.

For the employee, being made redundant is rarely a pleasant experience. One of the meanings of the term 'redundancy' is 'surplus to requirements'. In organisational terms it is the function, not the person, which is no longer needed. Despite this, however, it is hard not to feel hurt and rejected when the axe falls on you. You may need to make a sustained effort to regain your self-esteem before you can face the challenge of continuing your career. It is important to remember, though, that redundancy does not carry the stigma it once did, not least because it has touched so many people's lives, either directly or indirectly. Early retirement can be less hurtful, because that sense of being surplus to requirements is usually absent – although some people feel they are being asked to leave when they still have a valid contribution to make.

All change can be seen positively or negatively. It is possible that redundancy or early retirement represents an opportunity you had been waiting for: for example, your redundancy pay or lump sum from your pension could provide the start-up finance you need to start your own business. Alternatively, provided your finances are fairly secure, you could be free to explore all sorts of different interests – hobbies, doing freelance work, working part-time, or doing voluntary work.

Whether you are taking redundancy or early retirement, the first step is to examine thoroughly the financial implications. Your employer – and this chapter – should help you to do this. A checklist is included below to help you work out your financial situation and to plan for the future. This chapter also looks at mortgage payments and rent, pensions, state benefits, the assistance offered by your Jobcentre, and training. Chapter 6 looks at self-employment. Chapter 7 looks at the financial effects of early retirement in detail.

Redundancy terms

Redundancy terms vary greatly, although minimum terms have been stipulated by legislation and good-practice recommendations have been made by prominent organisations such as the Chartered Institute of Personnel & Development (CIPD).★

Most employees who have been made redundant have the right to a minimum notice period, a redundancy payment and to claim unfair dismissal. They are also entitled to reasonable time off, if they work their notice period, to look for another job or to make arrangements for training for future employment. If you have been, or are being, made redundant, contact your human resources (HR)/personnel department straight away to find out what you are likely to receive by way of a notice period, redundancy pay and other rights.

The degree of help given by companies to redundant employees also varies considerably, but it is now widely accepted that, for example, redundancy counselling greatly enhances their chances of re-employment.

The least any company should do on making an employee redundant is to provide full details and advice about redundancy terms, including pension implications, and what is to happen to any 'perks' such as a company car, private medical insurance funded by the company, and so on. Companies are not legally obliged to do any more than this, but some are more generous, offering:

- personal counselling to help employees come to terms with the situation (see Chapter 3)
- the use of outplacement agencies, which give practical help (latterly to senior staff and now increasingly to all staff: see Chapter 3)
- information on social security benefits, mortgages, pensions and other personal finance matters
- advice about job-seeking, such as how to write a good CV, letters of application, job choices and sources of jobs, and interview skills
- facilities to assist in job-seeking, such as typing and photocopying, and access to relevant directories
- recommendations on opportunities for further education or vocational training, including information from the local Learning Skills Council (LSC) in England and Wales or Local Enterprise Company (LEC, in Scotland). In England and Wales, 40–50 LSCs will replace the old Training and Enterprise Councils (TECs) in April 2001. For more details of training in Scotland, Wales and Northern Ireland, see 'Training' at the end of this chapter

- facilities for the local Jobcentre to give information and conduct interviews on the employer's premises
- a guaranteed first choice on other jobs for which the redundant employee is suitable that may come up in the organisation
- advice and possibly direct assistance for redundant employees who decide to start their own business or operate as freelances.

Redundancy pay

Redundancy pay depends on how many years a person has worked in an organisation and his or her age. The number of complete years is assessed by starting at the date on which the notice period expires or when termination takes effect and counting backwards, for up to a maximum of 20 years.

The statutory minimum payments are:

Employees aged 41–64	1½ weeks' pay per year worked
Employees aged 22–40	1 week's pay per year worked
Employees aged 18–21	½ week's pay per year worked

Many organisations choose to make more generous payments than the statutory minimum requirements: not only might the amount of money be greater, but also, for example, it may be possible for someone made redundant to purchase his or her company car or continue private health insurance at a lower rate for a certain length of time. Matters such as this, if not covered by the organisation's written policy, usually derive from accepted custom and practice.

If you are made redundant, earnings your employer owes you when you leave your job – for example, normal wages, pay in lieu of holidays, pay for working your notice period and any commission – are taxed in the normal way under PAYE, but a few items are tax-free, as is your total redundancy package if it comes to less than £30,000. Check with your HR/personnel department for details.

Basic financial considerations

Whether you are changing your career or job or returning after a break, you will have to work out how much money you need and balance it against how much you think you will make in your new position. If you intend to start a business, you must work out how much investment needs to be made, and plan for your income to increase only gradually over time. If you are taking early retirement and do not propose to work again, you need to plan for what could be a good many years – perhaps 30 or more – without a salary.

This section cannot cover comprehensively everyone's individual circumstances, and should be consulted for guidance only. Whichever situation you are in, you will need sound professional and independent financial advice. What to do with your mortgage/ rent and pension if you are changing careers is covered in separate sections below.

Personal budget

It is probably worth doing a cashflow forecast of your likely income and expenditure for the next 12 to 18 months. Major change takes time to happen and to adjust to. If you have a written forecast it will help with budgeting, and give you an idea of when any shortfall might happen. You can also work out the minimum income you and your dependants need to manage on.

If you are married or living with a partner, you should construct your budget together so that you can see what you jointly need to keep the household going. This has the added benefit of including him or her in what is – for you both – a major life event. Do not waste too much time arguing about what is 'essential' and 'non-essential' expenditure: everyone has their own priorities and you will probably want to add and discard items from the lists below. But you should find them useful, none the less, as memory prompts. Do bear in mind that this is likely to be a stressful time for you and you have much to accomplish. If you normally smoke or drink alcohol as part of your daily routine, this may not be the best time at which to try to give up such 'non-essentials', so in assessing your outgoings make some allowance for the fact that you should not have to change your lifestyle totally in order to adjust to your new situation.

Income   £

(1) after tax and National Insurance:
   * salary   . . . .
   * freelance/self-employment   . . . .

(2) any pensions you have started to draw
(e.g. on taking early retirement), after tax . . . .

(3) from savings and investments, after tax . . . .

(4) any other income, child benefit, state benefits,
alimony or child maintenance payments,
income from investment property, etc. . . . .

Total income: _____

Expenditure £

(1) Essentials
- Food . . . .
- Mortgage or rent . . . .
- Water rates . . . .
- Council tax . . . .
- Electricity . . . .
- Gas . . . .
- Other fuels . . . .
- Telephone . . . .
- Pension contributions . . . .
- House maintenance/appliance repairs, etc. . . . .
- Buildings and contents insurance . . . .
- Travel to work . . . .
- Car maintenance . . . .
- Car insurance and road tax . . . .
- Childcare . . . .
- Clothes . . . .
- School or college fees . . . .
- Loan repayments . . . .
- Bank and credit-card interest charges . . . .
- Other, inc. hire purchase payments and
  other essential financial commitments . . . .

Total essential expenditure: _____

(2) Non-essentials
- Holidays ....
- Drink and cigarettes ....
- Entertainment and meals out ....
- Presents ....
- Petrol ....
- Other travel ....
- Home improvements ....
- Professional fees/subscriptions ....
- Trade union dues ....
- Life/health insurance ....
- Regular savings plan ....
- Newspapers, books, periodicals ....
- TV licence, TV rental ....
- Hobbies ....
- Children's pocket money ....
- Your pocket money ....

Total non-essential expenditure: _____

Total expenditure: _____

**Difference between income
and expenditure:** £ _____

Life and/or health insurance
Check whether you are covered under any schemes by your organisation, and whether the cover ceases when your employment ends. If it does, you may need to arrange alternative cover (temporary, if you are looking for another job), and include the premiums in your cashflow.

Holiday arrangements
If you have booked your holidays already and your financial circumstances have unexpectedly changed, it might be a good idea to check whether there are any penalty payments if you cancel. Holidays may be a luxury you cannot afford at the moment. Also, using money you may need for later may increase your anxiety, which should be considered against the short-term pleasures of a

holiday. Again, only you can decide, but remember to talk it over with anyone else who will be affected.

School or college fees

If you are contributing financially to your children's education, you may be entitled to grants and other help, so talk to your bank manager, your local Benefits Agency, the Local Education Authority and the school.

Loans

If you have any loans from your organisation which will need to be repaid before you leave – say, towards some training or a season ticket – you will need to find out how the repayment is to be made. If you are being made redundant it may be deducted from your redundancy payment or need to be settled separately.

Mortgage payments and rent

If you are facing redundancy and have an outstanding mortgage on which you fear you cannot keep up the repayments, talk to your lender as soon as you can – do not ignore the issue in the hope that you will be able to manage somehow. Lenders will be more understanding if you discuss the options with them earlier rather than later when you may have run up some arrears.

In the early 1990s an unprecedented number of homes were repossessed by building societies and other lenders. Lenders are now very wary and keep a close eye on people who seem to be getting into difficulties with their payments. If you find you cannot keep up your mortgage payments, do not assume that you will automatically lose your home – a lot can be done to help the situation. Different considerations apply depending on the type of mortgage you have. Solutions could include taking a short payment 'holiday' while you sort out your finances, extending the term of the mortgage, or making reduced or interest-only payments. In the last resort, your lender could repossess your home but this would be considered only when all the other possible solutions had been exhausted. Larger mortgage lenders may run their own debt-counselling services which will look at your whole debt problem and help you to sort out other aspects of your finances as well as just coping with the mortgage payments.

Possible options

Repayment mortgages

The lender may agree to extend the term of the mortgage – for example, from 20 to 30 years – if you are finding it hard to keep up your repayments. This will not necessarily reduce the monthly payments by very much (especially in the early years of the mortgage, when interest forms the largest part of each payment). Alternatively, the lender may agree to your paying interest only for a short period, particularly if your problems are likely to be short-lived.

You may find that if interest rates rise, you may be able to extend the term of the mortgage rather than have to increase your monthly payments.

If you get into arrears, and there is sufficient value on the home, the lender may agree to capitalise the arrears (i.e. add them to the loan). Be careful about borrowing your way out of debt.

Endowment mortgages

With endowment mortgages, extending the term of the mortgage may not make any difference to the payments you have to make because the amount of interest you owe will still be the same. Further, unlike the case of a repayment mortgage, you will not have the option of reducing payments by paying interest only, because that is what you have been doing all along. Moreover, you have to keep paying the endowment insurance premiums – otherwise the loan is not covered and the lender may foreclose on the mortgage or force you to sell your home. The only course of action open to you, therefore, is to consider changing to a repayment mortgage. Consider surrendering only as a last resort. The penalties for surrendering a policy in the early years can be so high that you might not even get back what you paid in. A better option might be to sell or auction the policy – several companies specialise in this.

Pension mortgages

Like endowment mortgages, a pension mortgage is an interest-only loan, so simply extending the mortgage term would not reduce the amount of interest due each month. However, the lender might be prepared to let you switch some or all of the mortgage on to a repayment basis (see above), giving you more flexibility.

With regard to the pension plan, you might be able to reduce or suspend your contributions, but check whether the plan provider makes extra charges for this (see 'Pensions', below) and be aware that the plan will then probably no longer be on track to pay off the mortgage in full at the end of the term. So reducing or stopping the pension contributions should be viewed only as a temporary measure.

Once your finances are back on an even keel, you will need to pay extra into the plan or build up other savings to meet the shortfall.

Current-account mortgages

Recognising that people may not have a stable income over the lifetime of their mortgage, some lenders have introduced current-account mortgages. These allow you to use your loan like a current account, topping it up with surplus funds when you can, and withdrawing when times are difficult.

This is clearly an option to go for when you have been made redundant, and may also help if you are studying and unable to earn the same level of income for a while.

The negative-equity trap

Owing to the fall in house prices in the late 1980s and very early 1990s, some people were left burdened with mortgages that are higher than the value of their houses. This problem of negative equity presents problems for those who want to move – even those who have maintained all their monthly payments and are not in financial difficulties – because lenders usually insist on loans being repaid as a condition of agreeing to a sale of a house.

Some lenders have introduced schemes to help those with negative equity and more are likely to follow suit. If you have to move – for example, because of your job – you may transfer the negative equity from your present home to your new one (but you will not be allowed to increase your loan).

Insuring in case of hard times

Some lenders which were hit hard by many repossessions are now demanding that new borrowers take out some form of mortgage

---

How to avoid repossession of your home

Here are some tips on how to ensure you do not lose your home:

- if you are unemployed and/or are claiming Income Support, ask for assistance from the Department of Social Security (DSS)* to help with interest payments (not capital repayments)
- if you fall behind with your payments, contact your lender at once (before it contacts you) and explain your position. Some lenders now have helplines. Ask for advice on what can be done
- contact the National Debtline*
- do not ignore letters from your lender. Respond promptly to each one
- if you are retired, get advice and information from your local Age Concern* branch
- consider going to a debt counsellor. Many Citizens Advice Bureaux (CABx) offer this service free of charge
- be very wary of borrowing more to pay off the arrears, particularly if you are being offered a loan by a finance company. Interests rates are often much higher, and you could find that you are simply getting deeper into debt
- if court proceedings are issued, comply with the time limits and go to all court hearings. Writing a letter to the court explaining your circumstances is *never* sufficient. Courts do have wide powers to suspend possession orders if there is a reasonable prospect of the arrears being cleared.

---

protection, a vague term which can mean different things to different people.

Although insuring against unemployment and long-term illness seems a sensible thing to do, make sure you read the small print carefully before agreeing to have one of these policies. Some policies are merely forms of life assurance which will repay the mortgage only when you die and will not cover unemployment or illness.

Check also how long you have to wait before the policy will begin to make your mortgage payments. Many do not start to pay out until two months after you lose your job, get ill, or have an accident. So if you get another job or recover within that time, your premiums will have been paid for nothing.

The wider the circumstances in which you can claim the better. Some policies pay out only if you are unable to work because you are ill or have had an accident. Others include redundancy – though not always if you volunteer for redundancy, so check your policy carefully. A few policies cover a wider definition of unemployment, for example, if you are sacked or lose your job but are unable to claim a redundancy payment, perhaps because you have not worked for the organisation for long enough. Some policies do not pay out on redundancy or unemployment if you have been with your employer for less than a certain time.

Most policies will only pay out for mortgage payment for 12 months, a few will pay for two years; you are extremely unlikely to find policies paying out for longer than this.

Help from the state

Some help from the state may be forthcoming as far as mortgage repayments go. Under the rules that were introduced in October 1995, support on mortgages taken out after that date can be claimed only if a person has been out of work, or otherwise unable to pay the mortgage, for nine months. In such a case, the full costs of the mortgage payment (on a maximum loan of £100,000) would be paid. If the mortgage was taken out prior to 1 October 1995, the person would have to wait only two months before getting any form of state assistance. Anyone with assets totalling £8,000 or more will not qualify.

This is an area that is likely to be subject to politically motivated change, so seek out the most up-to-date information from your local Benefits Agency.

Paying the rent

If you fall behind in your rent, try to resume the current payments and pay at least something towards the arrears. If you are a council tenant and you do this, you are unlikely to be evicted. Private land-lords may take a tougher line. If you receive an eviction notice, seek help from your CAB immediately.

Pensions

If you are changing careers you have to think about what to do with pensions you have been contributing towards. These days, there are several different types of pension arrangement you might be offered through your workplace. This section looks at all the issues involved in detail, and describes the rules which apply from 6 April 2001 onwards. The effects on your pension of your taking early retirement are covered in Chapter 7.

Stakeholder schemes

The name 'stakeholder' is given to pension schemes which meet certain conditions, such as flexibility and low charges, and have been registered with the Occupational Pensions Regulatory Authority (OPRA).★ Stakeholder schemes can be either personal pensions or occupational money purchase schemes. Broadly speaking, anyone can have a stakeholder personal scheme, but a stakeholder occupational scheme is run by an employer for his or her employees.

If, from April 2001, you have the type of stakeholder scheme which is based on a personal pension, refer to 'Changing jobs if you have a personal pension or stakeholder scheme', below. If your stakeholder scheme is based on an occupational money purchase scheme, it is largely covered by the same rules, but, as with other occupational schemes, no further contributions can be paid into it once you have stopped working for the employer running the scheme – see below.

Changing jobs if you belonged to an employer's pension scheme

This section deals with occupational pension schemes. If you belong to a group personal pension scheme, the same rules apply as for any other personal pension (see below). For simplicity, the term 'stakeholder scheme' in this section refers to a stakeholder personal pension, unless stated otherwise.

Keeping the scheme going

In general, when you leave an employer, you must also stop being an active member of that employer's pension scheme. This means no more contributions can be paid into the scheme either by you or by your employer on your behalf. However, some schemes apply to a group of employers or an industry. Provided your new job is within the same group or industry, you can usually continue in the scheme without interruption. This applies, for example, if you are a teacher in the state sector and move from one school to another, or work for the NHS and move from one NHS trust to another.

Preserving your pension

If you have been a member of the pension scheme for less than two years, you might not be eligible for a preserved pension. Instead, you will usually get a refund of any contributions paid by you (but not your employer), less tax at a special rate. Provided you had been in your last employer's pension scheme for at least two years, you do not lose your right to the pension and other benefits (such as a tax-free lump sum at retirement and widow's or widower's pension) you have built up so far.

There are two types of occupational pension scheme.

- **Money purchase**. In this type, your own pot of money accumulates: contributions are paid in and invested to build up a fund. At retirement, the fund is used to buy a pension. If you leave the scheme before retirement, the fund which has built up till then can remain invested and still be used to buy a retirement pension and other benefits. The eventual pension will obviously be less than if you had stayed on until retirement because fewer contributions will have been paid in and invested.
- **Salary-related**. Alternatively, your pension and other benefits depend on a formula. For example, your pension might be $1/60^{th}$ of your pay when you leave the scheme multiplied by the number of years you were a member of the scheme. If you leave before retirement, the formula will produce a lower pension because your pay is likely to be less than it would have been had you stayed on, and you will have been in the scheme fewer years (see example overleaf). However, pensions built up since 1 January 1986 must be increased in line with inflation up to a maximum of 5 per cent a year between the time you left the scheme and the date you reach retirement age.

Bill belongs to his employer's occupational salary-related scheme which pays a pension equal to $1/60^{th}$ of his leaving salary for each year of membership. If he stayed on until retirement, he would have been in the scheme 24 years and, assuming his salary then were £40,000 a year, his pension would be: $1/60^{th}$ × £40,000 × 24 = £16,000 a year.

If instead, Bill leaves after 14 years in the job, his pension will be based on his current salary and the 14 years' membership he has built up to date. This gives a pension of: $1/60^{th}$ × £25,000 × 14 = £5,833. If inflation averages 2.5 per cent a year between now and his retirement in ten years' time, the pension from this scheme at retirement will have grown to £7,468 a year.

Most public-sector jobs offer membership of a salary-related scheme. If both your old and new jobs are within the public sector, you may be able to avoid or lessen any reduction in your pension by using the 'transfer club' – see below.

Transferring your pension rights

If you choose, you can give up your rights to a pension and other benefits from your old employer's scheme and instead transfer them to another pension arrangement, such as a new employer's scheme or a stakeholder scheme. If the old scheme is a money purchase one, the transfer value is simply the value of the pension fund less any transfer charges. If the old scheme is salary-related, the transfer value is a cash sum that is deemed to have the same value as the rights you are giving up. The scheme's actuary has to work out this value and does so making assumptions about how earnings, prices and investments might grow in future.

If your old job and your new job are both in the public sector – for example, you work as a teacher, for the NHS or for a local authority – you may be able to use the 'transfer club'. Typically, this lets you switch the years' membership you have built up in your old employment direct to the new as if you had always been a member of the new employer's pension scheme. You cannot take a transfer value as cash – it must be paid into another pension scheme or plan.

In general, you can transfer your pension rights at any time before retirement – your old scheme can remain where it is, although no more contributions can be paid into it once you have left your job. So, you do not have to make a decision at the time you change jobs; you can review the situation later on.

Deciding whether or not to transfer a pension is complicated. Get advice from the administrator(s) of the employers' schemes involved and/or an independent financial adviser. Note that financial advisers need extra qualifications before they can give advice about pension transfers. You can check whether an adviser has the appropriate qualification by contacting the Financial Services Authority (FSA) Central Register.*

Changing jobs if you have a personal pension or stakeholder scheme

This section considers your position if you have been contributing to a personal pension, a retirement annuity contract (individual pension plan started before personal pensions were introduced in July 1988), or a personal pension which is registered as a 'stakeholder scheme'.

Keeping the scheme going

Changing jobs has no effect on any single-contribution plans to which you have paid lump sums in the past – they just keep on growing as normal. If you have been paying regularly into a personal pension or stakeholder scheme, you can also keep this going without alteration, provided your contributions to this and other pension arrangements do not exceed the contribution limits (see below).

If your old employer had been paying into the scheme on your behalf, check what the effect of those payments coming to an end will be. For example, can you keep the plan going with lower contributions? Must you pay in extra? Can you persuade a new employer to make contributions?

Different rules apply to retirement annuity contracts. Usually, you can carry on paying regular premiums, but not if you join a new employer's occupational pension scheme, because the rules do not allow you simultaneously to pay into an occupational scheme and a retirement annuity contract.

You might have a rebate-only personal pension or stakeholder scheme – in other words one which is being used to 'contract out' of part of the state pension. Instead of building up additional state pension (through the State Earnings Related Pension Scheme, SERPS, or its successor, the State Second Pension), part of the National Insurance you pay each year is returned and paid as a rebate into the plan or scheme. This arrangement has to stop if you cease to be eligible to contract out. You are no longer eligible if:

- you become unemployed
- you become self-employed
- you join a new employer's pension scheme which is itself contracted out.

Stopping the scheme

With personal pensions and retirement annuity contracts, charges are usually levied in a variety of ways and some – for example, a regular flat fee – have a hefty impact on your pension fund if you stop paying in regularly. In the worst cases, your pension fund could be reduced well below the value of the contributions you have paid in so far, so get advice from an independent financial adviser before deciding to stop your contributions.

To qualify for the name 'stakeholder', schemes must meet certain conditions. One is that charges can be levied only as a percentage of the pension fund you have built up, and that they can be no more than 1 per cent a year – which is much lower than most personal pensions and retirement annuity contracts have charged in the past. This low percentage charge applies to all schemes, however small your fund – there are no flat-rate fees to eat up a disproportionate amount of your savings. The money you have paid in so far carries on growing as normal. You can restart regular contributions or make single payments at any time you like. Some providers are reducing the charges on their personal pensions and retirement annuity contracts to bring them into line with stakeholder schemes.

Whatever the type of pension arrangement, if you stop paying in, your eventual pension from this arrangement will be smaller. If possible, make sure you build up pension through an alternative arrangement (such as an employer's scheme) or you restart your contributions as soon as possible.

Transferring the scheme

With personal pensions, stakeholder schemes and retirement annuity contracts, the money paid in is invested to provide a pension fund that is eventually used to buy your pension. Before that happens, you can usually transfer the fund to a different pension scheme if you want to. Stakeholder schemes must let you transfer your pension fund out of the scheme without penalty. By contrast, with personal pensions and retirement annuity contracts, there may be hefty penalty charges which reduce the value of the fund transferred.

Deciding whether or not to transfer a pension is complicated. Get advice from an independent financial adviser. Note that advisers need extra qualifications before they can give advice about pension transfers. You can check whether an adviser has the appropriate qualification by contacting the FSA Central Register.

Contribution limits 2001–2

From April 2001, new pension rules called the 'DC regime' apply. (This stands for 'Defined Contribution', which is the more technical term for 'money purchase'.) Whether or not you have any earnings, you can pay up to £3,600 a year in total into the following types of pension arrangement:

* personal pension
* stakeholder scheme
* employer's occupational money purchase pension scheme, if it has opted into the DC regime.

If you are earning, or have been during the last five years, you may be able to pay in more than £3,600; for example, up to 17.5 per cent of your earnings if you are aged 16 to 35; 20 per cent of your earnings if you are aged 36 to 45; 25 per cent at ages 46 to 50; 30 per cent at ages 51 to 55; and more at higher ages.

Retirement annuity contracts are not included in the DC regime. The amount you can pay in depends on your earnings and age; for example, 17.5 per cent of your earnings if you are aged 16 to 50; 20 per cent if you are aged 51 to 55; and more at higher ages. If you join an employer's occupational money purchase scheme which has not opted into the DC regime or an employer's salary-related scheme, broadly speaking, you can pay up to 15 per cent of your earnings into the scheme each year. In addition, you can pay up to £3,600 into a stakeholder scheme and/or personal pension provided you earn less than £30,000 a year and you are not a controlling director of the firm.

If your employer's scheme is wound up

If your company goes bust or your organisation is taken over by another which does not wish to continue the scheme, your pension entitlement depends on the scheme's rules. Some are fairly generous to members in the event of the scheme being wound up, but with others you may be *entitled* only to the minimum required under the law – i.e. the benefits that an early leaver would get. The scheme rules may give the trustees discretion to decide what benefits over and above the legal minimum are provided, in which case you will be dependent on the health of the pension fund and the priority of paying or increasing the benefits of different types of members. If funds are short, usually those currently receiving pensions will be given top priority.

From April 1997, in accordance with the Pension Act 1995, salary-related schemes have to meet a test called the Minimum Funding Requirement (MFR). It requires the pension fund to have a regular check-up by an actuary to ensure that, if the scheme is wound up immediately, it would have enough assets to pay the legal rights of all the members. The MFR does not apply to money purchase schemes or unfunded schemes. At the time of writing, the MFR is being reviewed by the government and the rules may be changed.

State benefits

Help, advice and incentives are provided by the state to all unemployed jobseekers. Jobcentres (see below) offer a range of programmes and services, such as Jobclubs or help with the cost of travel to interviews, to help people find work. In addition, certain financial benefits may be available to those who qualify, determined by factors such as number of National Insurance (NI) contributions paid, low income, proven need and length of unemployment.

Benefits you may be entitled to

Jobseeker's Allowance (JSA) was introduced in October 1996 to replace Unemployment Benefit and Income Support for unemployed jobseekers. The emphasis is firmly on job search. To qualify for JSA you must:

- be under 65 (for men) or under 60 (for women)
- be capable of, actively seeking and available for work, usually for up to 40 hours a week
- have paid enough NI contributions (see below) or have income and savings below a certain level. For more information ask to see a Benefits Agency Adviser
- be out of work or working on average less than 16 hours a week
- (normally) be 18 years old or over and under pensionable age
- have a Jobseeker's Agreement signed by you and an Employment Service Adviser (see below)
- not be in 'relevant' education (but see below)
- be in Great Britain.

To receive JSA based on your income, you must also:

- be habitually resident in the UK, the Channel Islands, the Isle of Man or the Republic of Ireland, or
- be treated as habitually resident in the UK.

JSA can be either contribution-based or income-based, and is taxable, just as wages and salaries are. However, tax will not be deducted from your allowance before you get your money. You may get a tax refund when your claim for JSA ends or at the end of the tax year, whichever comes first. Leaflet IR41 (*Income Tax and the Unemployed*), available from your local Inland Revenue office or Jobcentre, is a useful source of information. Redundancy payments and other money you get when a job ends may affect JSA and the date from which you can get JSA.

Contribution-based JSA

You must have made a certain number of NI contributions to qualify for contribution-based JSA. The benefit year runs from 6 April to 5 April. Your NI contributions are based on what you have paid in the last two complete tax years before your claim is made. For example, if you make your claim on 20 April 2001 you are making a claim in the 2001 *benefit* year. Your qualifying contributions are based on the last two complete *tax* years, i.e. 1999–2000 and 2000–1.

If you have paid enough NI contributions you will receive a personal rate of JSA for up to 182 days (six months). As contribution-based JSA is based on how much *you* have paid, it can be made only to you personally. No additional benefit for dependants is paid, and if you have a partner who is working, his or her work does not affect your contribution-based JSA. You cannot get contribution-based JSA if you have been paying NI contributions for self-employment, but you may be able to get income-based JSA. Contribution-based JSA is reduced if you are drawing an occupational or personal pension over a certain amount. If you are unsure whether you qualify, seek advice from your local Jobcentre.

Income-based JSA

If you do not qualify for contribution-based JSA or if you need more money to live on, you may qualify for income-based JSA. This takes your income and savings into account, and depends on how old you are, whether you have a partner, any dependent children and how old the children are. Unlike contribution-based JSA, there is no limit to how long you can claim income-based JSA for, but you must continue to be available for work. It can be made up of three parts:

- a personal allowance for yourself and your partner (if you have one) and one for each child or young person you or your partner look after
- premiums for groups of people with special needs, such as families with children, people with disabilities and people who are getting Invalid Care Allowance
- housing costs to help with mortgage interest and certain other housing costs not met by Housing Benefit. Mortgage interest may be paid direct to the lender – see leaflet IS8 (*Homeowners – Help with Housing Costs*).

For current rates of JSA see leaflet GL23 (*Social Security Benefit Rates*). If you have a partner who works an average of 24 hours a week or more you cannot usually get income-based JSA. If he or she works less than 24 hours a week, those earnings will usually affect the amount of income-based JSA you can get.

JSA and education

You are not usually entitled to JSA if you are a full-time student. However, if you and your partner are both full-time students and one of you is responsible for a child, you may be able to get JSA during your summer vacation, but you must be available for, and actively seeking, work. If you are studying part-time you may still be able to get JSA provided again you remain available for, and actively seek, work. How much allowance you get will depend on the number of hours you are studying. If you are aged 25 or over and have been unemployed for two years or more, you may be able to do a full-time employment-related course, or an Open University course, and still get JSA. Whether you are a full- or part-time student, discuss your situation with your Personal Adviser. (This is your contact at the Jobcentre, who will be allocated to you during your job search, to provide continuity of support and advice.) If you are studying and are a single parent or have a disability, you may be able to claim Income Support.

Part-time earnings, occupational and personal pensions

You can earn some money (approximately £5–£20 per week in 2001–2) before your JSA is affected, but check with your Personal Adviser on the precise figure. Occupational and personal pensions can affect the amount of JSA you can be paid. You can receive an occupational or personal pension of up to £50 per week before your contribution-based JSA is affected. However, these pensions are taken into account in income-based JSA.

Income Support

You can claim Income Support if you are:

- a lone parent with a child under 16 living with you
- a disabled person whose earnings are reduced because of your disability
- a student who qualifies for benefit
- caring for a severely disabled person or a member of your family who is temporarily ill
- pregnant, within 11 weeks of your expected date of confinement
- aged 60 or over.

Ask at your Jobcentre for leaflest IS20 (*Guide to Income Support*).

National Insurance credits

If you are not working the state usually gives you a credit of an NI contribution for every week you get JSA. You may also get a credit if you satisfy the conditions for JSA (see above) but do not get JSA because:

- you have not paid enough contributions
- you have received your full entitlement of contribution-based JSA already
- your income is too high for you to get income-based JSA.

You will not get NI credits if you are:

- a married woman or widow who has chosen to pay a reduced rate of NI contributions
- receiving a reduced rate of JSA under the hardship provisions – see leaflet JSA9 (*Jobseeker's Allowance Hardship Provision*).

Your Personal Adviser will help you if you need any advice about credits.

Jobcentres and how they can help

A wide range of help is available from Jobcentres, which are run by the Employment Service, an executive agency of the Department for Education and Employment (DfEE),★ for people seeking work. The assistance offered falls into two main areas: helping people find a job and improving their prospects through training. According to DfEE figures (1998), 70 per cent of jobseekers find work within six months.

Contacting the Jobcentre

As soon as you become unemployed or know that you will be unemployed and looking for work, contact your local Jobcentre (details in the telephone book under Employment Service or Jobcentre). It is best to do this straight away because if you are eligible for JSA (see above for criteria) you may lose money by not claiming it at once.

When you first visit the Jobcentre you should take your P45 and NI number (which will be on your National Insurance number card, your P45 or P60) with you. On this occasion you will be asked about your situation, and be given information about what you have to do to claim JSA and advice about other courses of action you can take. If you decide to claim JSA you will get an appointment for a New Jobseeker Interview and be given a claim pack to complete before the interview. The pack includes the claim form for JSA and the Jobsearch Plan.

New Jobseeker Interview

At the New Jobseeker Interview a Personal Adviser will:

- make sure you understand the conditions for receiving JSA
- discuss the sort of work you are looking for and the best ways of finding those jobs
- give you information about jobs, training and other opportunities that are available
- discuss with you and draw up a Jobseeker's Agreement (see below)
- check that you have completed the claim form correctly and provided all the information needed to work out your JSA claim.

To get JSA you must have a Jobseeker's Agreement which is signed by you and your adviser; it will be drawn up at your interview and will set out:

- your availability for work and any agreed restrictions, such as caring responsibilities
- the type of work you are looking for
- what you will do to look for work and specific actions you will take to improve your chances of finding work
- what you must do to remain entitled to JSA (your adviser will tell you about this)
- the services provided by the Employment Service to help you back to work. Again, your adviser will tell you about this.

While you are claiming JSA, either you or your adviser can apply to alter the Agreement as your circumstances change.

At the New Jobseeker's Interview you will be given a booklet, ES40. This gives you important information about:

- what you must do to carry on getting JSA
- some of the changes you must tell the Jobcentre about. Other things you must tell staff about are mentioned in the leaflet INF 4, which is included in the claim pack
- the help that is available to enable you to get back to work
- what to do when your JSA stops – for example, when you start work.

You are welcome to use the Jobcentre services at any time. The opening hours are displayed at each centre. Normally you have to go to the Jobcentre at least every fortnight to sign a declaration to show that you have, among other things, been actively seeking work and are still available for work. Each time you attend, Jobcentre staff will discuss how your job search is progressing and whether you need any extra help, and will ensure that you still satisfy the entitlement conditions for JSA. It is a good idea to keep a record of what you are doing to find work. Apart from satisfying the conditions of JSA, it will also help you to see that you are making progress. Everyone has their own system of record-keeping, but try to keep a note of what you have applied for, the date of application, contact details, response, and the result of your follow-up letter or phone call.

Finding work and getting help through a Jobcentre

Your local Jobcentre will have details of jobs both in your local area and in other areas of the country. In addition, Jobcentres can help job-seekers in many other practical ways. There is a wealth of recent initiatives under the government's Welfare to Work plan. These work incentive schemes are designed to assist people – in all sorts of different circumstances – with the transition from benefit to full-time work. Some are for everyone seeking work, some depend on where you live, and others apply to people in specific groups. The information given here provides an overview of benefits and schemes available at the time of writing, and is therefore subject to change.

The situation is made more complex by the devolved administrations of Scotland, Northern Ireland and Wales taking on initiatives that were formerly the responsibility of central government. In the case of benefits and all social security matters, there are agreements, known as Concordats, between the National Assembly for Wales and the Scottish Executive, and the DSS.

There are also changes afoot to combine the relevant parts of the two ministries that deal with people of working age: the Employment Service (of the DfEE) and the Benefits Agency (of the DSS). The plan is to create a new Working-Age Agency, by the summer of 2001, as a 'one-stop shop' to support anyone looking for work. The ONE initiative (see below), is similar and will initially be running in parallel with the Agency.

General initiatives
Travel to interviews
The Travel to Interview Scheme (TIS) aims to encourage jobseekers to widen their job search, by providing financial assistance so

they can attend job interviews beyond a normal day's travel. In addition to the cost of travel, you may be entitled to a maximum of two nights' overnight subsistence. If you have been seeking work and claiming benefit for 13 weeks or more you may be eligible; the job applied for should be for 30 hours or more per week, and expected to last for at least 12 months. You must apply to your Jobcentre for the financial help before the interview.

Programme Centres/Jobclubs

Programme Centres perform a similar role to Jobclubs and are gradually superseding them. Their objective is to provide practical help and a supportive environment to help you with your job search. You could, for example, have access to newspapers, a computer, fax, telephone and photocopier, and use of stamps and stationery. A centre leader will provide one-to-one support with interview practice and help with applications, and you will also find you can benefit from the support of other jobseekers at the club. You can be a member for up to six months, and your fares to and from the Jobclub/Programme Centre will be paid for. Jobclubs/ Programme Centres are available for people who:

- have been unemployed for six months or more
- have been on Work-based Learning for Adults/Training for Work (see below)
- have a disability
- have spent time in prison
- are an ex-regular (in HM Forces)
- are returning to the job market after a break of two or more years.

Jobclubs offer an initial two weeks of guidance and training in a variety of job search techniques, such as telephone skills, writing a CV, interviews and research. Programme Centres have a more tailored approach, offering modules that can be adapted to the individual rather than fixed-length courses.

Work Trials/Employment on Trial

It can be difficult for both an employer and a potential employee to gauge from an interview, no matter how in-depth, whether that person could become a permanent employee. Work Trials, also known as Employment on Trial, are a chance for people to try out and demonstrate their suitability for a job, for up to 15 working days while remaining on benefit. You would also have your travel and meal expenses paid during the period. To qualify you must be over 18 years, have been unemployed for the last six months, or be receiving JSA and/or NI Credits, Incapacity Benefit, Income Support or Severe Disablement Allowance. These conditions may be waived if you:

- are returning to the job market after a break of two or more years
- are part of a large-scale redundancy
- are an ex-regular (in HM Forces)
- have spent time in prison
- are disabled (you would only need to be unemployed)
- have severe literacy or numeracy difficulties (you would only need to be unemployed)
- are on New Deal for Partners of Unemployed People
- are on New Deal for Lone Parents.

Jobfinder's Grant
This is a one-off payment of £200. It is payable to people who have been getting JSA for more than two years, and who get a job of more than 16 hours per week which is expected to last more than six months and pays less than £200 a week before tax. The aim is to encourage the jobseeker to take the job and give it a chance. Apply to your Jobcentre.

Business Start-Up
The Benefits Agency is the first port of call for information on Business Start-Up, and to qualify you need only be unemployed and wanting to start your own business. There are many different schemes, run by a wide variety of organisations. These include the 40–50 local arms of the LSC (in England and Wales), LECs (in Scotland), local councils, Enterprise Agencies, the Prince's Trust,★ Chambers of Commerce and others.

Area-specific initiatives
ONE Service
To increase collaboration between different agencies, and to help job-seekers have access to a wider range of services in one place, a scheme called ONE is being piloted, to conclude in spring/summer 2002.

ONE provides a common entry point for claims to, and information on, work, benefits and childcare for people who are not in full-time work. Check with your local Jobcentre for details of the pilot areas.

Under the scheme, you will be offered a tailored package of support, with a Personal Adviser to facilitate access to a range of opportunities. If you live in a part of the country where ONE is not being piloted, you have access to these things *only* if you have been receiving JSA and participating in one of the New Deals (see below). The package includes the following.

- At 'start up', you will have an interview where you provide personal details, your reason(s) for claiming benefit and information about your employment history, and discuss what sort of support will be appropriate.
- From 'start up', you will have a meeting with a Personal Adviser, which replaces the New Jobseeker Interview, and will include the signing of your Jobseeker Agreement (see 'Contacting the Jobcentre', above).
- For people considered to be ready for employment, a search of suitable vacancies will be made, with immediate referrals to prospective employers.
- You will work with your Personal Adviser on a personal action plan and meet him or her regularly. He or she will be your main point of contact, and will continue to work with you while you remain unemployed.

Employment Zones

For a two-year period from April 2000 the government has set up Employment Zones in 15 areas (details from your Jobcentre) where long-term employment is 'particularly high and persistent', with the specific aim of 'helping 48,000 people towards sustainable employment and independence'. Initiatives in these zones are run by consortia drawn from the local public, private or voluntary sector, which work with participants to develop an action plan to increase their employability. This can include education, training, work experience or help in becoming self-employed. Each person on the scheme has a Personal Job Account, which can be tailored to his or her individual needs.

If you are eligible you are obliged to be involved. You are eligible if you:

- are receiving income-based JSA
- are aged 25 or over
- live within the geographical boundaries of the zone, *and*
- have been continuously unemployed, without a break of more than 28 days, for 12 or 18 months (depending on the zone).

Action Teams for Jobs

Action Teams for Jobs started in October 2000, and operates in areas where, for a variety of reasons, people struggle to get into and keep jobs. This is a flexible programme based around local needs, and local Action Teams will decide on targets and how they should be met. The 15 Employment Zones (see above) are included, with 25 additional areas. There are also pilot schemes running in a further 29 areas (see New Deal for people aged 25 and over, below).

Initiatives for specific groups

Some help is directed at particular groups, determined by age or situation. Full details are given below. Many schemes are available nationwide, while some are based in areas of especial need.

New Deal brings together local employers, local authorities, training providers, LSCs, LECs, Jobcentres, and the voluntary sector in 36 areas in England, Scotland and Wales (details from your Jobcentre). The idea is that local partnerships of these organisations will deliver New Deal in a way that is appropriate for their area. As we go to press, new skills tests have been announced.

Employers benefit both from the filtering of referred candidates – who are screened for compatability and necessary skills by the Personal Adviser – and a financial incentive. So the employer knows that the applicant will be employable, motivated and committed, and right for the job – and if employers take on a New Dealer, they receive a weekly subsidy for six months. For further information on New Deal and self-employment on New Deal, contact your local Jobcentre, visit the New Deal web site or call the information line (see DSS in addresses section).

There are separate New Deal schemes for specific age groups and for other groups with particular needs:

- young people aged 18–24
- people aged 25 and over (and under 50)
- people aged 50 and over

- Partners of Unemployed People
- Lone Parents
- Disabled People.

People aged 18–24

New Deal: For people in this age group, New Deal begins with four months of individual help, called Gateway, during which you have access to a range of services and opportunities to help you prepare for and find work – including access to independent career advice and guidance, and expert help with jobsearch techniques such as interview skills. A Personal Adviser will provide help and advice, and assistance with action planning. If you do not find unsubsidised work during this time, there are further options available to you.

People aged 25 and over

There are a variety of different schemes, access to which is mostly based on how long you have been unemployed.

Job Plan and **Jobfinder Plus** are for people aged 25 and over who have been unemployed for 12 or 18 months respectively. Job Plan is a five-day programme of individual assessment, job search guidance and confidence-building. The programme includes: identifying skills and strengths, matching preferences to possible careers, developing techniques for getting back to work, and increasing awareness of employment and training options. Jobfinder Plus is similar to Job Plan, but instead of a programme there are a series of job-focused interviews, tailored to the individual.

New Deal for people over 25 years starts when you have been unemployed for two years or more. It is another chance to look at your position, skills and experience, and what jobs are available to match your circumstances. It can last from a few months to a year or more. As with Jobfinder Plus, you will have a series of individually tailored interviews with a Personal Adviser, who will give advice on drawing up an action plan, intensive help with job searching, and continuing support while you are on New Deal. The range of options includes: practical help with applications, confidence-building courses, interview techniques, and grants to help meet the costs of starting work or travelling to interviews. You can also re-train while remaining on benefit. Most courses are to refresh skills or learn new ones, and must therefore be vocational.

There are also pilot projects running in 29 areas of England, Scotland and Wales, concluding in April 2001, to determine whether placing participants on New Deal earlier would be effective or not. These are the same areas in which Action Teams for Jobs (see above) is being piloted. If you are in one of these areas, you can get on to New Deal after either 12 or 18 months of unemployment, depending on the area.

Work-Based Learning for Adults (**Training for Work**, in Scotland) helps unemployed adults into work or self-employment by enabling them to get the occupational skills they need to fill local skills shortages or to help them make a success of self-employment.

Self employment: A Personal Adviser will put the jobseeker in touch with organisations that run sessions on the realities of being self-employed. This is followed by a course, usually one day a week for four weeks, or one-to-one counselling to decide whether self-employment is the best choice for you, to get further information, and to write a business plan. An allowance of £15 per week on top of benefit is payable for six months.

People aged 50 and over
New Deal 50 Plus was launched nationally in April 2000, to help older people who want practical help to find work. It is voluntary. You are eligible if you are 50 or over, are not working, and:

- have been claiming JSA, Income Support, Incapacity Benefit, or Severe Disablement Allowance for at least six months
- if your spouse or partner is claiming benefit for you
- if you have been signing on at the Jobcentre as eligible for work.

You can choose to have tailored one-to-one personal advice from a Personal Adviser. This can include help with: job search skills, costs for travelling to job interviews, Work-Based Learning for Adults (Training for Work, in Scotland), or Work Trials. The scheme offers the following:

- an extra £60 a week, tax-free, on top of your wage if you take a full-time job; £40 for a part-time job. This is called an Employment Credit. It is paid straight to you, not your employer
- a guaranteed take-home wage of at least £170 a week (£9,000 p.a.) for your first year of full-time work

- the option to use the Employment Credit to help start your business, if you are thinking of self-employment
- a possible in-work Training Grant of up to £750 when you start work.

The government has issued a non-statutory Code of Practice on Age Diversity: details are available on the DfEE web site.*

Training

Because so many people are chasing the good jobs and employers can often take their pick, improving existing skills or gaining new ones can be a way to better your chances of finding work. Training or re-training can also confirm that you are already fully or partially competent at something, which will give you confidence in your skills and talents. As we have already seen, employability is a complex mix of generic and technical skills, experience and achievements, and personal attributes such as enthusiasm, commitment, flexibility, etc. Going in for training proves you have a commitment to continued learning and shows employers that you are prepared to improve your skills.

In England, Wales, Scotland and Northern Ireland all aspects of education and training are under review and change. The government has introduced new initiatives to promote 'lifelong learning', whereby people are continually developing the skills that employers need.

Much of the information provided below applies to England only. The devolved administrations in Wales, Scotland and Northern Ireland have responsibility for education and training (see below). In England and Wales, as described at the beginning of this chapter, the Further Education Funding Council and TECs are in a process of transition to the LSC.

Adult education and training opportunities

There are a variety of agencies providing information, advice and guidance to adults about education and training opportunities. This can range from factual information to in-depth careers guidance. Fees may be charged for some of the in-depth guidance services. Many agencies hold local and national databases of education and training opportunities that you can use. To reinforce existing provision and provide a more comprehensive service, the DfEE has set up local Adult Information, Advice and Guidance (IAG) networks. These will be developed over the period 2000–3.

Listed below are a number of sources of information on training. Training and sources of support for self-employed people is dealt with specifically in Chapter 6.

- **Jobcentres**. From April 2001, the Employment Service (ES) has assumed responsibility for work-based training for unemployed adults. Individual Learning Accounts (ILAs) are now operational throughout England, and the DfEE is working with the devolved administrations in Scotland, Wales and Northern Ireland to extend ILAs nationwide. ILAs are accounts that hold funds from the account holder, employer or the government, and can be used to pay for eligible training courses. As well as being able to advise on government schemes, some Jobcentres hold a small collection of careers information and databases of information and local opportunities.
- Your local **LSC** (in England and Wales) or **LEC** (in Scotland). LECs in Scotland have responsibility for training and enterprise services; from April 2001 local LSCs will have responsibility for training in England. The 40–50 LSCs and 22 LECs offer education and training services through many different organisations in their local area, and can provide you with training or re-training opportunities, irrespective of your age.
- Your local **Small Business Service (SBS)**★ for business and enterprise services, including training in all aspects of self-employment. The SBS provides a single point of advice and support for small and medium-sized enterprises (known as SMEs).
- **Learn Direct**,★ a national telephone helpline that helps callers with learning and career enquiries and provides information on a range of learning opportunities across the UK. It can also provide information on the costs of training and on childcare provision, and can direct enquirers to their local guidance service.
- Your local **careers service**. These contract with the DfEE to provide services in a particular geographical area, and offer information, advice and guidance to anyone in full-time education (except Higher Education institutions, see below) and to young

people for about two years after they leave full-time education. Many careers services also offer a range of services to adults: you can discuss your education and training needs, browse freely in their careers information library, and make use of their databases. Other services, which you may have to pay for, include one-to-one interviews, psychometric testing, and help with CVs and jobsearch skills. The national professional bodies for adult guidance are the Institute of Careers Guidance★ and National Association for Educational Guidance for Adults (NAEGA).★

- Your local **Learning Partnership**. These bring together a range of local partnerships into a single body to cover post-16 and lifelong learning. They have four key objectives: to widen participation in learning, to increase attainment, to improve standards, and to meet the skills challenge. All 100 local Learning Partnerships include representatives of local education authorities, LSCs, Further Education colleges and careers services, and many have extended their membership to include Higher Education institutions, schools and employers. At the time of writing, the relationship between the local LSCs and local Learning Partnerships is still under discussion. More information about Learning Partnerships is available from the DfEE web site.

- **Adult Learners Week**. This is an annual event, usually held in May, focusing on opportunities to learn. For information about the week and local events, contact the National Institute for Adult Continuing Education (NIACE).★

- **University for Industry (UfI)**.★ At the time of writing this is the working title of a new idea for making learning easily accessible to all, at a time and place convenient to the learner. It was launched in autumn 2000, with the aim of being fully operational by 2004. The intention is to have a thousand Learning Centres/Hubs established across the UK by 2002. During its first four years, The UfI has four priority learning areas:

  1. basic literacy and numeracy (it is estimated that around 7–8 million adults in the UK have low basic skills at present)
  2. ICT (Information and Communication Technology) skills for the workplace
  3. business services and management skills for small and medium-sized businesses

4. four employment sectors currently expected to have skills gaps or with low levels of training activity: automotive component production (70,000 companies nationwide), multimedia, environmental technology (5,000 companies), and distributive and retail trades. For more information contact Learn Direct (see above). Once the Learning Centres are set up, you will be able to go into your local UfI centre to meet an adviser, become a member, and so on. For more information visit the UfI web site.★

- **Community Education Centres**. These are funded by the Lifelong Learning Section of their local County Council (or equivalent) Education Department, and offer a mix of vocational and non-vocational courses. They produce booklets listing all the courses they run, which vary from area to area.
- **Higher Education careers services**. HE institutions usually have a careers service to offer help to their graduates and undergraduates. Some are members of a scheme called 'mutual aid', whereby graduates of one university or college can get help from another's careers service. Priority will be given to the institution's own students.
- **Further Education colleges**. All FE colleges offer advice and information to prospective and current students.
- **Guidance shops**. Some areas have high-street centres, providing information and advice on education and training opportunities. The range of services varies – not all provide in-depth careers guidance; some provide help with CVs and job search. Some have mobile centres for outreach work.
- Your **local library**. Some or all of the following will be available: local information on further and adult education, general careers and reference books, open learning materials, access to the Internet.
- **Citizens Advice Bureaux**. The advisers are not experts, but will probably have some information, or be able to direct you to a local source of information on training.

Differences in Scotland, Wales and Northern Ireland

Scotland
The education and training system in Scotland is quite separate from that in England. The present arrangements are that Scottish

Enterprise and Highlands and Islands Enterprise contract with the 22 LECs which are responsible for the delivery of government training plans. For information on vocational qualifications contact the Scottish Executive Enterprise and Lifelong Learning Department.*

Wales

The provision for post-16 education and training in Wales is currently similar to that in England. The Welsh Assembly published its report *An Education and Training Action Plan (ETAP) for Wales* in 1999. The Further Education Funding Council for Wales (FEFCW) and the TECs will be replaced in April 2001 by the Council for Education and Training for Wales (CETW). For information on vocational qualifications contact the Welsh National Assembly Education Department.

Northern Ireland

In Northern Ireland, the Training and Employment Agency is responsible for vocational training, other general training and enterprise. Training and work experience programmes include the Jobskill Training programme and the Youth Training programme. Further education is funded directly through the Department of Education Northern Ireland.* Northern Ireland also has a unified Education and Training Inspectorate, responsible for school, further education and training programmes. Northern Ireland ministers have recently published an economic strategy review, *Strategy 2010*, which outlines their proposals for lifelong learning in Northern Ireland.

This chapter has concentrated on practical and financial considerations. The next chapter looks at how to deal with change. It addresses particularly the emotional and personal aspects of changing careers.

Chapter 3

Change and new directions

- If you are facing redundancy, returning to work after a career break or simply seeking a change, you need to think about your motivations and circumstances when making career decisions for the future.
- The emotional consequences of redundancy and its effects on you, your family and close friends can be far-reaching and have to be resolved.
- You may benefit from counselling and support, and the practical suggestions in 'Sanity savers'.

If you are considering a career change or are having change thrust upon you, you will need to think hard about your priorities and motivations, your current domestic and financial circumstances, and how you and your family and friends will be affected by your decisions. You must consider what you can do to help yourself, and how to make the most of the help available to you.

Do take the time to pause. In busy, crowded lives, it is all too easy to rush on to the next thing without stopping to think about what is really important to you now, whether your circumstances have changed, or where the current path is leading you and whether that is what you want. What everyone wants is different, so do consider the points made in this chapter, and perhaps use someone whose opinion you value as a sounding board. Sometimes, when deciding where you want to go, it can help not to think about the job you want right now, but the one you might want next. This view may help you to see whether the first is leading you into an area that you want, be that a challenge, a refuge, renewed confidence, new skills or financial security.

This chapter looks in some detail at the psychological and personal consequences of changing career for people in three sorts of circumstances: those made redundant, those returning after a career break and those wanting to move in a new direction.

At the crossroads

As we saw in Chapter 1, the workplace has altered, almost beyond recognition in some respects, from what it was even a few years ago. One of the most striking aspects of this is that people now move jobs and change careers more frequently – out of both necessity (say, from being made redundant) and choice (wanting to do something different).

An increasing number of workers find themselves facing an uncertain future and many of them will realise that they are ill-equipped to deal with the perceived or actual job insecurity. The case studies in this section, which focus on people in different circumstances, demonstrate how others have coped and should help you through the various stages of coming to terms with your situation and planning for the future.

Redundancy

As we saw in Chapter 2, people are made redundant from organisations for a number of reasons. Your job could be under threat if your organisation or industry has been adversely affected by recession; is part of a sector which is in general decline; is introducing significant changes in work patterns or is facing the challenges of increasing globalisation. The writing could be on the wall if, for example, your company has had a wage or recruitment freeze for some time; the traditional hierarchical structure has been flattened, leaving fewer steps on the career ladder; and, of course, if some redundancies have already been announced.

Emotional responses to redundancy

Stephen Johnston was 52 and had been with an IT company for 29 years. It had faced stiff competition for some years and eventually made him redundant. He was very angry. He had always felt that the company and he had almost grown up together, because they had seen and survived so many changes. He could look back at the small team in the early days, the rapid growth, the buy-out, the boom-and-bust years of the 1980s, some recovery, some setbacks – and now it was his turn for the dreaded envelope. The last few years had been difficult: there had been a change of ownership, frequent changes in direction and lots of new financial targets to meet.

Perhaps you are in a similar situation? Maybe, as in Stephen's case, the change has been forced upon you – the company has made you redundant or 'proposed' early retirement. You will feel some sense of loss, and possibly be angry with your manager and/or the company because you feel they have broken the unwritten contract you had with each other. You will also find that when you are made redundant a number of other people will also be affected, some more severely than others: your partner, children, close relatives and even ex-colleagues (the 'survivors' of redundancy). Realising this will help you appreciate both that you are not alone in your predicament and that others close to you need reassurance and help too.

If, on the other hand, you are in a situation where voluntary redundancies are being sought by the company, you may wish to put your name forward. An overriding reason for this may be that when you go you will be leaving behind you all the bad situations, the frustrations and poor decisions which are irritating you. However, if you leave in these circumstances without any positive reasons, when you leave the building for the last time you can be walking into a future that may soon feel empty, after the initial euphoria has evaporated. If you decide to take voluntary redundancy, make sure your decision to do so is based on good and positive reasons.

Loss of a job is rated as one of the most stressful events that you can experience. Warning signs that you may be under more stress than is physically or emotionally good for you include changes in eating or sleeping patterns or an increase in smoking or alcohol intake. Another sign is an intensification of existing personality traits. For example, a person who is naturally defensive could become suspicious, and a careful person over-meticulous. Alternatively, existing personality traits could be reversed, so a naturally extrovert person could become withdrawn, while a creative person could lose his or her drive and vision. Ways of helping you cope with the boredom and lack of social contact and routine that follow the loss of a job are discussed later in this chapter.

Strong feelings are part of the process of change. Change is very tiring, both emotionally and physically. You may feel fine one day and low the next. You can expect to feel any or all of the following: uncertain, lacking in confidence, sceptical and cynical, suspicious, incompetent, averse to taking risks, angry, stressed, grieving, thirsty for information, hopeful, in a whirl, enthusiastic, confident, buoyant or positive.

People undergoing major change or loss in their lives – not just losing a job, but divorce or bereavement, for example – go through several different stages, each of which takes time to adjust to:

(1) **shock** at hearing the news, and then a range of feelings in a short time, which can be bewildering and immobilising

(2) **disbelief or denial** that what has happened has happened. It is easy to become stuck here, particularly if 'what if . . .' fantasies take over, which often precipitate panic as the deadline for leaving looms. You could find yourself saying things like, 'I cannot believe they would do this to us'; 'It cannot be true, we must fight these crazy changes'; 'Surely things are not as bad as Michael says they are'; 'We will be all right, won't we?'

(3) **anger** – at the system, the management, maybe your partner, ex-colleagues, yourself, etc. The overwhelming emotion may be one of depression or loss, and of needing lots of time, attention and understanding. At this point, people also need encouragement to accept that the change is inevitable and to look forward rather than back

(4) **acceptance** of what is happening. This is a major positive turning point because it is at this stage that an individual begins to take control of what is happening to him or her rather than just reacting to events. Counselling and support are still appropriate, but what is important now is that you put your energies into activities related to your understanding of the situation and its gradual resolution. Likely questions are: 'What do I do now?'; 'When do I go?'; 'Whom can I talk to?'; 'What is my redundancy package?'; 'When will I hear about the alternative jobs I can apply for?'; and 'What support service is in place to help me?'

(5) **testing/experimenting/exploring** new possibilities. This is the time to focus on self-assessment, goals, your CV and applications

(6) **understanding** the need to get on with the full-time job of finding work, networking, re-training and re-discovering unused skills and personal potential

(7) **recovery** – finding a new job, with new relationships, new circumstances, new challenges and new hopes.

The progress through these stages is not necessarily one-directional – you could feel that you are recovering from one stage when you find that circumstances or even a chance remark plunge you back into it.

If you have access to professional counselling, this is especially useful at stages 1–4. If this is not provided by your employer, contact the British Association for Counselling and Psychotherapy★ for a list of counsellors in your area or talk to someone at Relate★ (formerly the Marriage Guidance Council), which deals with individuals as well as couples, and not just with relationship problems. The services of an outplacement consultancy, with its practical and systematic approach to job search, will be most helpful for stages 4–7.

While it is true that time is a great healer, and your anger and sense of loss will lessen over time, sometimes it is useful to talk over these feelings with family, friends (if they are willing and able) or with a professional counsellor. Many companies have access to professional outplacement agencies or counselling services (see 'Counselling and support', later in this chapter). The former can help you with practical job-search skills and actions and the latter can help you to deal with the emotional changes.

Returning to work after a career break

People take a career break for a number of reasons: to bring up children, to care for elderly relatives, to travel, and so on. All of them face the problem of re-entering a world which has changed and moved on in their absence. Depending on how long they have been out of the work environment the changes (in terms of the kinds of skills needed, how the industry is structured, etc.) may be small or significant.

For example, Philip and Sarah George had their own business, which they sold up to travel around the world. After being away for

18 months they returned to the UK and began looking for work. During this time some of the old assumptions about what work people do and how they do it had probably altered significantly. Their knowledge of their occupation and industry, and possibly their skills, might have needed updating.

Penny James, on the other hand, spent seven years at home bringing up her three young sons, by which time the youngest was old enough to attend a local playgroup for a few sessions each week. Before giving up work entirely, she had worked part-time in her job in IT systems design for two years, and full-time for five years before that. In some ways the career break was good for her because it gave her the opportunity to re-consider her career choices. Originally, she had gone into IT systems design because she had studied computing as her degree subject so it seemed an obvious and well-paid choice. Moreover, it equipped her with skills that were easily transportable, so she was able to move from her native Australia to the UK, where her partner's job was relocated.

While these were valid reasons for her choice of career when she was in her twenties, to return to her old job after the break would have meant undergoing considerable technical re-training, which she was not keen on. In other ways, the career break was not so positive: the world of work seemed very unfamiliar territory, and Penny had lost confidence in her abilities. So she decided to change careers.

Being in a rut or seeking a change for some other reason

Some people drift into jobs and industries when they are young without really giving much thought to whether they want to build a career in the field or not.

Hilary Williamson, for example, took a summer holiday job with a major high street bank 20 years ago and is still there today. She is now in her early forties and wondering whether she wants to stay in banking or not. The banking sector has undergone immense changes in recent years brought about by the pace of developments in IT and the globalisation of the industry. Many of the routine functions are now carried out by machines, and much of the workforce now employed by the major banks is engaged in very different activities from those which predominated a decade or two ago. Consequently, Hilary is feeling much less sure about banking than she did a few years ago.

The first steps to altering your situation

If you are in any of the types of situation outlined above, you have a number of questions to ask yourself.

- If, like Stephen Johnston, you are facing redundancy or think it is a possibility, will you act now, look for a new job and resign when you have found one, take redundancy, or take early retirement? The last two options have financial and other implications, discussed in Chapters 2 and 7.
- If, like Philip and Sarah George and Penny James, you are returning to work, is your previous occupation still attractive? Is it in one of the sectors that is in decline (see Chapter 1)? Perhaps it has changed so much that it no longer appeals, or would now be difficult to re-enter without substantial re-training?
- If, like Hilary Williamson, you are in a rut and/or wanting a change, do you want to stay on and try to improve your situation? Would an internal transfer solve the problem? If so, what are the opportunities? Will your boss give you a sympathetic hearing? Can your human resources or personnel department help? Would another job within your industry satisfy you or do you need and want a complete change?

Whatever happens, you will need to be clear about what you want to happen. From a personal point of view, it is worth taking the time to sort out your own feelings so you do not transfer to a job or industry you will not like. In any case, simply from the professional angle, you will need to focus your objectives very carefully if you are to succeed in finding a job in a competitive market, and this means being confident of your skills, achievements and motivation.

Your family will be affected by the changes you decide to make, too, and you will need to ensure that they understand and are sympathetic to whatever you want to do.

Owing to the organisational and economic changes outlined in Chapter 1, employers are keen to take on people who will become self-sufficient and autonomous as quickly as possible, and/or who can become so with the minimum of coaching, time and fuss. Therefore, they will want to check the 'cultural fit', such as the sort of person you are, your values and motivations, and your generic skills (see Chapter 1) such as whether you can work as part of a team. They will also want to know in precise terms what you think you have to offer.

If you can be clear and focused on both these issues you will have a head start in finding a job because you are in a position to point out to potential employers what you can do for them. In this sense, the old-style chronological CV has become outdated: you will need to produce a rather different document (see Chapter 5) and be prepared to convince potential employers that you can and will do the job.

Whether you are facing redundancy, or increased uncertainty and insecurity; returning to the workplace after a career break; or are in a rut and/or seeking a change, 'What next?' needs a good answer. As discussed in Chapter 1, to manage change well you need to be flexible, positive and proactive. Bearing this in mind, consider your options under these four headings:

- What is important for you now?
- What will be the effect of your career change on your family and friends?
- What is happening in the job market?
- What are your skills and achievements?

What is important for you now?

Whether the change has already happened or is imminent, you have a chance now to think about what is important for you at this point in your life and career. A significant change from the 1980s to the present decade is that many people are questioning whether long hours in stressful situations in return for a high salary are what they want from their working life. Many are looking for more balance between their career and their life outside work. Viewed positively, this could be because they want to have more time at home with their families or for leisure interests. Viewed more negatively, perhaps it is because they are simply exhausted from the long hours and the conflicting demands made upon them.

So, when making a decision to change career or to change whatever you are doing at present, the best place to begin is with yourself. If more balance is what you want, then now is the time to achieve it. You need to think about you, your feelings and your motivations. People often drift into jobs and careers without really thinking about whether they like or suit them. Discovering what you really want to do with your life can take time. Reading about or listening to the experiences of people who have made the move from situations similar to your own could help.

For example, William, who worked in advertising, and Suzanne, a solicitor, became fed up with commuting into central London. They also felt they were in a rut after seven or eight years in their respective careers. They gave up their jobs, but stayed in their professions, and moved to York to see if it was living and working in London that was the problem. Although they preferred York, they still felt restless, so they went travelling for a while and ended up working in Australia. William stayed in advertising, but Suzanne made a career change, moving into the travel industry. Although she did not have any qualifications, it was her own experience of travelling and evident enthusiasm for the places she had visited which got her the job. By now she was in her early thirties, but was happy to re-train as a travel consultant because she knew this was what she really wanted to do with her life.

The effect on family and friends of your career change

Your immediate and extended family, friends and colleagues – in fact, anyone who is important to you – will be affected by any changes you choose or are forced to make. It is important to be aware of this, but also that they may be able to offer help. You can ask their opinions about their experiences in similar industries and talk over how they would be affected by your decision to make a major change such as accepting redundancy or taking on a new career. They could be an important source of information: an ingredient that is crucial to successful job search.

A change of employer and/or career may mean you have to move house and leave an area you have lived in for many years. You may need to re-train, which could involve lots of study, probably at home, and have financial implications. If you decide to take early retirement you will suddenly have plenty of free time. What will you do with it? Self-employment may be your chosen new direction. Again, this will affect those close to you, especially if you work from home. Spending more time there – say, if you decide to become self-employed or work part-time – could put pressure on existing relationships. Discuss this potential problem in advance with those involved.

What is happening in the job market?

As you think about the personal questions discussed above, you might want to turn your mind to the practical question of 'what is happening in the job market?' – so you can see *how* your motivations could fit with what is available or may be happening soon. This will help you become focused on the real possibilities that you can consider and begin to actively pursue.

Chapter 1 will have given you some ideas about which industries and jobs are expanding, and which are in relative decline. So, think first about your industry and where it is going. What are the new trends? How is product development handled? Who are the movers and shakers? In what ways will globalisation and technology affect it?

Secondly, think about your particular job function. Is it/has it/will it change? And if changes are afoot, what are they likely to be? How will jobs be affected by the way work is being conducted, and any consequent changes in the skills needed – e.g. the new service culture?

You can also think about your local area, assuming you plan to stay. Are there new industries coming in? If so, who are they, and what sort of workers do they need – both now and in the future? Has the infrastructure (e.g. a new road system, large retail park) altered the sort of organisation that is attracted to the area? If you plan to move, for whatever reasons, how would you answer these questions for your new area? The issues raised by these questions are dealt with in detail in Chapter 4.

What are your skills and achievements?

Following on from the above questions, it is natural to begin to think about how your skills and achievements might fit with new industry sectors, new ways of working, a new job function, etc. Chapters 4 and 5 will help you prepare a CV that makes the most of your transferable skills, your potential contribution to an organisation, and so on. At this early stage, a preliminary think about skills and achievements is worthwhile; your ideas can be refined later.

It is extremely hard to see ourselves as others see us. So, try to find out how you are regarded by others, such as your colleagues: what skills you are valued for, what people think your contribution to the organisation has been, and so on. This research will help you stand back from what you may have done for some years, and put it into context. It will be invaluable as you consider your next move(s), because you will be able to draw on more than your own personal opinion.

You can also analyse your current job tasks and responsibilities to draw out the skills you use. For example, perhaps you work in human resources (HR), and one of your key tasks is to make all the arrangements for people coming for job interviews. The skills you might identify would be communication skills and organisational skills. Thinking about achievements, you might be particularly proud of how quickly you arrange reimbursement of expenses and despatch the acknowledgement letters, how few interviews need to be re-arranged because you plan everything so well, and so on. These ideas are taken further in Chapter 4.

Factors influencing career choices

When you are facing change, for whatever reason, it is important to allow time to make a well-informed decision about what you want to do. Motivation and circumstances are the two main factors influencing career choices, so both must be taken into account when you are evaluating your options. For advice on how to choose an occupation, industry or organisation, see Chapter 4.

Motivation

The reasons people have for doing the work they do vary enormously. Some motives may remain valid throughout one's working life, others may be significantly affected by circumstances and will therefore change over time. The following list is based on the concept of career drivers expounded by David Francis in his book *Managing Your Own Career.*

Affluence. You want material possessions, to be rich and to have a high or reasonably high standard of living. You might be prepared to take an unpleasant job or work very long hours because of the material rewards the job brings.

Being in charge. You want control of people and situations. You enjoy getting things done, and deciding what is to be done, by whom and how. You are likely to be in a management job, at the hub of an organisation, where you can use your initiative and power to make things happen.

A purpose in life. You want to do things because they fit with what you think is important, i.e. your personal beliefs and values. You seek self-fulfilment and want to contribute to what you think is worthwhile. Likely applications for this motive are very diverse, for example, nursing, training, teaching, voluntary work, working for a charity, writing, or practising complementary therapies.

Mastery of skills. You like to feel technically expert in what you do. This could involve mechanical, sporting, crafts, intellectual, scientific or practical skills, so the application of this motive will be very varied. You work hard to get qualifications and relevant experience and to keep up to date with your specific area of knowledge.

Innovation. You want to be creative and be acknowledged for it. You may prefer to work on your own or in a small team because you think larger organisations do not value your creativity or give you the space to work on it. For some people this can become an important motive as they get older, especially if their confidence in their skills grows.

Human contact. You want to be close to other people. Sometimes you may stay in an unfulfilling job because your work relationships are so important to you. People with this as their primary motive will, unsurprisingly, want to work with people. This might be in a customer- or client-facing role, such as sales or customer service.

Independence. Being free to make your own decisions is very important to you. You probably feel boxed in by bureaucracy, and see procedures and systems as irritants. What you want above all is the freedom to choose, so you may decide to work as a freelance or to run your own small or medium-sized business.

Dependability. You want a solid, predictable and secure future, so you are probably attracted by well-known companies and large institutions. This may depend on what personal or family responsibilities you have.

Recognition. You want to be admired and respected by people. If this is an important motive you will want to work at the best, the biggest or the most prestigious organisation in your field, and be in a high-profile job with high status.

Here are some examples of how motivation affects career and job choices.

- Do you live to work, or work to live? In other words, do you work to finance your hobbies and social life or do you really enjoy your work for its own sake?

Joe, for example, was keen on very active outdoor sports. His three main hobbies were mountain biking, skiing and orienteering. His middle-management job was important to him because it gave him the money he needed to pursue these hobbies. He wanted to do one or all of these professionally, but with a young family to support he decided that at this stage in his life they would have to remain as hobbies.

- Are you prepared to earn less money and make a major life change?

In the popular 1970s BBC TV series *The Good Life*, a couple played by Felicity Kendal and Richard Briers made a radical life change. Tom Good, with the support of his wife, Barbara, left a well-paid company job to live off the land at their house in Surbiton.

This was of course fiction, but if your circumstances were to allow, and/or your main reason for working is not material wealth, you too could decide you want to lead a simpler, if less affluent, sort of life. Before you give up everything and take the plunge, however, it may be worth trying out your new lifestyle for a short period (at weekends, or while on holiday) to see if it would suit you.

Sometimes giving the proposed change a trial is not feasible, and you just have to take the plunge. Graham, for example, was a chartered accountant with a major London practice and had a smart car and a salary to match. He read Latin and Greek for pleasure. After about eight years he decided he would give up this particular 'good life' and go to Oxford as a mature student to read Classics. Now in his final year, he is considering his career choices. One thing he is very sure about is that he will not be returning to chartered accountancy. Graham accepts without regret that if he wants to pursue his love of Classics in his job he will not therefore be able to resume his former lifestyle.

- Do you want to continue at the same level in a different industry or job?

Colette was made redundant from her middle-management job in the knitwear industry at the age of 39. She enjoyed knitwear and was experienced and knowledgeable about it. As a qualified accountant she wanted to find a job at a similar level, preferably in the same industry. She started to look, but could find nothing suitable or interesting.

After about five months with no success she decided to cast her net wider and to look at jobs in other industries. She worked hard at becoming known in recruitment agencies and at networking among friends and associates. She eventually heard of a comparable job at a similar level in the travel industry. Before attending any interviews, she did a good deal of research. At her second interview she had to give a presentation on travel to senior managers, which she found very hard because the industry was so new to her. She got the job and not only settled into it very well and very happily, but found the industry itself much more fun than the one she had left behind.

- Do you want a position that is comparable, more senior or less senior than the one you are in now?

Brian retired from a senior job in insurance in the City of London in his early fifties. Having worked all his professional life in the City, he decided that it was time to stop commuting from Hertfordshire every day. However, he found quite quickly that he really missed the pace of working life, and felt he still had a lot of experience and energy to give, so he looked around for something to do in the local area.

He found a lower-status and less well-paid job as full-time bursar in a local secondary school where he could use his business skills, and is now thoroughly enjoying his 'retirement'. The benefits have not all been one way, as the school has gained from his commercial skills. His projects have included improving the recruitment and induction procedures for non-teaching staff and introducing appraisals for them, both of which initiatives have improved staff retention.

- Could you turn an interest into paid employment or self-employment?

For about five years, Caroline took time off work and worked at weekends because of her interest in training, particularly in women's development. When she was made redundant from her full-time job in the wine trade, she was able to turn her interest into self-employment. Within a few years, she had a successful training business.

• Are you clear about what you enjoy about work?

Jonathan started work as an apprentice mechanical engineer, and many of his jobs were highly technical. However, his employers encouraged his interest in, and aptitude for, people management skills, as a result of which he became a works manager. If he were to change jobs now, he would rely less on his technical skills and more on his abilities in dealing with people.

Circumstances

Circumstances can also influence your decisions about what is important for you now.

• Do you have a young family?

Robert is a computer engineer who has recently switched from an office-based 9am to 5pm job to one which entails travelling around a good deal of the south-east of England. He is often on call, but knows well in advance when that will be. He has made the change because his wife is studying part-time at the local university while continuing to work part-time, and the flexibility in his work patterns means he can share the early-morning and late-afternoon school run and childcare.

• Are your children at college or university, or have they now become financially independent of you?

When her two sons had finished university, found jobs and left home, Patricia retired from her full-time teaching job as head teacher of a state nursery school in her late forties, weary from many years at a tough inner-city school. The qualifying age for her pension was 50 years, so she had a few years before she could start claiming it.

She and her husband decided to return to their roots in rural Derbyshire, where they bought a house in a small village. Her husband was self-employed and in a field that was not dependent on where he is based, so he could easily move his business. She took a part-time job as an NVQ assessor, which made the most of her teaching experience and her ability to get on with young adults. From a situation where she was exhausted and run-down, the change in job and lifestyle gave her new vigour.

- Do you have caring responsibilities?

Another consideration for Patricia in her move from the city to the country was that she would be near her elderly, widowed mother. Instead of being a two-hour drive away, she is just around the corner. This proximity was useful recently because her mother had a fall, and Patricia has been on hand to help.

- What is your financial situation?

Brendan and Sue both have full-time jobs, a large mortgage and two school-age children. At one stage when Brendan was out of work for about nine months it became a struggle for them to meet all their financial commitments. They managed because Sue had her job and they had some savings. At the time, they found the large mortgage to be a particular burden, both financially and emotionally. They planned that once Brendan got back into work again Sue would work only part-time. However, when he did get a job they changed their minds because they decided that never again would they want to feel under such pressure from the financial commitment of a large mortgage. They both continued to work full-time so they could pay off some or all of the mortgage early. When they succeeded in paying off £10,000 they felt very relieved to be getting back in control of their financial situation.

- Are there reasons to stay in a particular location?

Jon and his wife Jeannie come from close-knit families living in the north-east of England. They married about five years ago and have two young children, whom Jeannie looks after at home.

Jon is very able and ambitious, but concerned to balance home and work. He works for an organisation with branches nationwide. If he wished to pursue his ambitions it would entail a move to the head office, in Bristol. At the moment, Jon is not prepared to uproot his family and disrupt the strong family ties. He has taken a good job at a regional centre that still signals his ambitions and abilities to senior management, but balances work with his home life. His career is still on track, and when both the children are of school age the couple plan to move to Bristol.

Deciding what is important for you

The overriding feeling of anger that Stephen Johnston (see 'Emotional responses to redundancy', above) felt at being made redundant was recognised by his company as being harmful to him and undermining his performance during his last few months at work. His employers arranged for him to see a workplace counsellor. Stephen realised that his anger was affecting his relationship with his wife and that he wanted, in his words, 'to do something more constructive with my feelings than hurt Anne'. He negotiated to work part-time for the last four months so he could start researching an idea he had for running a caravan park.

Stephen's research convinced him that the caravan park would work and he has re-trained in business skills for self-employment and done a business plan with help from his local Enterprise Agency. An added bonus is that his wife wants to be involved as well. Part of his lump-sum redundancy payment will be used to start the business.

Hilary Williamson is also thinking about what is important for her now. She is 42 and married with teenage children of 16 and 18. She worked part-time at the bank while the boys were small, and has been full-time since the younger one went to primary school. She has thought a lot about her motives and feels that they have changed from wanting financial security, when the children were young, to wanting to work in a smaller organisation where she can set the rules, rather than always following someone else's.

Philip and Sarah George had an exciting time abroad, enjoying various new experiences such as white-water rafting and scuba-diving. On returning to the UK they were surprised and bewildered by how much *they* had changed, and felt out of touch with the job market, particularly as they had been self-employed before their trip. At present, they feel so unsettled that they may go off travelling again. They have not really decided what motivates them and what is important now, other than that they would like to start a family soon – but that is a life decision, not a career decision.

Penny James's motives have changed from a mixture of wanting material rewards and security to having a purpose in life, in that she now wants to contribute to something she thinks is worthwhile. Her present ideas focus on working with people who have special needs, either because of social problems or emotional difficulties; possibly in a charity or not-for-profit environment.

Counselling and support

As we have seen, making changes in our lives is neither easy nor straightforward. Whichever situation you are in – redundancy, returning to work, or seeking a complete change – you will probably find that counselling and support will help a good deal. They come in many forms which we discuss here, and are often free, but sometimes you will have to pay for them.

Helping someone cope with the psychological stress of redundancy requires professional counselling expertise. Such support can be provided by suitably trained people, either in-house or from external organisations. In addition, the person made redundant may need advice of a practical sort, e.g. to do with finance, which may not be available within the firm or organisation shedding staff. If the information required is on financial matters such as personal pensions, tax and lump-sum investments, this must be given by properly qualified financial advisers. Similarly, few organisations will be able to provide a comprehensive job-search service from internal resources, and may harness the help of an outside agency. Indeed, this may work to the benefit of the individuals involved, who often find it easier to accept advice from an outsider perceived to be independent and therefore 'untainted' by any internal agenda.

Counselling services

A few companies have in-house counsellors who can offer help with personal problems and work-related issues, such as redundancy or the effects of a restructuring, or with someone at a career crossroads. If your company has no one in-house who can offer counselling, your HR department should be able to put you in contact with someone it knows and trusts. Personal referral is often the best way of finding a good counsellor as you can get some idea of his or her style, method of working, appropriate industry experience, and so on. You could also contact the British Association for Counselling and Psychotherapy for details of someone in your area.

Some large organisations have an Employee Assistance Programme (EAP) in place, so you can be referred to a counsellor whom the company has retained for the employees' benefit. This will be confidential even though the company is paying the bill. The usual practice is for the counsellor to submit a monthly bill which details the number of hours and only allocates a number to each person to ensure confidentiality is maintained.

Outplacement agencies

If a group of people is being made redundant, or if you are of medium to senior status, your organisation may engage an out-placement company. The range of services such a company can offer is wide. The full service (and the most expensive) includes counselling, workshops on finding a job, psychometric testing, help with writing your CV and applications, interview practice, and the provision of secretarial support and a fully equipped workspace with a desk, telephone, computer and printer at its premises.

The advantage of the full service incorporating workspace in an office environment is that once you are out of work you can continue to travel to a place of 'work' which probably replicates surroundings that are familiar to you. Many people find that this familiar type of environment and the routine help them make the transition from 'worker' to 'jobseeker' because it gives their days some structure. Others may find it irksome precisely because it reminds them of an organisation where they may have been unhappy, perhaps felt undervalued, and which in the end did not want/need them any more.

The best agencies offer a personal and caring service. In the past the outplacement services on offer were often prescriptive. The run-of-the-mill organisations could make you feel you were being processed through programmes which had been designed more for their convenience than your benefit. Nowadays, programmes are often tailored to the needs and budget of the client company. Clients pick from a 'menu' of services, and the consultancy will tailor the choice and duration of seminars and one-to-one help to reflect their particular needs.

Following a major restructuring of one of its divisions a large charity organisation chose a mix of one-to-one counselling and group workshops for the employees directly affected. The sessions were preceded by management briefings on the cycle of change and the feelings following restructuring and redundancies, plus some tips on how to lessen the blow and reduce the impact on people's performance. The workshops on all aspects of job search were followed by team training for those who were staying, to pull the new teams together.

Outplacement is usually offered while those being made redundant are still with their organisation, and for some people that is too early, as they may be still too traumatised by events to take proper advantage of what is on offer. Some organisations extend the offer of outplacement help beyond the leaving date. If you do not feel able to benefit yet, do keep your options open – some counselling and help with job search will be useful later. Although opinions vary on just *how* helpful outplacement and/or training on job search skills are, what is not in question is that having someone to help does increase the speed with which people return to work. Most organisations do feel bad about having to make people redundant, and you can sometimes use this to your advantage. So even if nothing is initially offered by your employer, it is worth doing some private research, and making a case to your management for some form of help. Most outplacement consultancies claim that between 65 and 95 per cent of their clients find new employment within six months.

Choosing an outplacement agency

If your organisation cannot provide you with help from an outplacement agency, you could contact one yourself. You can also ask your HR department for recommendations. The criteria to look for in such an organisation, according to the Chartered Institute of Personnel & Development (CIPD),* are:

- corporate membership of the CIPD (companion, fellow or member)
- registration of the appropriate staff with the British Psychological Society as a chartered psychologist
- staff with other qualifications in psychology, vocational guidance or counselling recognised by a professional body.

You should expect the consultancy to be aware of, and adhere to, the guidelines and regulations in the CIPD's Code of Professional Conduct and Professional Conduct Regulations.

Sanity savers

Whether you have been made redundant, are re-entering the job market, or are changing career, you could be out of work for some months. To minimise the effect of the uncertainty and tension of finding work – on you, your family and friends – you need to prepare yourself in a number of ways. Thinking positively, having a support network, using a dedicated workspace for pursuing your career, structuring your time, combating physical inactivity and doing temporary or voluntary work could all help.

Take a positive approach

One important aspect of our lives that gives many of us a sense of identity is our work. Often the first question we are asked on being introduced to someone new is, 'What do you do?' When you are out of work, you need to find a way of answering this question without feeling too uncomfortable.

If you are unhappy or unsettled in a job and looking for something new, it is all too easy to slip into something like this: 'Oh, I'm pretty fed up at the moment. I've probably been in my job too long, and I need to move, but it's a difficult time because of . . .' If you are planning to return to the job market, and it is some time since you worked outside the home, you may say something self-deprecating such as, 'Oh, I'm only at home at the moment.' If you have been away from the UK job market for some other reason, perhaps because you have been travelling, you may say, 'We've been away for some time, and I feel rather out of sync with everything.'

Every time you shift about looking embarrassed or simply evade the issue, you are losing a good opportunity to enlist the help and support of someone who could have useful contacts and knowledge. Although this is easier said than done, try to get out of feeling low and sounding negative, which can become a habit. Turning the response into something positive can be quite productive. For example, instead of saying, 'I've just been made redundant,' you could say 'I have just left XYZ Limited, and am looking for a new job in such-and-such field.' A response like that acknowledges your situation, but does not stop there – it shows you are looking ahead and moving on in a positive way. It also gives the other person the chance to pick up on that positive response, and suggest ideas and offer help. Remember also that few people will have been un-affected – directly or indirectly – by job loss at some time or other, and that the help offered could take many forms, such as putting you in touch with someone who has information on the new area you are interested in, or an organisation that is recruiting, etc. This is equally useful if you are not in the situation of being made redun-dant, but are returning to work, or changing direction.

Get support

Although it is possible to survive a prolonged spell of being unem-ployed or searching for a job with better prospects without ever feeling low, most people in such a situation find that they experi-ence periods of dejection. You will probably need support, and not just from your immediate family and close friends, who themselves will be affected by your predicament. Many formal and informal networks, such as Jobclubs (see Chapter 2), offer different sorts of support for people seeking work. Your local Jobcentre, CAB, library or Learning Skills Council (Local Enterprise Company in Scotland) will all be able to refer you to facilities in your area. Meeting people in similar circumstances to your own, catching up with what is hap-pening in the job market and having access to re-training opportu-nities can all be very useful.

You will need the support in various ways, from people who:

- know your industry
- are honest in their criticism
- know how to find things out
- usually help you
- challenge you
- can be trusted
- can help you when you have bad news
- are good at giving practical advice.

Try to fill in a name against each of the eight roles above. A word of warning: do make sure that nobody takes on more than, say, two of these eight support jobs. If someone has to do more than his or her fair share, the friendship may become stretched, and he or she may resent the fact that you are taking too much.

Take heed of a cautionary tale. An executive was made redundant from her high-powered job. In some ways, it was probably a good thing as she was beginning to suffer considerable stress. But once she had worked her notice and stopped work, she became an emotional and mental wreck. At this time, and over the next six months until she found work, she relied – over-relied – on two friends for all the support she needed. In the end, she lost their friendship as the friends felt it was 'all take, take, take, and never any give, give, give to us'.

Needless to say, apart from trying not to impose too heavily on those who are helping you through your bad patch (one of whom is likely to be your partner, if you have one), never forget, once you are back on your feet, to thank the people who have supported you when you most needed it.

Have a designated workspace

It may seem obvious, but you will find that searching for a job – no matter what sort it is – is easier if you are organised and efficient. This is true whether you are currently in work, or unemployed. One way of ensuring this is to have a work area at home which is yours, and where you can have ready access to the telephone, files to keep your job applications and papers in an orderly fashion, space to work and spread out the newspapers and journals, a PC and printer (or reasonable access to them), a notepad, pen/pencils, and your CV to hand so you sound on-the-ball when someone telephones you. You do not have to have a large area but ideally it should be somewhere exclusive to you which you do not have to clear away every night, and where you can think of yourself as being 'professional' in this new job of finding work. Indeed, you may find it helps your self-discipline to refer to this workspace as your 'office'.

If you have a young family who are around for all or part of the day, make sure that they do not answer the telephone and are not making a noise in the background when the telephone rings, in case a potential employer is on the line.

Structure your time

If you have been made redundant or have been out of work for a while for other reasons, you may find that the lack of structure to the day has odd side-effects, which make you less efficient. It is easy to end up drifting around the house rather than being disciplined and focusing on the job search. Some people in such a situation find that they need to have the structure of 'clocking on', so they set themselves a time to start work, timed tea/coffee/lunch breaks, and a time for clocking off at the end of the day.

When you are outside the externally imposed structure of regular work, you need to pace yourself. If you are shut in your new workspace day in, day out, with no one to chat to, have a coffee with, or spur you on with news or gossip – all of which happens in most external work environments – it will not be long before you are metaphorically climbing the walls and finding excuses not to go into the 'office'. Accept that you will not be able to look for a job for 37 hours each week, and that you are likely to get low and depressed because your work lacks structure, you may suffer from loneliness and you are likely to be physically inactive. A practical solution to this problem is to schedule your week.

For example, Bob gave up a regular office job to run a small office cleaning contract company, working from his own basement. During the first month he appreciated the fact that because no one interrupted him he got much more work done than he had expected: in his previous job he had spent so much time in meetings and on the telephone that he felt he never completed anything. Gradually, he began to wish that the telephone would ring, and became distracted thinking about all the people who could be ringing him, and why they were not ringing, and whether he should call them.

Bob solved his problem by having 'meetings' – a coffee or lunch with friends – on Tuesdays and Thursdays so that the week was broken up. Gradually, as the months passed by and his business got going, these social 'meetings' were replaced by genuine meetings with customers and suppliers.

You can also keep a chart of progress, on which you plot the number of telephone calls made, letters written, agencies contacted, and friends and acquaintances renewed. You may even find it helps to report your progress to someone else as a way of maintaining the discipline and spurring yourself on. People vary in their reactions to the lack of structure when looking for work, so experiment and choose the strategy which will work best with your temperament and situation.

Bob's story shows that it pays to split the week up. You could, similarly, divide up a day based on the different tasks that searching for a job entails. For example, you could read the daily newspapers and trade journals first thing in the morning, take a tea/coffee break, then do some research on particular industries, occupations and organisations by telephone, letter or on the Net; visit a friend for lunch to find out about his or her company or industry, compile a network list/work through the list (see Chapter 4 on networking), telephone contacts in mid-afternoon, visit the library, and so on. Again, try out various permutations and combinations to see what suits you best.

You may find that you can make proactive telephone calls only on days when you feel buoyant and confident. See how many hours you can sustain yourself for. Between five and six hours a day is a reasonable figure to work towards. Commit yourself to the number of hours that will suit you, and produce results, and then be disciplined about sticking to them. This may sound rather prescriptive, but if you approach your job search in a business-like way, you will feel more confident and professional.

Combat physical inactivity

One other problem that someone looking for a job is likely to face is inactivity. To avoid being desk-bound all day, you could do some housework, or get up and stretch at regular intervals, but these may not be sufficient. Of course, looking for work is not just about trawling through advertisements for suitable vacancies, surfing the Net, writing application letters and going for interviews, and therefore does not have to be sedentary. You could plan your day to take in other essential activities such as going to a local or specialist library to research an industry or company, or visiting a Jobclub. Alternatively, you could decide to network and meet a friend who works at one of the companies you have targeted, or research a company's products, especially if you wanted a job in, say, retail, banking, catering or construction.

Other options include:

- taking regular exercise. This could be a bike ride or a swim at lunch-time, walking the children to and from school instead of using the car, or visiting a gym. Many council-run and private gyms and health clubs have cheaper off-peak membership rates and cut-price sessions for day-time use, and the council-run ones usually have concessionary rates for unemployed people
- cultivating a hobby. This could be gardening every lunch-time, or painting or writing for some time each day
- meeting friends purely as a social activity to help keep buoyant and sane.

Do temporary or voluntary work

While you are looking for a job it may help your self-esteem and preserve your sanity if you do work of some kind. Besides, it will also look good on your CV.

Ranjit, for example, worked as a volunteer one day a week in his local charity shop. He chose a Thursday mainly because it was the busiest day in the shop, and it made him feel very useful. His previous job had been as a stock controller, and he had an enjoyable time re-organising the room where the donated goods were stored and sorted prior to going into the shop for sale.

Everyone benefited from the arrangement. He knew that what he was doing was valuable and was pleased that he was helping the charity. Moreover, he could add the experience to his CV and discuss it at interviews. Employers could see he had not stagnated during his unemployment and were impressed by his initiative. The charity shop manager was also pleased to end up with an orderly stockroom.

Jane, on the other hand, was an archaeologist who had been made redundant from her research job because the funding had come to an end. While looking for work, she gave short talks to children at her local primary school. Their questions made her look at her work with fresh eyes, and she used this insight at interviews to put herself into the place of the people who financed the research.

Another example is Andrew, who had been running a successful marketing consultancy for some years but had always planned to retire in his mid-fifties. At 51, he was planning for what he would do in his retirement. One idea was to teach. He approached his local university and did some part-time lecturing and seminar work for the marketing undergraduate course, taking an afternoon off work each week to do so. Although he had a lifetime's experience in the subject, he found the students' relative lack of knowledge and of relevant work experience quite a challenge. At the beginning he struggled to make the concepts clear without using too much jargon. He also had to work hard to create good case studies which would make sense to people 30 years younger than himself. Andrew certainly benefited from the experience. He had experimented in a relatively risk-free way to find out whether university teaching would suit him or not. Overall, he came to the conclusion that he should try out some other ideas for his 'retirement' before making any decision.

Doing short-term contracts is becoming increasingly popular. These are also sometimes called interim contracts, so you would be known as an 'interim'. Employers often need someone for a short period for various reasons: to do a one-off project or provide cover for a maternity leave, while they wait for someone to serve their notice or for seasonal reasons. Taking on such employment can be beneficial to you because you have something concrete to put on your CV. It may be in a sector where you were previously employed, or may be in a different sector. In either case, it augments your CV, and in the latter case, may help you with the transition into a different industry sector or different sort of job.

For example, Michaela was made redundant from her accountancy job in food retail. She registered with an agency, which dealt with both temporary and permanent work. Her first contract was initially for just seven weeks as an accountant in home retail. As she proved her worth to the company, so the contract was extended and eventually lasted six months. It augmented her existing retail knowledge, and extended it into another sector. The second contract was as a bid manager for a company specialising in facilities management (FM). So this gave her the opportunity to learn about FM, a growing sector, and to use her financial skills in a new way. She still used her numeracy skills, and gained the new skills of client management, taking a brief, etc. Both jobs gave her renewed confidence, and added to her CV. In particular, the second contract gave her the confidence to go for more commercial jobs away from her 'comfort zone' of accountancy. In the end, she got a permanent job as a commercial manager in logistics.

The work you choose to do may be directly related to your job function – as in the case of Ranjit – and can therefore augment your existing skills and experience. Alternatively, you could, like Jane, use the opportunity to give you a fresh perspective on your work. Or, like Andrew, you could view the experience as an experiment to see whether the work might suit you on a more permanent and/or full-time basis. Another option is to use temporary or voluntary work as a chance to practise a newly acquired skill which needs honing before it can be used professionally.

This chapter has been about personal motivations, the emotional consequences and likely implications of major career change, and the sort of help and support which is available. It will help you to start thinking, 'What next?' Chapter 4 is also about decisions, but is more factual and information-based; looking at changes in recruitment, how to research industries, occupations and organisations, and ways of making the most of your skills and achievements.

Chapter 4

Looking for a job

> • Recruiting practices have undergone radical changes, so those looking to change careers now have to market their transferable skills much more actively than previously.
> • As networking has become more important as a recruiting tool than advertising, it is up to the jobseeker to show initiative and make the first move.
> • Researching an occupation, industry or organisation is a crucial first step in making any long-term decisions.

Changing jobs and/or career is a complex matter, and you need to know the rules of the game to succeed. Today, jobseekers have to be clear, focused and determined as never before. This chapter examines the changes in recruitment practice, including new ways of getting into the job market, gives advice on how to research an occupation and industry, encourages you to think about your skills and achievements, and explores the factors that may make it harder for you to get a job and how to minimise their effect.

How recruitment has changed

Most organisations now recognise the need to reduce the risk of taking on someone who will not fit into their culture and/or will not be able or willing to do the job in question. A major bookselling chain has estimated that recruiting a new sales assistant for one of its branches and getting him or her established in the post costs the company £2,500. The search for someone to fill a senior position in a large organisation could run up a bill of about £8,000; the services of a headhunting consultancy could bump it up to as high as £30,000.

Because recruitment is so expensive and time-consuming, employers are keen to avoid mistakes. Rather than concentrate entirely on what a candidate has already achieved, they now want to try to assess his or her future potential more accurately and to judge whether they will get good value for money from the new person and whether he or she will fit in with the rest of the department, team or organisation.

This and the other changes in recruitment practices examined below have consequences not only for those seeking jobs in a new field but also for those who are opting for self-employment, because they too will need to be up to date with the job market: for example, they may wish to fill, in a freelance capacity or on contract, one of the many gaps in larger organisations that have downsized. Like those looking for salaried jobs, they will need to be aware of what is needed and by whom, and to pitch their skills and services accordingly.

Leaner organisations

One of the results of the cutbacks of the 1980s and 1990s is that new recruits to an organisation are going to find few people with the time or the ability to coach and nurture them. They therefore have to find their feet very quickly, on their own. No organisation, whether it is public or private sector, small, medium or large, can afford the time or money to have people who are not functioning to their full capacity. This means that you have to demonstrate to the organisation – both during the hiring process and when you are a new employee – how quickly you can become fully useful to it.

Increased 'people' skills

As we have seen, people skills have become more important, even in jobs that do not entail direct customer contact. This is especially true in de-layered organisations because people can no longer rely on a chain of command to get things done, but must use interpersonal and influencing skills instead. Businesses are increasingly aware of how crucial both customer service and team-working within the organisation are, and will try to employ people who can meet these needs. Good communication skills and the ability to motivate oneself and others are now seen as essential to your employability.

This is true even in technical jobs, with many employers ranking team and people skills alongside or even ahead of technical skills.

As a jobseeker you need to be confident and articulate about what sort of person you are. Be prepared (and able) to demonstrate your people skills to prospective employers and the ways in which you can benefit any organisation you work for.

Broader range of skills

Research commissioned by the Department for Education and Employment (DfEE)★ during 1995–96 confirmed that most employers (74 per cent) expect individuals to have a broader range of skills than has previously been the case. As a jobseeker and career changer, you may have to re-train and/or improve your skills to prove your potential worth to employers.

Cultural fit

Management gurus have given us an increased understanding of the importance of 'culture' in an organisation, often referred to as 'how we do things around here'. This idea of company culture benefits organisations because:

- it encourages cohesiveness and helps people to feel part of their unit or team. This is especially important in de-layered organisations with less clear lines of command, and/or 'matrix' management (as opposed to conventional hierarchical management)
- many now rely on every single employee to be flexible and reliable so he or she can step into someone else's shoes if that person is away.

Cultural fit means a closer match between you, your ideals and skills and the organisation for which you work – the notion of 'a round peg in a round hole'. One of the precepts of this book is that when you are looking at particular industries, occupations or organisations you should check whether the cultural fit will work – for you and for the organisation employing you. This is explored in greater detail later in this chapter, and also in Chapter 5.

Less dependence on advertisements

Advertising vacancies in the national and trade press is expensive, not just in terms of the cost of the advertisement itself but because of the demand it makes on management time. When there is high (or relatively high) unemployment, responses to advertisements rocket, and are very time-consuming, and therefore expensive, for employers to process. It can take weeks to go through all the applications, draw up a shortlist and then interview and test the candidates to find the best person. Inevitably, in the meantime some of the better qualified and more experienced applicants are likely to have found other jobs.

Recruiting in these circumstances has been likened to panning for gold – it takes time, there is a lot of unsuitable material, and you could find that, even after a lot of hard work, the precious metal you have been seeking slips through your fingers.

At present, because unemployment is relatively low, some industries and job functions are experiencing a skills shortage and finding that some positions are hard to fill. One publishing company, the market leader in its sector, advertised a post for a commissioning editor in maths – a senior career post – in a national broadsheet newspaper, and received only one suitable reply. Many organisations, if they found themselves in a similar situation, would quite rightly take the view that an advertisement would simply be a waste of money.

To cut down the effort involved in conventional recruiting methods, many employers are using other means – both formal and informal – to find suitable people.

The formal approach is for a company to brief a headhunting agency on the sort of person it needs. The agency then uses its database and/or contacts to find a suitable shortlist of candidates who meet the criteria. If, as a jobseeker, you want to use this route to a new job, you need to approach the various agencies (see 'Where jobs come from', below, for more on agencies) with your CV and suggest a meeting to see if there is a good fit between the sort of openings they have and your skills and experience. Some agencies use only a database, so you need to send in your CV and ask for your name to be put on the database to be considered for jobs. Others eschew databases and start each assignment afresh with a clean sheet and research using their contacts. Some use both. Whichever sort of agency you approach, make sure you are clear about how to project yourself and that you are articulate about your skills and achievements.

Agencies make their money by charging the employers whose recruitment requirement briefs they take on; the amount charged is usually based on a percentage of the initial annual salary (together, possibly, with the cost of any advertising placed).

The informal approach is for both employers and jobseekers to use industry, business and personal contacts. If you are looking for a job, let it be known to people in your network. Again, make sure you convey clearly and succinctly what you want to do and what your profile is. See 'Where jobs come from', below, for ideas on how to build up and use contacts.

The use of interim managers by organisations to fill gaps caused by take-overs, management buy-outs or major restructures is another way into employment for those at senior management level (see Chapter 1). The people taken on as interim managers are usually very experienced older workers who can be parachuted into difficult situations in the expectation that they will be able to turn the business around, keep an important project on track, or at least hold it together until a permanent appointment can be made or things settle down again. Often such temporary managers are offered short-term contracts of three months in the first instance which are then extended to six or more months.

Fitting your attributes to the employer's requirements

As a jobseeker, you will have to make a lot of the running yourself. In your letter of application, for example, you need to emphasise and demonstrate how well you fit the job profile, rather than merely hope that someone speed-reading CVs and covering letters at the company concerned (or an agency) will notice your key attributes. Another point to bear in mind – and this is a fundamental change from the past – is that your CV should not just describe the duties you performed in your different jobs, but show how well you achieved them (see Chapter 5 for details on how to do this).

The consequences of these changes in recruitment practice are that you need to be able to answer three basic questions in a CV, in letters of application, on application forms and at interviews:

(1) Can you do the job?
(2) Will you do the job?
(3) Will you fit in?

In an old-style recruitment process interviewers would have considered Question 1 in some depth, and part of Question 2. If all had gone well, the personnel department would have taken up references and then offered you the job. However, the interviewers would have information only on your past, which is not always a successful indicator of your ability to perform in the future.

That is why Questions 2 and 3 have come into play. They are useful because they try to determine more accurately how a candidate will fit in with the company's culture, his or her motivation and determination to succeed in the new job, the sort of person he or she is, and how he or she has handled things in the past. These factors do have a bearing on how someone is likely to perform in the future. For example, an interviewer asking you about mistakes you have made in the past is not interested in knowing whether you have ever made any (indeed, an answer to the effect that you haven't is likely to be greeted with some scepticism) but in how you have handled the errors and managed the consequences. Chapter 5 looks at each of these three questions in detail.

Where jobs come from

It may come as a surprise to those who think that responding to an advertisement is the most common way of getting a job that up to 50 per cent of management and supervisory posts are filled by networking, and the rest through agencies and speculative approaches as well as through advertisements. There are variations across different industries or occupations: for example, it is thought that recruitment agencies place a larger proportion of people in accountancy or computing jobs than in other areas. In the USA, the number of jobs filled through networking is even higher than in the UK, at 75 per cent.

The Internet is now an extremely useful medium for helping organisations and individuals to find each other. This is true at all stages of job search, whether in researching organisations or industries, looking for advertised vacancies, or networking. Both organisations and candidates can post their details on job sites, enter their criteria, and see what comes along. Many agencies now operate on-line, and some newsgroups can be used for networking or even for job offers and applications.

A survey by Reed Business Information in 2000 gives some indication of the degree of use and relative success in finding jobs via the Internet. The question was: 'Apart from searching for vacancies, have you ever done any of the following on a recruitment web site?'

Looked for information on a particular company	46%
Posted your CV on a site	41%
Applied on-line to a prospective employer	38%
Applied on-line and had a job interview	23%
Applied on-line and had a job offer as a result	15%

Networking

Researching an industry, occupation or organisation is, as has been pointed out, a crucial first step in making any long-term career decisions (more details later in this chapter). One simple but effective way of doing this is to tap into your network of friends, family, colleagues and ex-colleagues and ask them detailed questions about their jobs, the organisations they work for and whether any vacancies exist within their companies that would suit you. Being embarrassed to do this may result in the loss of vital opportunities.

Networking can be used in three aspects of job search: factual research, looking at trends and possibilities, and scouting for work. Depending on which of these three stages you are at, your approach to people will be different.

Factual research
You could use your network in addition to web- or library-based research to seek facts about specific industries or companies to expand your knowledge of them. This could involve talking to people or reading up on, say, the current level of salaries in a particular industry or companies starting up or diversifying.

Trends and possibilities
You could keep track of new trends in industries by reading trade journals and the business pages of the broadsheet newspapers or

asking for help from your network contacts. Staying aware of these things could give you an edge over others in a similar situation.

Work opportunities

This is the least factually based of the three sorts of research and is likely to be the one you feel least comfortable about. However, you could combine it with gleaning information on trends or expansion news by saying to your contact, for example, 'I thought XYZ always kept its projects in-house. I hear now that it is contracting things out . . .'

How to network

Building up your network could take a little time and effort but it will be worth it. You could plan it by first writing in a circle in the centre of a blank page a short phrase describing what sort of job you are researching. Think of its applications or the industries you could find such work in, and write them along little lines branching out in different directions around your original idea. You could then put the names of people you could contact to get information from along further lines joined up to the previous ones, and so on until you get a 'map' of your network spreading out from your central thought (see overleaf).

If you use the research interview techniques detailed in 'How to choose an occupation, industry or organisation' (see page 118) and keep in touch with your contacts – they are unlikely to consider an occasional telephone call from you intrusive – you will most probably hear of job openings. It is also worth talking to people regularly because your priorities may change such that your job search takes a different turn. They, or some of their friends and associates, may be able to help you more than they could before.

When networking, remember:

- you are not asking directly for a job, but gathering information on a company. A good way of establishing contact with someone you have never met but is known to someone you know would be to write a letter, email or telephone and say, 'I am interested in changing to ABC (the person's industry, occupation, etc.), but I really need to find out more about it. Jim Robinson suggested I contact you. Could you spare some time to talk to me about how you got started?' Ask to meet the person for no more than half an

How to build up a network

hour. Prepare some intelligent and open questions ('How did you start?'; 'It must have been difficult during the recession: what did your company do about . . .?'; 'I saw in the local paper that you have signed a new contract with XYZ. How will that affect your production capacity?')

- to start with someone you know and ask him or her about his or her job, industry, or company. Imagine you are going to write up what you discover into a short profile listing the highs and lows, the way in, the way up, career prospects, salary, perks, etc.
- to ask for two more names of people your contact knows whom you can talk to
- to write or telephone to say 'thank you'. A stock of attractive cards is useful for this
- to move on to the two new contacts you have, see them, ask for two from each of them, see the four new people, and so on.

If you would feel more comfortable making the initial contact in writing rather than by a telephone call, the following sort of letter can be productive.

Address

Date

Contact's name
Organisation's name and address

Dear [name],

Your name was given to me by . . . ., who suggested I write to you to find out more about . . . ., as I understand from [contact] that you may be recruiting soon/have recently been awarded a large contract. I am very interested in your organisation as I read recently that you . . .

I know [contact] from my time at XYZ Limited when we worked on the . . . . project together [mention achievement here]. My experience and skills have been in . . . . and . . . . I now want to broaden my experience/develop my work in . . . . Would it be possible to have a brief meeting with you to discuss the types of vacancy in your organisation that might be suitable for someone with my background?

I look forward to hearing from you.

Yours sincerely,

Your signature
Your name typed.

Do not despair if some of these letters are unsuccessful. It may be nothing to do with you, but simply that the organisation receives lots of similar requests and cannot acknowledge all of them. Even though you may not achieve a meeting, the person you wrote to may send you information about the company which will help with your background job search.

Networking works because of two truisms: 'people buy people' and 'it's a small world'. As has been pointed out, one of the vital questions interviewers need to answer is, 'Will this person fit in?' So if, while networking, you have made a favourable impression on someone and a job comes up in his or her organisation, it is possible that he or she will think of you first. An employer will use his or her networks to find a known, rather than an unknown, quantity. Moreover, the cost in time and money of conventional recruitment advertising, added to the risk of eventually hiring someone who does not fit in, mean that more and more companies are deciding that it is easier, quicker and less expensive to ask around their friends, associates, business colleagues, suppliers, customers, etc. and find someone suitable that way. Some organisations offer existing employees a 'finders fee' for successfully introducing someone to the organisation. In short, they put out feelers and use their networks. Of course, you will be doing the same. It is quite common for employer and employee to find each other using this method, because many networks interconnect, especially in certain industries and occupations.

It may seem that networking does not accord with best practice as far as equal opportunities policies go, but it is usually the case that organisations use their networks of informal and formal contacts merely to *identify* potential candidates and then go on to recruit in a fair way.

Different industries undoubtedly vary in the use made of networking. Because fitting into an organisation's culture is so important for the middle and senior management appointments, it is particularly likely that networking will be used to find these people. This is also because CVs and application letters may not give sufficient clues to whether someone would fit in or not, whereas a personal recommendation is more than likely to. So networking becomes more successful, and more crucial, the older you get and the higher you advance in your chosen field.

Advertised posts

Although it is true that networking accounts for the filling of an ever-increasing number of vacancies, it is by its very nature a hidden means of recruitment. For many jobseekers, especially those who have yet to establish networks, advertisements in newspapers, in the trade press and on the Internet are the first and most obvious means of discovering job openings in particular organisations. Jobs in different occupations are advertised on specific days by individual newspapers (see opposite page).

Job advertisements in broadsheet newspapers

	Daily Telegraph/ Sunday Telegraph	Guardian/Observer	Financial Times	Independent/ IOS	Times/ Sunday Times
Monday	N/A	Creative, media & sales/ New media & e-commerce/ Marketing & PR/Secretarial	Accountancy, banking & financial markets (up to £40,000)/Law	IT/Telecommunications/ Engineering	IT
Tuesday	N/A	Higher education/Further education/Schools/TEFL/ Courses	N/A	N/A	Legal
Wednesday	Education	Executive senior & management appts/ Finance/Housing/ Regeneration/Environment/ Health/Social care/Courses	N/A	Finance/Legal/Banking/ Secretarial	Secretarial/Education
Thursday	General	On-line (IT & telecommunications)/ Graduate appts/Science & technology/Courses	Accountancy, banking & financial markets (all levels)/General/IT	General/Graduate appts/ Education/Public/Media	IT, telecommunications & e-commerce/ Graduate appts & 2nd jobbers/General/ Senior managerial
Friday	N/A	N/A	N/A	N/A	Media, sales & marketing/Secretarial
Saturday	Music	Repeat of Monday– Thursday/General appts/ Courses	Law (repeat of Monday) and General/IT (repeat of Thursday)	N/A	N/A
Sunday	General (repeat of Thursday	Executive senior & management appts/IT & telecommunications	N/A	General (summary)	General managerial appts (£35,000+)
Web site	www.appointment-plus.co.uk *From May 2001:* www.jobs.telegraph.co.uk	www.jobsunlimited.co.uk	www.ftcareerpoint.com	N/A	www.thetimes-appoints.co.uk www.sunday-times-appoints.co.uk

How to read an advertisement

While a good advertisement deters all but the genuinely suitable, the converse is also true: a bad or indifferent one, which is vague about the job, the company or the kind of person needed, invites everyone to write in. However, responding to a poorly worded advertisement could be a complete waste of time for you because it will be next to impossible to write a letter of application that will match ill-defined requirements and therefore it becomes all the harder for you to get shortlisted.

Make sure that you are selective in what you apply for. Learn to 'read' the advertisement, what the company is saying about itself, and about the position. Is this really the job you want, or is it just vaguely in the right area? Try to match your aspirations with what is in the advertisement. A well-balanced, targeted application takes some time to prepare, so you might as well spend your time on a job you have a chance of getting, and want to get.

But how do you learn to distinguish between bad, indifferent and good advertisements? The three advertisements that follow are all for the same job.

Exceptional individuals   **Exceptional salary**

Our client, a subsidiary of a £multi-million multinational company, is seeking to further enhance its continuing success as an established market leader in its niche product area. To enable it to exceed its present high volume of sales, it needs fearless team managers, change managers and great opportunists to meet ambitious business targets.

To be successful each player will need to make valuable, high-profile contributions to a progressive, motivated and professional team. You will need quite exceptional business acumen, interpersonal skills, individual flair and creativity to meet the challenge of making our client one of the foremost business leaders in the next decade. If this level of challenge and opportunity appeals to you, apply now to . . .

This is an extreme example of a bad advertisement, because after reading it you would not be in a position to answer the following crucial questions.

- What is the job?
  The advert is so clogged with jargon and cliché that it is impossible to work out what the job is. Reading between the lines, you could assume that it is a sales or business development role, but you cannot really be sure.
- What industry is the organisation in?
  It could be something you find uninspiring and in which you have no experience. On the other hand, it could be your industry, and you could be extremely well qualified, but you cannot tell . . . You may be tempted to put in an application just to make sure you are not missing a good opportunity.
- What experience does it need from the successful applicant?
- How many vacancies are there?
  The advertisement mentions 'team managers, change managers and great opportunists'. Is it in fact for three or more jobs – a team manager, a change manager and a great opportunist – or several of each?
- What competencies, skills or attitudes does the organisation need?
  It is clear that it wants people who are creative, but in what field? A fashion designer is creative, as is a software developer, and a trainer, a promotions and marketing manager . . .
- Where is the job based?
  There is no mention of the location.
- What is the salary package?
  If no indication of the likely salary is given, you cannot immediately see whether the job is too senior or too junior for you.

Some advertisements are simply indifferent, but could turn out to be more of a drain on your resources and time because you may be tempted into responding to them. On the one hand, the advertisement may not be bad enough for you to dismiss out of hand, but on the other it may not be worded clearly enough for you to feel you have a good chance.

Sell only the best to the best!
Senior Account Manager   Scotland   Excellent package

We are a world-beater in our field with a unique product, the xyz software for the extractive industries. As a multinational player with a blue-chip client base, we pride ourselves on the cutting-edge quality of our product development and marketing.

    We are seeking to appoint a core account manager with excellent communication and people skills. No stranger to frequent travel, you will be comfortable in international environments. We need a competitive team player with industry knowledge who is hungry enough to keep chasing new business. Interested? Contact . . .

This advertisement gives some useful information, but slips into jargon and unclear language. What can you extract from this one?

- Location: you know it is Scotland, but not precisely where. If you were to apply for the job but discover that relocation would be necessary, this could be an impediment to your accepting it. For example, if you have to be within one hour's travelling time of Penrith because of family commitments, you could not apply for a job in Aberdeen.
- Salary and benefits: they are not spelt out, only promised as 'excellent'. The job looks quite senior, so you could hope it is enough, but you are not sure, are you?
- Travel: you can see some travel is involved, but how much is not made clear.
- The job: it is difficult to work out the scope and responsibilities of the job. Excellent communication and people skills are needed, but in what context? Would it be with customers, suppliers, staff?
- Skills and achievements: what is stated ('competitive team player with industry knowledge who is hungry enough to keep chasing . . .') is rather clouded by jargon.
- The company and the culture: the language is clear ('we are a world-beater', 'blue-chip client base', 'we pride ourselves', 'hungry enough'), so you can form an opinion about how this organisation sees itself. Does it match what you want?

Senior Account Manager, IT   Aberdeen   c.£45,000 + car
Company's name and logo   + benefits + re-location

The company
XYZ develops and markets xyz software, with clients in 25 countries and over 130,000 installations. Our core customers are in the petroleum, gas and oil industries.

The job
We need an experienced account manager who can manage large accounts and prospect for new ones in our core business areas in Europe and the Middle East. Based in Aberdeen, you will lead a team of six account executives, who are based in northern Europe and the Middle East. There is some international travel, averaging two months a year. We are a small company; as we grow, so will this job.

And you?
If you can show us core skills and achievements in account management, customer service, new business development, people skills and knowledge of our industries, we would be delighted to hear from you. Please send your CV and a short letter explaining your potential contribution to the company to . . . (name, address) by (date).

Visit our web site at: www.gasandoil.org.uk to find out more about us.

This is a good advertisement, because it would deter everyone but the genuinely suitable. For people who do have the right skills and achievements, it is an excellent job, with prospects. The advertisement gives you some clues about the organisation's culture ('We are a small company; as we grow, so will this job'), it is informative ('you will lead a team of six . . .') and the language is quite open and informal ('if you can show us . . .'). Any applicant can judge whether to apply or not after checking the match on important details:

- skills
- achievements
- the company and the cultural fit ('as we grow, so will this job', 'we would be delighted to hear from you')

- duties and scope of the job
- career prospects
- the closing date
- what form the application should be in ('send your CV and a short letter explaining your . . .')
- industry
- salary scale and benefits, including relocation costs.

As these examples indicate, an advertisement can tell you a lot about an organisation by how clear its language is. Failing to be clear in an advertisement for which it is paying a lot of money can often be a warning sign of a general lack of clarity in the organisation. So beware!

Evidently, language can repel or attract applicants, and can provide clues about the culture of the organisation. You might want an interesting job, but not at any price. Recruitment is a two-way process, and you and the employer are both buying and selling. The sort of people you will work with, how the company is organised, the opportunities for training and promotion, what the physical environment is like – these are important as well. A survey by PricewaterhouseCoopers in 2000 confirms that the formula for staff retention has three elements: a good remuneration package, opportunities for self-improvement and an enriching working environment.

In the last advertisement example the recruiter has used open and informal language, which can be very attractive. An exercise that you could find useful is to take two differently coloured highlighter pens and go through a range of advertisements, highlighting language which attracts or repels you. You can mark whatever you like, including particular phrases that you think are informative: such as 'hungry for', 'meeting the challenge', 'seeking to recruit', 'please tell us why you fit our remit', 'be part of'. Sometimes, adverts will give you information about the physical environment that may be important to you. For example: 'pleasant no-smoking offices', 'two minutes' walk from the station', 'staff restaurant', 'close to shops and parks', 'free parking'. After marking a number of advertisements, you can often see a pattern emerge.

The image an organisation has chosen to project is communicated through the design of the advert as well as its language. This includes the typographic style, size of headings, size of advert, use of colour, use of a border/logo – they all combine to create an impression. You could use your highlighter pens again, and mark those that you like or dislike. This technique can also be useful when researching industries and occupations (see later in this chapter).

Becoming quick at reading advertisements will pay dividends – with many organisations reporting a skills shortage, there are lots to read. A study by Cranfield School of Management in 2000 showed employers to be having difficulty in recruitment at all levels, from graduate entry to board level.

Replying to advertisements

This is covered in detail in Chapter 5. The main points to remember are that you should tailor your CV and write a targeted letter for each job you apply for, matching what you can offer with what the organisation wants.

Agencies

Agencies can help organisations in their recruiting procedures in a variety of ways. Some specialise in executive searches, or head-hunting. They use a database and/or their network of contacts to find suitable candidates for specific vacancies in client companies. In a way, it is a formalised method of networking, for which they are paid a substantial fee. Their research is highly targeted and they usually deliver only a small number of potential candidates for each vacancy to their clients.

The other activity agencies perform is recruitment, which involves managing some or all of the recruitment process on behalf of their clients. The minimum service is to place the advertisement, handle any telephone enquiries and open the applications, which are then handed on to the client. The next level of service is to sort applications into piles, such as interview/marginal/reject, suggest a shortlist, and hand the list to the client, without doing the interviews. Some agencies go further, shortlisting and carrying out the first round of interviews, of up to perhaps a dozen people. The client company would then do the subsequent interviews. Services such as psychometrics and the use of assessment centres are also offered by some agencies.

Agencies have to manage two sets of relationships: one with client companies, from which they need to get a clear brief about the jobs they are recruiting for – for example, the skills and experience required, seniority, reporting structure, some indication of the package and so on; and the other with the jobseekers. If you are looking for work, it is worth registering with a selected group of agencies.

Most agencies and organisations will now accept – and often encourage – applications by email, as this can speed up the process of selection. An emailed application will usually look better than a faxed version. Also, because the information arrives electronically, it can be easily manipulated into a form which best suits their system – again cutting down on time and effort at their end. Often there will also be a web site that you can visit. This can include details of current vacancies, how the agency or organisation operates, whom to contact and how to apply for a vacancy; and may contain more information than the printed advert, such as an expanded list of duties and/or competencies – after all, they are not paying for the number of words on a web site, unlike a printed advert. You can often apply directly via the web site. If a web address is given, it is always worth having a look.

Some agencies specialise in particular job functions and occupations. For example, they may be well known for working in the finance sector and have expanded into legal and marketing divisions. Others may specialise in not-for-profit organisations and charities. Some may have built up expertise in particular functions, and place, for example, programmers, office staff, catering and hotel staff.

Another kind of specialisation is to handle only specific levels of job, say, middle and senior management ones, and not be limited to any particular industry sector.

Choosing an agency

With so many agencies to choose from, you may find that it is difficult to know where to begin. It is worth taking the time to choose carefully the agencies you wish to use, and manage them well. Many advertise in *Yellow Pages* under Employment Agencies; it should be clear from the advertisements whether they have any specialised interests.

A number of agencies are listed in *The Executive Grapevine: the Directory of Executive Recruitment Consultants*. This is published annually and is expensive to buy; however, it is available in most public libraries. Bear in mind though that agencies choose to be included in it, so it is not an independent or objective listing. None the less, it is very detailed, with numerous cross-referenced indices (by sector, salary band, and location of job and agency).

Personal recommendation is also very useful. Ask around your friends and colleagues and find out what their experiences have been of particular agencies. You could, of course, just walk into an agency and judge for yourself how efficient and friendly it appears, depending on how you are dealt with. The way agencies receive you if you make a personal visit *is* instructive. Even details such as whether you are invited to take a seat in a waiting area, whether the waiting area is attractive or horrible, whether you are offered a drink, how long you are kept waiting, etc. will vary from agency to agency. It may seem petty to judge an agency on whether its staff give you a coffee or not, but a lack of customer care in small details may betray a similar attitude in how it handles the whole process. You could also respond to advertisements placed by these agencies, and see how they deal with your application. As with applying directly to an organisation, remember that you and the agency are both buying and selling. Choose only those you think you can work with.

Staff at some agencies are extremely professional. For example, when they see you they may take a digital photo for reference; take great care to do in-depth interviews; have sophisticated software to record your details, and to keep track of conversations and interviews; and be speedy and polite.

Using an agency

The first step in making contact with an agency is to send a good letter or email and your CV.

The following is an example of a suitable letter with which to introduce yourself.

Contact details

Date

Agency's name and address

Dear [named person],

I enclose my CV. You will see I am working at XYZ Limited where I have been . . . . [job title] for the last . . . years. Prior to that I worked at . . . . I am a qualified . . . . ., with . . . years' experience of the . . . . industry.

[Optional] Because of cutbacks/business difficulties my department has been closed down/my team has been made redundant/a number of people have been made redundant, and I am among them. I am now looking for similar employment in the . . . . industry in the . . . . [geographical area] at a salary in the range of £. . . . . .

I understand your agency specialises in . . . . posts, so I should like to see you to discuss any suitable vacancies you might have on your books. I will telephone your office in a few days, or if you would like to contact me my telephone number is . . . . . .

Yours sincerely,

Your signature

Your name typed.

Follow the letter up with a telephone call about seven to ten days later. This is partly because some of the larger agencies receive hundreds of unsolicited letters each week, but also, whatever the size of the agency, this is a good length of time – not long enough for your information to have gone astray, yet long enough for it to consider what you have written. Consultants in agencies are busy people, so you have to be persistent to get through to them. The purpose of the call is not merely to check if the agency has received your CV; you should also ask whether it has any suitable jobs for you. Make sure that you do not waste the consultant's time: be focused and clear about what you have to say. Any consultant worth his or her salt will use the telephone conversation as an impromptu interview – he or she will probably say, 'Tell me a bit about yourself,' so you must be prepared for that invitation. Do not be caught on the hop by this. First impressions count, so make sure it is a good one.

Alternatively, you may be called in for an interview. In many respects, this will be like any initial job interview – a 'let's meet and get to know each other' meeting. The consultant will probe your competence, motivation, and try to gauge possible cultural fit with clients. He or she will try to judge your commercial 'worth' to the agency because it has to 'sell' you on to the client. Afterwards, the consultant will probably ask you to keep in regular telephone contact. This will be especially important if any of your details change. Consultants often have assistants who will handle the day-to-day candidate–client contact, so make an effort to get to know this person as well. Give the agency feedback on any interviews you have been for, your impressions of the client and what the job was like, and whether you liked the company or the job. The agency may be retained by the client company to do the first round of interviews; even if it is not, consultants at the agency may be asked for their opinion of the candidate. Either way, it is worth your while to invest some time and effort to get to know the agency.

Increasingly, agencies have networked databases on which they record client information. As the whole agency will be networked in this way, once you are on its books, you can be sure that when you telephone and give the consultant or his or her assistant any new information, it will be input directly to your candidate record. The better agencies will update your information as you attend interviews, using feedback from you and from the employing organisation, so that any consultant anywhere in the agency can log on and look at your information. This makes it doubly important for you to treat the first telephone call you make to the agency as an interview, as someone will record his or her judgement of you on the database, and not necessarily in the politest of terms.

Keep a note of when you first got in touch with the agency, the name of the person to whom you spoke, a summary of what you discussed, any jobs you may be suitable for, and any other relevant information. You may find it helpful to have a single sheet for each agency, which you can update periodically. Some agencies will send you a letter of rejection if there is nothing suitable on their books.

Sadly, some will not have the courtesy to reply at all – but at least you know they are not worth spending any more time on! Some will ask to see you for an interview even if nothing suitable is on their books. This is because they may like to get some sense of your personal qualities, what motivates you, your interpersonal skills and so on – in other words, aspects of you which cannot be conveyed very well in a CV. This makes good business sense. When an agency recommends a candidate it wants that person to fit the job and personal profile as closely as possible, otherwise it will have an unhappy client, who will not return to the agency in the future.

If for any reason you are unhappy with the way you have been treated by an agency and wish to complain about it, contact the Employment Agency Standards Office★ helpline.

On-line job search

Opportunities for job-hunting on the Internet are growing rapidly, with an ever-increasing number of sites advertising jobs. Organisations may advertise their vacancies on their own web site, a job site, or use an on-line recruitment agency. Although the medium is different, job-hunting on-line is basically the same as with the traditional method of scouring newspapers and other publications – you look for job adverts, contact the organisation or agency, and send out your CV – but it is quicker and simpler and you have access to a far greater number of vacancies. Until recently the kinds of jobs which were advertised on-line were predominantly in IT and computing, but this is changing.

The immediacy of the Internet is useful to recruiters as well as jobseekers: a vacancy can be posted on the Net as soon as it becomes available. For this reason, and also because it is much cheaper than advertising in the press, advertising on-line is becoming increasingly popular. A list of job sites and recruitment agencies is given in the addresses section, but do remember that dotcom companies are appearing and disappearing at an amazing rate, and that these are no exception.

To compete with agencies that operate exclusively on-line, most of the traditional recruitment agencies have added on-line recruitment to their range of services. The advice is as before: shop around, ask around friends and colleagues, try out a few – you need to find agencies you can do business with. Many agencies have a searchable database which you can browse, gaining a snapshot of the job market in a particular country or sector. Job sites or agencies may offer an email 'job agent' facility, whereby you are automatically notified as soon as a suitable vacancy occurs. You simply post your details, specifying fields of interest (type of job, level/seniority, location, etc.), and the job agent selects jobs that match your criteria and sends them to your email address. Of course, as in any such system, the keywords you choose are important. If you are too general, you end up with lots of jobs you would not be suitable for. If you are too specific, then you will not receive anything. You can alter your criteria, depending on the response you get.

The Internet also offers an unparalleled opportunity to research an organisation well before you apply for a position or go for an interview – assuming, of course, that it has a web site that contains useful information! A web site acts as a 'window on the world', and it is used actively to promote the organisation to its visitors, whoever they may be. Increasingly, web sites are used for recruitment as well as marketing, and many have a 'working for us' button on which you can click. Of course, the organisation chooses what goes on the web site, so remember that you will not be getting impartial information.

As we have seen, networking is an important research tool. You can also network on the Internet, using newsgroups. There are around 30,000 discussion forums, some of which are at best unsavoury or at worst illegal. Do not be put off by these few bad apples; remember that newsgroups can put you in contact with people all over the world, in your industry or area of interest – a potential mine of information. If you do decide to log on to a newsgroup, be specific about your goals, search for your fields of interest, and post one or two intelligent questions – someone will respond.

Direct cold-calling

Direct cold-calling or making a speculative approach involves contacting an individual manager and/or the HR/personnel department in a company and asking if any of its job vacancies are suitable for you, or requesting to be kept on a vacancies mailing list, or on file for future reference. Once you have researched an industry and organisation (see 'How to choose an industry, occupation or organisation', below), you will be in a good position to choose a few companies that you would like to work for. Write to named individuals – you can get their names from trade journals or newspapers (local and national), or by asking friends and colleagues who may know the companies, or even by telephoning and asking for a relevant name – and make sure your letter and CV are properly targeted.

Many organisations, both small and large, receive unsolicited letters and CVs each week. The following mistakes guarantee swift disposal into the bin:

* heading up the letter 'Dear Sir/Madam'. This makes it perfectly obvious that this is one of a batch of unfocused applications sent out by you
* compounding this by going on to say how much you would like to 'contribute to your organisation's success' without specifying how or showing that you know what the company does
* sending a letter where the main body of the letter is in one type-face, and the organisation's details and the date are in another, demonstrating once again the 'scattergun' approach
* sending a letter and CV which details experience you have in industries completely unrelated to the organisation. Again, the message is loud and clear: 'I could not be bothered to check whether what I have is relevant to what you might want, but here it is anyway'
* writing in a very feisty or aggressive manner, along the lines of 'Have I got a good deal for you!' At best, this is misplaced humour; at worst it is ill-judged and crass
* demanding to know the salary package and perks you would expect to get.

Some focused research will ensure you do not make these sorts of mistakes. Concentrate on the industry or industries you are really attracted to, and jobs which you are at least partially qualified to do.

How to choose an industry, occupation or organisation

If you are looking to change career, you need to address various general issues about work before homing in on a particular job or even a specific organisation.

- Do I want a full-time or a part-time job?
- Am I prepared to job-share?
- Am I working to replace a full-time salary, or am I working to supplement a pension?
- Am I prepared to move?
- Do I want to change job function?
- Do I want to change industries?
- Do I want to start my own business or franchise?
- Do I want to do voluntary work?

The income/expenditure calculation in Chapter 2 will help you assess what level of income you would ideally need to earn. Industrial and occupational trends, including changes in working patterns (flexible working, increase in temporary and part-time work and self-employment), as described in Chapter 1, may have set you thinking about what you would like to change to. You will also need to examine your motivations and circumstances (see Chapter 3).

Research

In addition to the financial and job opportunity aspects of choosing a new career, you also need information, and lots of it. 'Research interviews' are an increasingly popular way of finding out more about an industry, occupation or organisation. They do not replace web-based, desk-bound or library-based research, such as that generated by reading relevant journals, the financial and business pages of newspapers, directories, yearbooks and statistical surveys – instead, they supplement it, and add a dimension of real-life experience which you really need to help you decide whether a particular industry, occupation or organisation would suit you.

Research interviews work like this: you look around your friends, relatives, colleagues and acquaintances and think about what they do – the industry they work in, the job they do, the organisation they work for. If something appeals, you arrange a structured talk with the person who does it. A chat would probably feel more natural, but it needs to be planned well to be sure you get the information you need. One way to think about the talk is, 'Could I write this up as a short profile of this industry, this job, this organisation?'

Researching an industry

Using the structured-talk approach with individuals who work in a particular industry is a good way of researching it. For example, if you were interested in the tourism industry you could:

- write to the head of the trade association for information on the industry and possible career pathways
- join the trade association. Many have local groups, and often you can attend talks organised by them as an unqualified member, for example, with associate or student status. There is usually an opportunity to talk to people – including the speaker – afterwards
- write/talk to staff at the relevant Industry Training Organisation (ITO), a government-recognised body which all industries have. They exist to encourage professional qualifications and training, so ask them about qualifications and suitable courses. There will also be useful information on their web site
- write/talk to tutors and students on relevant courses, which you can research at your local reference library or via your ITO. Many introductory-level books on specific industries will list appropriate courses in a reference section
- use any contacts you may have (local or otherwise) to talk to people at local tourist attractions. Volunteer as a guide, work in the teashop or sell souvenirs
- contact nationwide organisations such as the National Trust, and visit their local properties
- go into travel agents, see the sort of jobs people do, the type of holidays and tourist attractions which are promoted and how they are promoted (cheap package tours, expensive tours, tailored tours and so on)
- contact and visit your local Tourist Information Centre.

You can try the structured-talk approach with some of the people you meet. The more experienced people are likely to have a broader industry-wide view, so choose carefully. Suitable questions include:

- What are the pros and cons of working in the tourism industry?
- What are the career pathways?
- What qualifications/relevant experience would I need?
- What are the sort of jobs people start in, and at what salary?
- What are career prospects like?

- What are the current and future trends within the industry?
- What is very popular, what sort of attractions will be developed in the next ten years, and how will that affect the jobs, skills and experience of people working in the industry?
- What sort of people work in tourism?

This will yield plenty of useful information, much of it peppered with personal views from individuals, but it will not be enough. You will also need quantitative information, so:

- read the trade press for the news, gossip and job advertisements in the tourism industry
- look in the local and national press for jobs and information on the industry
- read relevant books on the industry
- collect travel brochures from different companies: does any one company attract you and, if so, in what way(s)?
- look at the different sorts of tourist attractions, for example, historic towns or houses, heritage trails, ancient monuments, woodlands and gardens, working farms, industrial archaeology sites: does anything particularly attract you?

Researching an occupation

Once you have taken a good look at the industry as a whole – and you like what you see – you will be in a better position to start homing in on a particular job within it. For example, you may decide that you would like to be a tour guide. Does anyone you know have a contact who works as a tour guide? You may find someone within your network to whom you can talk. If not, can you find someone from your earlier research, for example, in the Tourist Information Centres or the local tourist attractions you visited, whom you could approach for a short talk? The sort of questions you should ask include:

- What are the pros and cons of being a tour guide?
- How did you get started?
- What qualifications or relevant previous experience did you have?
- How did you get those qualifications/experience; where, and how expensive are the courses?

- What are your future prospects like?
- What skills do you use most?
- What, for you, makes a good day, and what makes a bad day?
- What are the salary levels like? (at the start, mid-career and end-of-career)
- What are the perks of the job?
- What is a typical day like?
- What are the hours?
- Based on your knowledge of me, do you think I might be happy and good at doing a similar job?

With all this information you will get a real sense of whether being a tour guide might suit you. You can improve the quality of your information and extend your network by asking the contact for the names of a couple of other people who are tour guides or in a related field. Go for a structured talk with them as well. Use your first contact's name to open the door to these new contacts: they probably have a lot of people they do not know approaching them. Ask them for a couple of names, and before you know it you will have sought information from as many tour guides as you want.

Researching an organisation

When you are researching an organisation you can repeat the exercise of having a structured talk with someone who works there. Most organisations put effort into presenting a good face to the public. If you are serious about working there and want the cultural fit to be right, you need to get behind that public face, and preferably before you start a job there. Talking to an employee is one way of doing this. Again, think to yourself, 'At the end of this talk, could I write up my information as a profile of this company?' This time the questions might be:

- What is the company like to work for, really?
- How are people promoted?
- What does the company look for in new recruits?
- What is the prevailing company culture?
- What is the company's policy on training?
- What is its policy on developing staff?
- Based on your knowledge of me, do you think I might be happy there?

- How is the company structured?
- What are individual people like to work for? (you may not get an objective opinion, but it might be useful)
- How does the organisation define 'success'? (e.g. is it market share, profit, happy customers, efficient systems?)
- What is good/admirable about it as an employer?
- What is bad/less than admirable about it as an employer?

If the organisation is large, you will get only an individual's view of a limited aspect of it, so try to talk to a few other people. If the organisation is small or medium-sized, then perhaps talking to one person will be enough for you to form an opinion. If the company is local to your area, keep an eye on the local press for information about it to supplement your knowledge and ask around your friends and contacts for news about it. Also read the trade press and national press to pick up useful news.

Again, an organisation's web site is another very valuable source of information. In addition to details of current vacancies, it can tell you about the company culture, how it is organised, its products, recruitment procedure, and so on. You may not have access to a PC at home, but there are now internet cafes in many towns, where you can have a coffee and surf the Net. You may also be able to use the Internet at your local library.

Research using advertisements

Advertisements can yield a lot of useful information to the career changer, at all the levels of occupation, industry and organisation.

Start by looking at an industry or occupation. As previously suggested, take two highlighter pens, one of a colour you like and the other one a colour you dislike. Go through the job advertisements in a broadsheet daily, Sunday newspaper, or a local one. With the colour you like, highlight the advertisements which appeal to you, owing to either their content or their style of presentation (typographic style, size of headings, ease of finding the relevant information). Then repeat the exercise with your 'dislike' pen, picking out industries or occupations you do not like. Look back over what you have highlighted: are there any features common to those you have marked? Do certain sorts of industries or occupations stand out as being more interesting than others? Once you have established this, you can do more detailed research in a library or the trade press, or by conducting research interviews.

Next, look at specific organisations within the occupations or industries you have narrowed the field to. Again, highlight with one colour those advertisements that attract your attention, and with another those that turn you off.

Advertisements are an organisation's PR tool – as we saw earlier, they telegraph a lot of revealing information to the outside world, sometimes inadvertently. Can you judge how they see themselves? Some organisations write verbose advertisements in which it can be difficult to find the job title. They take up so much space telling you about themselves that you cannot find out what they need you for. Would you want to work for an organisation which cannot marshal its thoughts sufficiently well to write a succinct piece of copy? An organisation which does not understand that potential candidates need to know about the job not just the company? An organisation which cannot be brief and comprehensible?

The wording of advertisements is very revealing. It can show whether the style of the organisation is formal or informal (e.g. 'we are looking to recruit' *vs* 'we need'), and what it values (e.g. 'customer satisfaction is our ultimate goal' *vs* 'we strive to maintain exceptionally high quality standards'). Bear in mind, though, that this may reflect the style not of the employing organisation but of a recruitment agency.

Review what you have highlighted. Do certain sorts of organisation or particular companies appeal? Do you like smaller companies, which are likely to be more informally run, or do the larger organisations, which may (or may not) be more highly structured and relatively formal, appeal more? Or would you prefer something in between? Once you have reached some conclusions, you can begin to research them in more depth by talking to people in the companies or using your local library. You could keep a close watch on what sort of jobs the organisations are recruiting for, and perhaps even make a speculative approach. Start keeping files and cuttings on what you are researching. Make KISS (Keep It Short and Simple) your watchword. You do not need an elaborate filing system, otherwise you will spend more time administering it than doing the job research, which is clearly counter-productive.

Do not ignore local newspapers: they are very useful sources of information for the career changer. Obviously, they will have only local jobs advertised in them, but they will also have news and articles on local organisations. You can find out which organisation has had planning permission withheld, which is expanding, which has just won a new contract, etc. This will be useful background information if you reply to a job advertisement or make a speculative approach ('I would be interested in working for you because I saw in the *XYZ Times* you have just been awarded the ABC contract, and I have a lot of experience of working with them.') You will also make a good impression at interview if you can ask well-informed questions such as 'I read that you have just got planning consent for an extension to your factory. How will this affect production/shift patterns/the packing department?' This technique can also be used with national papers and the trade press.

Recognising skills and achievements

As this chapter has emphasised throughout, jobseekers need to be clear about their skills and achievements to demonstrate competence and future potential to prospective employers. A skill might be defined as 'expertise' or as 'ability combined with experience', and achievement as 'accomplishment' or as 'application of skills to given situations'.

A CV can very easily just end up as a chronological listing of your life, but nowadays your CV, which will be in competition with many others, needs to be a real selling tool, and recognise that those doing the selecting do not have much time. For advice on how to write an effective CV for today's job marketplace, see Chapter 5.

Defining and describing yourself

One way of making your application stand out from the crowd is to use a short descriptive phrase about yourself which will stick in the mind of the person reading the CVs. Start by devising a short phrase (a thought bubble) that you feel describes you accurately. It could combine a personal attribute (e.g. friendly, informal), a skill (e.g. skilled trainer), and knowledge (say, with X years' experience in hotel/catering). 'Knowledge' can include industry experience as well as experience in particular jobs. The thought bubble needs to be short to capture the essential point. Depending on your experience, you might find you need two or three bubbles. You can use these pithy phrases as the basis of your CV.

For example, Brendan, aged 39, has a degree in economics and qualified as a management accountant (CIMA) in 1984. His jobs in the 1980s were in financial analysis and pricing in the IT and car rental businesses. In 1989 he moved to the auto-part industry and took on more commercial work such as due diligence and contract negotiation. He became interested in marketing and his company sponsored him to study for the Chartered Institute of Marketing's Diploma. Outside work, he especially enjoys food and wine and entertaining friends.

What could be in Brendan's bubbles? You could define him by occupation, by industry sector or by interests. He decided that his bubbles would be:

financial analysis	marketing	'commercial'
in IT or leisure	in IT or leisure	(defined as a mix of other two)

He wrote three different CVs to reflect the three bubbles, and began to look for jobs in each category. He found that the 'commercial' one kept attracting business development jobs which he thought were too sales-orientated to suit his skills or temperament. So he dropped the 'commercial' bubble to concentrate on the first two. In the end he got a job carrying out financial analysis in food retail, which also includes more commercial work such as looking at business propositions and marketing ideas. So he has managed a very felicitous fit for his skills, achievements and personal interests.

The thought-bubble approach works to your advantage because:

- you can write your CV based on those few words so it reflects that bubble, and it gives your CV focus
- it helps you to cut out details which do not fit the thought bubble, again, keeping your CV focused
- you can identify easily the jobs you are interested in because they do or do not fit the bubble. Therefore, you spend your precious time (and energy) on the jobs you have the greatest chance of getting

- interviews become much easier. Because you are clear about your vision of what you want, you can answer the questions more confidently, and you can also look at the organisation with a cooler head to check whether you like what you find
- if you use your network to look for work, you need to send a clear message so that people can link you with possible vacancies quickly and easily.

Compare these two statements:

> I have worked for a large charity for five years in a development job in South America. I have lost my job because of a recent restructure so I need a new job. Because of the uncertainties about what might happen, I have not had much feedback recently. I am not sure what I want to do next.

What is the bubble for this person? It could be 'Charity development worker'.

> I have been XYZ's regional manager in South America for five years, working closely with producers of fair trade goods. I enjoy working with people in a practical way, and have improved the quality and appeal of the goods. As a result of a restructure my job has been made redundant. I am looking for a job as a regional manager or director in fair trade where I can use my practical, people-based skills and fluent Spanish.

What is the bubble for this person? Possibly 'Fair trade manager, Spanish-speaking'.

In fact, it is the same person. If he puts out the first message on his network, he may hear about work, but whatever comes back will be vague. This is because the message was itself unclear in two fatal ways. First, it was woolly about his experience, and second, it did not clarify what he wanted to do next. The second message will be much more productive because people will be able to match what this person wants with any opportunities they hear about. The quantity of responses may be fewer, but the quality should be much higher. The power of the message would be increased even more if he could prioritise still further and define the non-negotiables, i.e. the things he must have in a job.

It is clear from the example of Brendan looking for work that you may need to broaden your view when you think about what work you do and what you want to do. It is very easy to become institutionalised and defined by a job title or your company.

For example, a very bright and able corporate manager working for a high-street bank saw himself solely as a Bank Manager for The XYZ Bank (his capital letters). He felt trapped, partly by his own description of himself but also because he had only ever worked at that particular bank. After career counselling and feedback from people outside the bank, he decided he was a manager who happened to work for that particular bank – a fundamental change in his view of himself. He has not left the bank, but, ironically, feels much more settled as he sees he has more options now – he could find work elsewhere because he has skills and accomplishments which are valuable and valued beyond the world of the bank. Nothing has changed except his perceptions.

People facing redundancy

If compulsory redundancy has affected or is likely to affect you, it may be difficult to see your abilities in a positive way. As described in Chapter 3, a person experiencing job loss goes through seven stages, ranging from shock and disbelief to understanding and getting a job. Stage 4 – acceptance – is the major turning point in the cycle, because it marks the phase when the person changes from being reactive – acting in response to events – to being proactive and taking charge of what is happening. If you have reached this stage, you should start taking stock of your skills and achievements.

Because you are likely to be looking for work from a position of being out of work, it is important that you are clear about what you are capable of doing and what you would like to do. This will help you to remain positive and focused on what you need to do next, and that means you can present a more confident face to the world. The example of Stephen Johnston in Chapter 3 showed that because he was helped by a counsellor to channel his energy more positively, he was able to pursue the caravan park idea with gusto and enthusiasm. These attitudes undoubtedly helped him when it came to convincing others, such as his wife and the bank manager.

People returning to work

Philip and Sarah George (see Chapter 3) decided to go travelling again because they were still uncertain about what to do next in terms of a career. However, before setting off they both took career advice so they could mull over their options while travelling. Before they left, Philip's bubbles were:

self-employment in catering   food retail management

DIY retail management

Philip has dual South African/British nationality so another option was to leave the UK and start a business in South Africa. Sarah is an experienced children's reference editor, so publishing was in one of her bubbles. Her other option was to join Philip in their own catering business.

Returning from their trip, they researched self-employment in catering for them both, looked at many possible sites, considered leases, and wrote plans for businesses in Bath and Norwich. Nothing seemed to gel – the location was wrong, or the price of the lease was too high, etc. Their second line of enquiry was the food retail management thought bubble. After some interviews and lots of research, Philip got a regional manager's job for a chain of American coffee shops. The organisation was new to the UK, and needed experienced local managers. Because there were teething problems, it was a good challenge for Philip, and after a year in the post, it has proved to be an evolving and involving job. Philip and Sarah also decided to make the life choice they had been considering earlier, and now have a young daughter, Ellie.

What you end up putting in your thought bubbles could change the longer you reflect on it. Penny James (see Chapter 3) did not want to return to her well-paid job in IT systems design after being a full-time mother for seven years, and was considering working with people who are disadvantaged. When she first considered the options, her thought bubbles were:

voluntary work   paid work

She and her husband looked at their finances and decided that they could manage if she wanted to do voluntary, rather than paid, work. She then had to re-define her bubbles again, and this time they were:

working with adults   working with children

Penny was aware that even if she worked outside the home in some capacity, she would still be the primary carer at home, so she discarded the option of working with children because it would be too similar to her regular work as a housewife and mother. This left working with adults. At this point she thought about her motivation. She realised that she really enjoyed using technology to help people find solutions to problems, hence her original interest in IT. She asked around her friends and acquaintances, and someone mentioned the social deprivation in an area of the city she lived in. This struck a chord in her, and she began to think seriously about how to help. She went to visit the Community Education Council in the area, and talked to staff there about her experience. They had plenty of people who wanted to help with the literacy programme, but no one who had good IT skills, so they were delighted that she had approached them. She found something she really loved doing, she knew that what she was doing was really needed, and took extra training to qualify as a paid adult literacy tutor.

Sadly, soon afterwards, her marriage failed, and Penny returned to her native Australia. Changed circumstances mean she now needs well-paid work. The re-training she had done in the UK enabled her to get to where she is now, namely doing cutting-edge programming for the Internet, in up-to-date languages. She is certain that if she had not done the basic skills work with adults, she would not have learnt the Microsoft PC products (such as Word, Excel and Access), and therefore would not have been able to start her current work, which is based on an Access database. She is very pleased with the career returner path she took.

Penny has successfully changed career: although she is still applying her original computing and IT skills, she is doing so in a very different context.

People in a rut and/or seeking change

If you are staying within your present industry or occupation, the context for your skills and achievements remains the same. Hilary Williamson (see Chapter 3), who drifted into banking and has stayed in this field ever since, has built up a lot of experience, so she could stay there. If she does, she can write and talk (in her CV and at interview respectively) about achievements such as her increasing financial competence, her involvement with corporate and personal customers, her particular interest in foreign currency/letters of credit, etc. For Hilary, one bubble would be:

> Experienced corporate banker,
> especially with multinationals

She has another option. She is now in her forties, and her motivations have changed such that she wants more independence – to play less by someone else's rules and more by her own. She has visited Brittany a number of times with the family over the years, and collects Breton-style pottery. Her French is reasonable. She gets on particularly well with one of her corporate customers, who imports and sells fine pottery from Limoges by direct mail and to well-known stores. She could research any possible convergence of interest between herself and this company. She has international banking experience and has some knowledge of the product (Limoges pottery). Her own collection (Breton pottery) is different from the company's standard line, but she thinks that it might be an interesting diversification for the company. She has decided that her second bubble is:

> importing and selling pottery

This bubble is quite vague at the moment and she needs to do a lot of research, and not just of the company's business. She has not defined a job function. She needs to look at the whole business sector in considerably more detail and refine this bubble much more before she could hope to write a CV.

Feedback and self-assessment

As discussed briefly in Chapter 3, it is extremely difficult to stand back and be objective about what you have done in your career. To see yourself as others see you is essential, so you need to get as broad a range of good-quality feedback as you can. If your organisation has an appraisal system you could get useful information from your most recent one. However, appraisals are usually held only once a year, so you cannot rely on your appraisal document exclusively for feedback on your performance and your career development. You should receive regular comments from your manager and others around you – if you do not, begin to ask for them. Some organisations encourage mentoring of junior people by more senior people. Even if your organisation does not have a formal system, there is no reason why you should not identify someone and begin to use him or her as a mentor. He or she will also be a reliable source of feedback.

Some good 360-degree competency questionnaires which rate skills and achievements are available. Your HR or personnel department should know how you can get hold of them. A number of key competencies are defined in the questionnaire, and each respondent – your manager, your peers, those who report to you, and you yourself – is asked to rate you on each competence using a scale from 1 to 5, with 1 indicating 'having little competence' and 5 'fully competent'. Usually, the identity of the respondents is not revealed to you so they are encouraged to be more open in their feedback. You could extend the net still further and include customers or suppliers: this is sometimes called 540-degree feedback.

If this seems over-formal or too elaborate, you could ask each key person to write just a paragraph or two (and you could offer to reciprocate). He or she could use headings such as:

- three things this person does well
- two things he or she needs to improve on
- his or her communication style
- setting clear objectives
- giving praise and criticism, when appropriate
- overall impression.

Again, good-quality feedback is very useful to someone changing career because it gives information which is both objective and personal. The objectivity of that feedback can, of course, be open to interpretation, as an individual's feedback is coloured by his or her own perceptions of you. Therefore, try to get a good cross-section of opinions, whatever method you choose to collect the information. Feedback that is personal is also invaluable because then you will know the person has your best interests at heart and is trying to help you with your career.

Transferable skills and achievements

If you are going to change career you need to think about your skills, accomplishments and achievements. If you decide to change industry and/or job function, you need to know which of your present abilities are transferable and which are out of date. Start scanning the job pages of the quality national papers and highlight the talents which are mentioned most frequently. How do yours compare with what is needed?

An updated and well-presented CV (see Chapter 5) to 'sell' these skills and achievements to your new employers will be essential. It may help to think of your CV as having hooks, like Velcro, and the reader or interviewer as the fabric that adheres to the hooks, so make sure that you give enough interesting details in it for the latter to become hooked. You will be attending interviews, and given that it may be some years since you have been on the side of the desk on the receiving end of penetrating and detailed questions, it will be worth thinking about your transferable skills beforehand.

- What are you good at?
- What would you like to be better at?
- Which skills are transferable, which need updating, which are of limited future use?
- Do you need any new skills? (See Chapters 1 and 2 for details.)

Generic skills were covered in detail in Chapter 1. They are: communication, numeracy, IT, working with others/team working, improving own learning and performance, and problem-solving. Most of these are subsumed under the headings below. It may help to think about your skills and achievements under these headings.

Technical skills

These are the basic skills required to do your job, covering knowledge of how to do what you have to do, i.e. fulfilling the duties and functions of the job description. Whatever you do, you must be technically competent. If you are staying in your current industry, you need to research the new technical skills that are required. If you are changing career, you will need to be as fully competent as you can be through re-training, taking opportunities (voluntary work, during leisure time) to get the skills in an environment outside your job, demonstrating that existing skills can be transferred to the new environment, and so on.

John Sharpe, for example, had been a quality control manager for a company which specialised in manufacturing deep-mining equipment. Many of Britain's deep mines are nearly exhausted and are viewed as too unprofitable to mine any longer. So in his late forties John was made redundant from his employer of more than 20 years. When he started to look for work he found that many companies in the field had suffered in the same way because of the industry's decline. Although his experience had been in a particular industry, his quality-control knowledge and experience were transferable to related fields. John wrote his CV to reflect this. He is now employed by an engineering company.

Management skills

These skills are to do with how to lead, motivate, direct, delegate, supervise, plan, organise, control, administer, monitor and reward your work and that of others. Think of examples and stories to illustrate your competence in these areas.

Janice Sutcliffe was able to do this. She had been a British army officer for 17 years. With the ending of the Cold War and the increasing use of computerised payroll systems, her job supervising the payroll section in the former West Germany had become redundant. She was used to managing a department of 12 people, which gradually reduced to two full-time staff and one part-timer. This is how she covered this part of her career in her CV: 'For 10 years I supervised a department of 12 staff in the payroll section. When I started, the department had just been relocated from elsewhere in West Germany, and we had lost many local civilian staff. I was able to recruit and train 8 new people, and our error rate dropped from 8 per cent to 3 per cent in the first 18 months.' Janice did give information about her duties, but also illustrated her competence with specific achievements to bring her CV to life. When she is interviewed for work, this scenario will – like Velcro – give the interviewer something to latch on to: 'I see from your CV that you were able to reduce your error rate significantly. How did you achieve that?'

Strategic skills

These skills are concerned with vision, knowing where you are going and what is needed to get there. They involve an understanding of the context of your work and your role within that context. With strategic skills you can see the implications of your work and the options that it presents to your organisation and yourself.

The personal insurance industry has altered a good deal since the mid-1980s, mainly because of the boom in direct telephone-based services. Brian McCarthy worked in the personnel department of a large insurance company. He became concerned about the organisation's ability to compete with the newer players and the staffing implications if it failed to compete effectively. He looked in detail at what the direct services offered and wrote a paper on it for his departmental head. The paper was referred to the main board for discussion as part of a broad strategic review of their business.

Brian needed to write this up well for his CV. This is what he wrote: 'While planning our long-term staffing needs, I surveyed the direct telephone services to compare their staffing with ours. Among other things, I found their call success rate was X per cent higher than ours although we had the same staffing levels. If this is carried through into overhead charges, our staff overhead is considerably higher than theirs. I gave a range of options for the main board to consider as part of a broader strategic review of our business. I was very pleased that a planning paper intended for my departmental head was referred to our main board.'

Brian gave lots of information to any potential employer, and established plenty of hooks for a prospective interviewer. Obviously, he had to judge how much confidential detail to give. He showed his strategic skills not by saying 'I have strategic skills', which is dull and tells us nothing, but by giving specific examples of how he applied his skills. Without saying so, he also showed that his skills could be applied in a variety of situations. For example, he would have been useful to any new employer, firstly, because he had the technical skills to do the job. Secondly, because he could also see the future implications of business issues, write papers good enough to go to the board, research competently, look ahead beyond the everyday unbidden, use his initiative, and so on.

Interpersonal skills
These skills are all about getting on with others and how to influence them appropriately.

Rowena worked as an administrative secretary for a company which made carpets. It was a medium-sized company, and she worked for four different managers who had responsibility for specific parts of the business. Because she worked for four people, she was always busy, and as she did not have much knowledge of the carpet industry, she felt she was very reactive all the time, only responding to what each manager wanted. She knew she had other talents which were not being used, and she became bored and fed up.

Rather than looking for another job, she approached each manager and asked for a 30-minute meeting each week to plan that week's activities and to talk about what might be coming up in the next few weeks. She felt that this meeting would make her more proactive because she would be able to plan the work better. She sold the benefit of the weekly meeting to each manager by saying that she would be able to help him or her more with his or her particular area of responsibility and take on some of the administrative parts of the work. Two of the managers jumped at the chance, and two did not. Rowena kept detailed notes so she could prove whether the idea was a success or not. Also, she was disciplined about not exceeding the 30 minutes allocated to the meeting so the manager would not see the meeting as a chore. After four months, she was able to prove the experiment had been a success because she had streamlined some of the administrative tasks, so that the departments of the two participating managers ran more smoothly. One more manager asked for the weekly meeting. Rowena benefited too because she felt much more involved in what was happening, and could make use of skills which had been under-utilised.

How to overcome possible disadvantages

Leading outplacement agencies advise that it could take a middle/senior manager an average of six to seven months to get a new job. Individuals may discover, however, that certain factors – such as age, for example – alter the odds, and that it consequently takes longer for them to find employment. This section looks at some of these considerations and gives advice on how to minimise their potentially adverse effects.

Your age

A study of the views of candidates and employers by an outplace-ment consultancy in the early 1990s revealed that candidates believed that their career prospects started to become limited at age 42. As explained in Chapter 1, employers often prefer to take on young, inexperienced people because they can pay them a great deal less than they would have to pay a more experienced worker. Also, a widespread perception exists that older workers are looking for a gentle slide into semi-retirement, and will therefore not contribute wholeheartedly and productively to the aims of the company.

However, the situation is beginning to improve for older work-ers. The government has now published its non-statutory Code of Practice on Age Diversity for employers, to signal its opposition to age discrimination in employment, and to encourage employers to adopt age diversity in all aspects of employment. The Code is intended to help employers, employees and applicants by setting a standard, and gives guidance to employers on how to eliminate age discrimination. Details are available from the Department for Education and Employment (DfEE) web site.★ At the time of writing, the EU has a draft directive on discrimination in employment, including age, which may become law during 2001.

The demographics make compelling reading. In 2000, 35 per cent of the labour force was aged 45 or over. By 2010, that figure will rise to almost 40 per cent. The implications are stark: if employers make decisions about who to recruit based on irrelevant factors such as age, they restrict their choice unnecessarily, and in ways which could limit their business. This does not mean that older people should be employed simply because they are older. As the Code of Practice states, 'age diversity is about getting the best person for the job, regardless of age, and making sure they have the skills or the life experiences they need to do the job'.

In general, research indicates that ageism is waning. Organisations are starting to realise that if they dismiss their 'grey heads', they stand to lose a lot: in-depth experience of their processes, customer and product knowledge, and so on. Older employees also tend to stay longer, give greater commitment and loyalty and have less absenteeism.

Chapter 1 referred to the experiment by B&Q, the DIY retailer, in staffing a store entirely with people aged over 50. The results were striking: staff turnover was six times lower than average, absenteeism was 39 per cent lower and profitability was up 18 per cent. For the sake of balance, B&Q now has an 'age diverse' work-force in its stores. This means it deliberately has a mixed-age staff.

Moreover, as described, the population profile for 2000–10 reflects that there are fewer young people, so if employers need skilled workers they will be forced to recruit older staff, many of whom are prepared to work flexible hours or part-time. An additional benefit of employing older workers is that older customers, clients and suppliers often prefer to deal with employees of a comparable age in traditional service industries such as retail, hotels, insurance and banking. Mixed-age groups provide balance in the workplace and are more likely to reflect the customer base.

It is clear that service industries in particular welcome older workers. You will help your case especially if you:

- are prepared to be flexible about the hours you work
- have specialist skills and could therefore be a valuable adviser to staff and customers alike
- have specialist knowledge (for the same reason)
- act naturally, because mixed-age groups help create a family atmosphere (for example, in restaurants).

Do not wait for jobs to be advertised. Stay on the look-out, and keep up to date on what is happening locally, learn which employers welcome older workers, and approach those who are likely to be recruiting. Being flexible will help you to adapt to different sorts of people and jobs, which will make you much more attractive to potential employers. Prioritise your skills so you know what you can offer and what you would like to do.

Interim management (see Chapter 1), whereby someone senior is brought into an organisation for a short period to turn its fortunes around or take a stop-gap role during a time of change, is another option. If you have senior or middle management experience it is worth considering this. Project management experience is increasingly popular. Apply to the specialist agencies (many of which are members of the Association of Temporary and Interim Executive Services*) and use your networking to look for interim jobs – they are increasing in number, variety and popularity. Interim management could become your preferred way of working, or may be the stepping stone to permanent work. It is certainly one way of overcoming age discrimination. This is because once you are in the organisation doing a good job, people can look beyond your age and realise how much you can contribute.

Your industry and occupation

If you are in a declining industry or occupation a glut of people with a similar work background to you will be on the job market, so new employers can afford to be choosy. This will also be true if particular local circumstances apply, such as a large employer making many people redundant.

To maximise your chances of getting a job in a new occupation or industry you will have to show that your skills are transferable and be willing to re-train, move area if necessary, and take part-time, interim or contract work rather than full-time work – in other words, to be flexible and positive.

Your skills

You could find that for various reasons – for example, what you do is being replaced by automation and you therefore need to change career, or you are returning to work after a long break – your skills need updating. Having and being able to demonstrate transferable skills is essential for any jobseeker, so you must ensure that you are not at a disadvantage in this area.

Acquiring new skills or polishing up old ones will make you more marketable. Opportunities for re-training abound (see Chapter 2 for details). Local initiatives vary enormously across the UK. To find out what is on offer in your area, it is best to contact local sources of information such as your library, the local Learning Skills Council (LSC) in England and Wales or Local Enterprise Company (LEC) in Scotland, your Jobcentre, the Local Education Authority/Education Department, and the community education services available through your county council or local colleges.

Community Education Centres, for example, offer a range of courses. Free courses teaching basic skills in English, IT and mathematics are usually available. Some councils provide courses for career changers and jobseekers, such as book-keeping, wordprocessing and computing for beginners, and even ones which are aimed particularly at people who are thinking about change, such as writing a CV and interview skills.

One way of learning new skills while still working would be to take up a 'bridging' job, i.e. one which helps you transfer out of one job function into another. For example, if you are a traditional secretary and have noticed that the demand for such a post is declining because so many people have access to a PC and can create their own professional-looking documents, you could become an expert in other related areas. You could learn desk-top publishing (DTP), book-keeping, or the skills needed for a broader administrative or client role. You will probably need further training. The bridging job (which might be called administrator/book-keeper in this example) would include some unfamiliar duties, such as book-keeping, but also some familiar ones, such as typing, filing, keeping diaries, making travel arrangements, etc. This bridging job could become the new job area for you so you continue to have a mixed role which combines the old with the new, or it could lead into another job which has more book-keeping or DTP, and thus into a change of career.

Proximity to home

If working close to home is a priority for you – say, because you have responsibilities as a carer which necessitate your being nearby, or are disabled and find commuting next to impossible, or are simply fed up with a long and tiring commute – your chances of finding exactly the job you want will almost certainly be reduced. Unless you are very lucky it is likely to take a long time for you to get your dream job within a short distance of your home, so you may need to alter your ideas and be flexible about what sort of job you will take. For example, you may have decided that a full-time job is what you want. That may not be feasible, and you may have to take part-time work instead. Perhaps you will have to take a less senior job, or work in a different industry. Only you can decide whether working close to home is an overriding consideration, or one which may have to change if it constrains your options too much.

Working from home

If you want to work close to home, you must learn to come up with creative solutions. Perhaps actually being at home would work well.

Given the increase in home-based working and improved communications, you may be able to negotiate with your new or present employer that you work from home a few days each week, so you can avoid the long and expensive journey to work every day. At present, this way of working is best suited to those who have computer- and desk-based jobs which require periods of concentrated solitary work, such as an architect doing designs and drawings, a system designer or an editor.

Lingering resentment

If you were made redundant, you may not have come to terms with the enforced change in your circumstances and may still feel angry and resentful. Prospective employers will probably pick this up at the application stage, and certainly when they interview you. They are likely to be put off because they will not want to employ someone who has not let go of the past. The obvious danger is that your anger may spill over into the new situation, and that you will not give your full attention to learning the new job and making new work relationships.

If you are returning to work after a career break, you are unlikely to feel resentful, but you may feel disoriented. If you are unhappy/unsettled/bored with your work, and are determined to change, you may feel you have been poorly treated. All prospective employers want someone who is forward-looking and enthusiastic, and who can be committed and involved in their business. It will help you considerably if you can demonstrate these qualities to them.

You may need help to get over any feelings of resentment you harbour against your previous employer. Seeing counsellors or outplacement agencies could enable you to start thinking positively and flexibly about the new phase in your life. You should also take time to consider the consequences of the change. The financial and emotional aspects are dealt with in detail in Chapters 2 and 3.

If you are returning to the workplace, depending on how long you have been absent, you will probably feel quite out of step with your smart, switched-on, networking, proactive and go-getting friends. Indeed, you may feel envious rather than resentful. Break down the process of getting work into small steps, one of which could be social visits to friends (particularly at lunch-time) just to get more in tune with what people are wearing, learn the new buzzwords, etc. These cultural issues can be just as important as having the right technical skills, as you will need to fit in as well as have the ability to do the job.

Unrealistic salary expectations

Your chances of finding work quickly will be affected if your expectations of salary and the accompanying package are unrealistically high. If you have been with one employer for many years, or are in a specialised and well-paid industry like computing, it may be that you have little idea of your external worth when you leave that situation. What you were paid could soon become 'what I should be paid', and that could lead to dangerously high expectations. For example, if you have worked in the services all your life, you may have only limited knowledge of civvy street, especially in terms of salary expectations, working conditions, and what are considered to be the 'perks' of the job. You will need to familiarise yourself with your new surroundings. The services do help their leavers with advice on CVs, and how to translate their experience out of service jargon into a language that will be understood in the commercial world.

If you find yourself in any of these situations, you must above all learn to be flexible and prioritise.

Think about whether you *need* as high a salary as you earned before. When you looked at your financial situation in Chapter 2 perhaps you concluded that you could now afford to take a job that paid less well than a previous job because your domestic circumstances have changed. Or it may be that if you take a job closer to home you will be spending significantly less on travel, so you could afford to take a drop. You may decide that you will hold out for a salary which exactly replaces or improves on your previous one. If so, think hard about what you need and what you would like (for whatever reason – comparability with peer group, ego, financial situation and so on). No matter what situation you are in, it is always better to have a salary range to negotiate within, rather than a precise figure.

It is worth remembering that other benefits such as a bonus or help with travel costs may raise what looks like a lower basic salary to more than what you received before. Many organisations have moved during the last decade towards profit-related pay, share options or bonuses as a way of rewarding and motivating their staff.

Membership of an occupational pension scheme is a valuable benefit because your employer must pay a substantial part of the cost of providing you with a retirement pension and other benefits. If, on the other hand, a group personal pension plan or stakeholder scheme is offered, will the employer pay anything into it?

If you are changing career or re-entering the job market, you will need to research salary just as thoroughly as everything else. Remember too that the salaries quoted in job advertisements are like house prices – employers state what they would like to pay, not what is eventually agreed upon.

Underselling yourself

In a competitive job market being over-modest about one's achievements is not an advantage: you must be able to show what skills you have and how useful they are to a new employer if you want to get work. Whether you have been made redundant, are re-entering the job market or are seeking a change, you will need to overcome this potentially debilitating habit to improve your chances of employment.

If you are concerned that you are underselling yourself, you can help yourself by:

- practising key selling phrases for letters of application and interviews, such as 'I have been most successful when . . .'; 'I feel very comfortable in teams which . . .'; 'What I am looking for in a job now is . . .'
- being enthusiastic and showing your commitment to the new industry, occupation or organisation. Employers and organisations have egos too, and want to believe that you have chosen them because they are the best, are very innovative, the most profitable, etc.
- preparing two or three thought bubbles and trying them out often, so they feel natural and are true of you
- using the thought bubbles to prepare a short career statement, which again sounds like you
- writing up your work achievements
- networking and researching well to help you feel more natural about some self-promotion
- seeking feedback from colleagues and friends.

143

You must remember that when promoting yourself you must always be yourself. Everything you write or say about yourself, your motivations and abilities should be consistent and be truly representative of you. You could ask someone to help you with your CV, but make sure the words are yours, not the other person's. Alternatively, ask a friend to read your CV and come up with a thought bubble based on it, and see how closely it matches the bubble you had devised for yourself. This sort of exercise will give you valuable feedback. It might also help you to accept genuine praise and to find your own ways of giving information about yourself to others in a natural and comfortable way. For example, it may sound boastful to your ears to say 'I am very good at . . .', but you may find it easier to say something like 'Friends have often said that I am very good at . . .', or 'during my last appraisal my manager spoke about my skills in . . .'.

Chapter 5 will show you how you to put all the advice given in this chapter into practice when actually applying for a job.

Chapter 5

Applying for a job

- An effective CV 'shows, not tells' that the candidate can do the job, is motivated and will fit into the organisation.
- Letters of application should match what the organisation wants with what you have done and have to offer.
- Questions asked in an interview usually have a sub-text that relates to one of three issues: competence, motivation and cultural fit, so you have to 'read' the question and pitch your response accordingly.

If you are changing careers or returning to work after a long break, awareness of changes in the job market, recruitment practices and the tactics you have to adopt to sell your skills and achievements effectively is vital. Chapter 4 will have armed you with this knowledge, but applying it in practical ways can prove difficult. This chapter shows you how to do just that: it gives advice on how to write appropriate and convincing CVs and letters of application, fill in application forms effectively, make speculative applications, and prepare for and conduct yourself at first and second interviews.

On-line recruitment

As discussed earlier, the new media of the Internet and email have brought about notable changes in recruitment practices and processes. In addition to job-searching, applying for jobs has also been made quicker and easier in many cases. Being able to email your application to a recruiter (in-house or at an agency) speeds up the process of delivering the paperwork. When people are busy, and anxious to recruit and appoint quickly, being towards the head of the queue could make the difference between being seen for interview and not being seen. Of course, certain areas of work – for example, IT – are more oriented towards on-line applications than others. Some organisations are well prepared for receiving CVs on-line, and have an automatic acknowledgement so you know yours has arrived safely.

If you are emailing your application, ensure that you personalise it as if you were sending a hard copy through the post. There appears to be a growing trend for companies that are receptive to receiving CVs electronically to be getting them in large numbers, partly because this is a quicker and easier medium. It is therefore important that you make your application stand out.

Despite these changes, however, in another respect the Internet and email have not made any difference to recruitment, and that is further on in the process, at the face-to-face stage – the interview. Of course, there are a few apocryphal stories circulating – mostly in the City of London – about someone being hired unseen in the afternoon after emailing their CV in the morning. But the old cliché that 'people buy people' is still true, and most people like to meet candidates to make their own assessment of their abilities, organisational fit, and so on.

The role of the CV in getting a job

A 'CV' (Latin *curriculum vitae*, meaning 'course of life') is a personal document which gives relevant information to a prospective employer.

Your CV should be relevant in two ways: firstly, it should be about you, your skills and achievements, what you have done and what you want to do next. It should not be just a list of the duties you performed in different jobs, as this could never be something personal to you: it is likely that if the job remained the same, the people who preceded and followed you will have performed the same duties. Personalising a CV (see 'CVs that work', below) makes it work for you, in a way that an old-fashioned strictly chronological record does not.

Secondly, your CV should be well researched and written in a way that makes it of interest and relevance to the recipient, your potential employer. So it needs to be targeted at each job and each employer. Perhaps this involves changing only a short section, but in doing so you avoid giving the impression that you have sent out dozens of identical CVs. Tailoring your CV and covering letter to the needs of a specific organisation will lead potential employers to feel that you genuinely want to work for their company, not just get a job with any organisation.

It is worth remembering that the personnel/human resources (HR) function has changed in recent years, especially in its role in recruitment. These people are usually unable to deal with recruiting all staff, and may act almost like a recruitment agency: as a post-box and acknowledgement service, passing on the applications to the recruiting manager for all subsequent actions, and being involved in some, but not all, shortlisting and selection decisions. So remember that your CV and application could end up on the desk of someone for whom recruitment is an occasional task, and who may regard it as an irksome distraction from their other responsibilities. This paints rather a bleak picture, but it could be the situation you face. If so, you need to make at least half the running. The manager will want to recruit a certain sort of person with a particular set of skills to do a specific job. Assuming their advertisement was well written in the first place, then you increase your chances considerably by making their job easy: pointing out the sort of person you are, how your skills fit what they need, and what you bring to the job.

'See me!'

No matter what sort of job you are looking for, the prime purpose of a CV is to be the selling device (together with the application letter) which gets you in front of the recruiter. Once at the interview, you become the selling device. The CV allows a prospective employer to judge whether a meeting would be worthwhile. In essence, a CV should open the door for you.

You have less time than you think to get your message across. Professional recruiters in the agencies, who read hundreds of CVs a week, usually allow each one a minimum of 15 seconds and a maximum of 45 seconds. Anecdotal evidence suggests that the attention span of people during the first skim-read is between 3 and 20 seconds. So make the recruiter's task easy. First and foremost:

- keep it to a maximum of two pages
- ensure that you point out how beneficial you would be to the organisation on the first page
- write short sentences: give your information in simple, active language
- make your CV easy to skim-read by setting it out in an accessible form.

These seem obvious points to make, but many people fail to follow even these basic steps. Your CV is intended to attract someone to see you, so its basic message should be an insistent 'see me, find out more'.

What your CV should tell potential employers

Earlier in this book the recruitment process was compared to panning for gold, not only because recruitment is hard and time-consuming, but because what the recruiting organisation really wants can so easily slip through its fingers, especially at the last moment. On behalf of their organisations, recruiters need to satisfy themselves on three counts:

(1) Will this person be able to do the job (competence/ability)?
(2) Will he or she actually do the job (motivation)?
(3) Will he or she fit in (cultural fit)?

It is important that all these questions are answered (see 'Show, don't tell', below) to the employer's complete satisfaction to avoid the expensive mistake of taking on the wrong person for the job. Your CV is the first tool in convincing potential employers that you fit the bill.

Providing a basis for an interview

Many interviewers, particularly if they are inexperienced, will use the CV as a convenient way to structure the interview. Even experienced interviewers sometimes work from the beginning of a career forward to the present. This is because they like to see the influences which have led you to make the particular career decisions which determined where you are now. To be on the safe side, make sure that the story told by your CV is progressive in terms of the positions you have held, the skills acquired, the responsibilities assumed, and so on. We talked about Velcro 'hooks' before in Chapter 4: do make sure there are plenty of interesting details with which to hook your reader.

Writing your CV

As a powerful self-marketing tool, your CV can be useful to you in many ways. If you are applying for advertised posts or making a speculative approach to an organisation, you will rely on your CV and accompanying letter to get the first interview. If you use networking to gain access to the job market, your CV will still be important to confirm initial impressions and provide detailed information. When you are completing an application form, your CV can be the draft from which you work. During an interview it can provide the agenda as it directs the interviewer to the specific assets and achievements which you are marketing and wanting to make the most of.

As a first snapshot of you, your CV is vital because it shows your:

- overall clarity of thought
- ability to understand and communicate clearly and concisely what you have to offer (note: *not* only what you have done)
- work experience
- assessment of your work experience
- education, professional qualifications and training.

One of the best ways of learning how to write an effective CV is to see some examples of bad CVs – learning what to avoid is as crucial as knowing what to include. A 1991 survey of US and multinational companies identified the ten most common mistakes that people make. Although this was some years ago, too many people are still guilty of these mistakes when writing their CVs:

- making them too long
- providing disorganised information scattered around the page, making the structure hard to follow
- typing or printing them poorly, such that they are hard to read and look unprofessional

- overwriting, using long paragraphs and sentences, and taking too long to say too little
- making them too sparse, giving only bare essentials of dates and job titles
- not orienting them towards results and not showing what the candidate accomplished on the job
- including too many irrelevancies, for example, health, marital status and ages of children
- spelling, typographical and grammatical errors
- trying too hard, with fancy typesetting and binders, photographs and exotic paper, all of which distract from the content
- not tailoring them: too many CVs arrive on employers' desks unsolicited and make little or no apparent connection to the organisation.

The reality of the job market today is rather a patchy picture. In some industry sectors and occupations it is a buyer's market, where each advertisement will attract many applications. In other sectors and occupations, organisations struggle to attract a good number of suitable applicants from whom to make their selection. In the former situation, whether they are in an organisation's HR department or in a recruiting agency, those going through CVs are looking for ways to reduce them from a large pile to a more manageable number, and will therefore look for reasons to reject candidates. In the latter situation, even though there is a much smaller pile of CVs to consider, recruiters must still check that applicants fit the job description/person specification; and a badly written CV and application will still be rejected. Ten good reasons for rejecting CVs are given above. Take a good hard look at your own CV: does it really clear all these hurdles?

Hard-pressed recruiters are sometimes forced by the volume of applications to screen CVs more on the basis of the quality and clarity of the presentation – because they need to be able to extract the relevant information as quickly and as easily as possible – than on the candidates' qualities. Although they do not intend this to be the case or like to be forced into it, you need to be aware that it can happen. There are two consequences of this: the negative one is that well-qualified people are sometimes passed over and not considered for jobs because their CV is not working well enough for them as a selling tool; the positive one is that if you develop a clear, well-focused CV you will greatly improve your chances of being interviewed and getting job offers.

The four essentials for an effective CV are:

- be clear
- write about the organisation, not just yourself
- focus on your achievements
- show, don't tell.

Be clear

Be focused on what you want and how you want to be remembered. The concept of thought bubbles, introduced in Chapter 4, is a useful starting point because many recruiters will summarise a CV into short, memorable phrases describing the candidate. You can help them by building your CV around one or two bubbles that are transparent to the reader. For example, if the thought bubble 'very experienced works engineer, excellent person manager' is appropriate, it can be expanded thus:

> I have been a works engineer and works manager for 15 years in the brick industry. During this time, I have solved industrial disputes, recruited and retained excellent middle- and senior-level staff, and commissioned green- and brown-field sites. I am now looking for a more senior job, preferably as a regional director with board-level responsibility.

This is a strong and positive career statement, leaving the reader in no doubt about how you see yourself and what you want next. Being focused in this way will help the recruiter to fit you into a suitable role. If your CV lacks this sort of focus, you are naturally more difficult to place. For a recruitment agency, where time is literally money, this is especially true. Agencies are retained because they can find good people – fast. So if you can show your focus, and almost suggest where you could be placed, they will be able to find you something suitable more quickly and easily – 'Aha, here's a square peg [you] I can fit into that square hole [the job] that came in this morning.' The same applies if you are making a speculative approach, for much the same reasons.

Write about the organisation, not only about yourself

If you are replying to an advertisement placed directly by an organisation or by an agency on its behalf, you can focus your CV and accompanying letter very firmly on what it wants. In recent years, many organisations have begun to write good adverts with a mixture of job-specific skills and personal attributes in a number of bullet points. Some invite you to respond to these in a specific (and for you, helpful) way. For example, they may say, 'Please state in your letter of application in what way(s) you fit our remit' – so in your letter you can easily answer each bulleted point in turn. This sort of request is deliberately asking you to make the link between what they want and how you could fit the bill. You may choose to rewrite only the career statement on your CV, or to re-state some of your achievements to match the job profile.

If you are either making a speculative approach (cold call), or using your network, it will be more difficult to be focused on the particular company and to show just how wonderful you would be because there is nothing for you to respond to. Therefore you may be tempted to talk about yourself, not the organisation. To retain the focus on the organisation, you will need to research extensively (see Chapter 4). This will give you the focus you lack, and enable you to write an effective CV. It will help if you are trying to transfer between job functions or industries, because you can show transferable skills and experience. As a career changer, if you can talk of your achievements as they relate to the new industry or job function, it will be especially beneficial because recruiters will get a sense of how you work, and what sort of person you are.

Focus on your main achievements

Your achievements are the best possible advertisement for you as they show not only that you have the ability to do the job, but also that you are motivated to do it. They need to be quantified in some way to show the scope of your responsibilities. For example:

When I took over as manager of Goods Inward, our staff retention was poor because another distribution centre had just opened nearby. I introduced NVQs and regular team briefings. Over a six-month period, the rate of staff turnover reduced from 10 per cent to 7 per cent, which saved the company an estimated £XX,000 in recruitment costs.

Giving some detailed information on each achievement makes your task at interview easier. This is because the recruiter will pick up on what you have said, and ask for further information.

Show, don't tell

A fundamental principle in writing a clear and easily assimilated CV is to 'show, not tell'. This means that your CV can no longer simply list your jobs with short descriptions of your duties – because that is telling, which does not make for an interesting read. You will end up with a CV either full of jargon and giving only the barest of details or, conversely, one that is immensely long and lists faithfully every single duty you have ever performed. Telling is symptomatic of an old style of hierarchical and autocratic management.

Showing proves competence, and a good match between what someone wants and what you have. This means you need in your CV to point out your best features and then link them to the benefits you can offer to the organisation you are applying to. For example, an electrician working at a large international show may say on his or her CV that he or she is:

- very committed to his work
- meticulous
- responsible.

These phrases do not help a prospective employer, who may say 'So what?', because they do not make the benefit to him or her crystal clear. The candidate can strengthen the statements by saying:

> I am very committed to my work so I will work through the night before a show to get everything working correctly.
> I am meticulous: I will re-do a stand revolve again and again to make sure it will not fail during the show.
> I had a chance to show I enjoy responsibility when I was 22 and was asked to be in sole charge of the electrics on the XYZ stand at the show in Geneva for four weeks.

As already mentioned, to make your CV work for you, you will have to show the recruiter that your application answers three crucial questions throughout the selection process. The first of these, 'Will this person be able to do the job?', is intended to discover whether you have the skills – strategic, technical, managerial or interpersonal – necessary to do the job well. To ascertain this, recruiters will look at your abilities and achievements, so you should use your CV to prove your competence, show your experience, and display your accomplishments in ways which are relevant to the organisation and the particular vacancy they want to fill – and showing, not merely telling, is essential to make your point.

Potential employers will also look for any clues you can give as to how you approach your work, because they have to form an opinion about how you might perform in the future. Remember that they need to feel confident, so ensure that your CV gives them this feeling. Giving detailed information and specific examples is the main way of doing this as this can be evaluated, investigated and discussed. It provides, as described earlier, 'Velcro hooks' that a recruiter can latch on to.

If, for example, one of your achievements is that you are very experienced and good at managing teams of people, you could say:

For some years I have successfully managed teams of people.

But this does not provide sufficient information for a recruiter to judge your ability to do the job. Let us say, for the purposes of this example, that the job is to lead a customer service team of two managers and 20 engineers. If your CV is full of bald statements like the one above you are very unlikely to pass the first hurdle of the initial selection process. So your application is heading for the 'Polite turn-down' (PTD) pile – even if you *could* do the job, because the recruiter cannot see beyond the short phrase. If you are very lucky and do get through to a first interview, the recruiter will have difficulty in asking you detailed questions because the CV has offered him or her no hooks. He or she could ask a fairly bland and open question such as 'I see you have managed teams of people. Tell me about it', which is not very likely to give you an opportunity to shine and give details to substantiate your claim. So to make your job – and that of the recruiter – easier, you should provide interesting initial information for you to discuss at interview and prove you are the right choice.

Strengthening your CV thus could make a difference:

During the last 12 years I have successfully managed teams of between 4 and 15 people.

At least now at the initial selection stage and interview someone has some concrete information. Your application is now probably hovering between the PTD and 'Possible' piles. Your CV can be made even stronger:

> During the last 12 years I have successfully managed teams of between 4 and 15 people in sales support, customer service and logistics functions.

At last, we can see a match between the job vacancy and you: you have some relevant experience, and may be able to do the job. Your application has definitely made the 'Possible' pile, but this is not the best outcome. To ensure that you make the 'Must see' pile, you could make the statement even stronger by supplementing the purely descriptive statements – the best way of doing this is to add an achievement targeted towards the specific job, which shows clearly that you are able to do the job:

> During the last 12 years I have successfully managed teams of between 4 and 15 people in sales support, customer service and logistics. At XYZ Ltd, I started as Customer Services Supervisor with a team of 4. As the company grew, we recruited 8 new people to cope with the extra work, and I was promoted to Customer Services Manager. As two teams we manage xxx contracts in xxxx installations nationally from our hub in ABC.

You are now in the 'Must see' pile because you have shown your abilities and good fit with the job requirements. At the next stage, the interviewer will have plenty of hooks to initiate a productive and worthwhile discussion.

The second crucial question your CV must address is, 'Will he or she actually do the job?', which is a test of your motivation. At an interview you may be able to show your enthusiasm and commitment, but first your CV has to get you to the interview – so it needs to convince people before they meet you that you are keen to do the job. This may be hard to do without sounding rather gushing. A sentence like: 'I have always wanted to be a . . .' sounds gauche and unconvincing. Proving that you are motivated can be done well, and again relies on showing, not telling:

> As an experienced Customer Services Manager, I have enjoyed the challenge of working with people who are remote

from the office. I find it can be hard for them to sustain their energy and enthusiasm. So at XYZ Limited I started a 'buddy' scheme where we placed our engineers in pairs or teams of three. It has been rewarding to see the improvement. The IT industry is highly competitive and I know that what sets companies apart is often their CS operations. I work with our sales and pre-sales teams to make our bids professional and personable. Efficient call-handling is an important part of any CS operation. I introduced a new system so that the call-handlers did some of the initial diagnosis. They also received feedback on how their contribution had helped the customer.

All these examples show how keen and committed this person is to his or her job, and would assure a prospective employer that he or she is motivated to contribute to the new organisation. It is clear that the candidate has thought imaginatively and performed beyond his or her job description to improve customer satisfaction, staff morale and motivation, and he or she has not conveyed this in boring and uninformative CV-speak, such as 'I am highly oriented towards results, bringing innovation and flair to all my customer and staff relations'. Much more importantly – and in a very revealing way – he or she has shown the qualities of commitment, enthusiasm, being a problem-solver, caring for staff and customers, and innovation, and not simply told the recruiter about them.

The third key question your CV should answer is, 'Will he or she fit in?' As with the second question, this one is also about making the recruiter feel comfortable with you, and *vice versa*. Cultural fit has become increasingly important for organisations and their employees in recent years as the workplace has changed so much (see Chapter 1), therefore candidates have to demonstrate the sort of flexibility and resourcefulness that will keep their new organisation functioning smoothly and ahead of the competition.

You can start acquainting yourself with the culture of an organisation quite early on in the process of job-hunting. When you look at an advertisement for a company, think about what it is saying about itself. If you are researching an organisation to make a speculative approach, what does the information you have, such as company reports, web site and product brochures, say about it? If you are using your network to gain access to the hidden job market, what do you hear on the grapevine about what a particular organisation is really like to work for? You will be able to form an opinion about its culture from all these clues, and decide whether you are likely to fit in or not.

Once again, convincing the eventual reader relies on showing not telling. You should always make sure that what you write matches with as much information as you have about the prospective employer. Say, for example, that the organisation you are applying to is a medium-sized hotel chain with 60 three- and four-star hotels around the UK, with a strong conference and business market, wanting to appoint a marketing director. If both the advertisement for the post and the literature the company sent out sounded quite formal, indicating a clear hierarchical structure, you may wish to word your CV thus to show that you can match the organisation's culture:

> When I worked with XYZ Hotels, I found that its centralised approach to marketing ensured we had a clear corporate policy on advertising and promotion. This helped me in my job as marketing manager because I could develop good working relationships with my business customers, knowing I had utterly reliable back-up from the central unit.

Presentation and layout

Imagine your CV is on someone's desk at the initial selection phase. As you cannot be in front of the recruiter yourself, looking your professional best, your CV has to create this positive first impression for you. Therefore presentation and layout matter a great deal. Follow these basic guidelines in putting together your CV.

- Hand-written CVs or even ones produced on typewriters are no longer acceptable in most areas of work. If you do not have access to a computer, try a Jobclub or ask a friend or relative to type it up for you on one. Alternatively, you could ask a commercial bureau to do it for you, but you will have to pay for it.
- It seems an entirely obvious point to make, but ensure there are no spelling errors. A CV that contains errors sends completely the wrong message to recruiters: 'I could not be bothered to check this', for example, which implies that 'you [the company] are not

worth bothering about'; or 'I cannot spell very well, and do not know how to use my spellcheck program', which implies 'I cannot use my initiative to overcome my shortcoming'.

- Observe the basic rules of grammar. A CV with grammatical mistakes in it is as bad as one with spelling errors. No matter what job you are seeking, expressing yourself well and clearly will be regarded as an important skill, and is therefore a good indicator for recruiters of your future work performance. Also, it is important to demonstrate that even though you are currently not working in that organisation – and are therefore an 'outsider' – you are able to make the transition and become a part of it. Many organisations are quite tribal with customs and fairly strong cultural behaviours – 'how we do things around here' – which could include language, dress, etc. Thus, being able to prove that you will fit in is an important part of recruitment. Poor grammar is a sure way of signalling that you are an outsider, especially for middle- and senior-level jobs.

- Use high-quality paper. Do not be tempted to use cheap photocopy paper. Apart from anything else, it may crumple easily, and it *feels* cheap. Instead, buy plain white A4 of the best quality you can afford. If you are applying for a job in which artistic creativity is called for, you might be able to get away with a CV slightly out of the ordinary, but even so it should not be too wacky – unless you are extremely sure of your audience's reaction. CVs are often photocopied for circulation to interested parties in the organisation. Coloured paper often copies very badly and looks smudgy.

- Laser-printed type looks much more professional than the output from older-generation dot matrix printers. If you do not have access to a good-quality printer it is worth seeking out a bureau which can take your disk and run it out using a good-looking font.

- If your industry or job function follows a particular style of laying out CVs, make sure you do too. These are often reflected in quite small details, such as the use of a border, or bold print, or certain buzzwords. If you are unsure what they are, check with people in your network. Academic CVs are an exception to the rule of limiting CVs to a maximum of two pages. They are much longer, and must list all publications, journal articles, conference papers and research awards.

- Make it look good. Although your CV should be restricted to only two pages of A4, do not be tempted to cram everything in. Leave reasonable-sized margins, and give a larger margin at the bottom than the top so that the page looks balanced.
- Make it easy to assimilate. This will include typographic details such as use of larger, bolder type for headings, the dates set out so they are easy to read, a clear, inviting typeface, the use of bullet points, and so on. A clean, easy-to-read CV can only help you.

If in doubt, leave it out

The one golden rule that everyone in the CV and recruitment business agrees on is that candidates must 'be honest'. Few people have a perfect career path. Most people have taken blind alleys, made bad career decisions, or suffered from a difficult work situation. It is not what has happened to your career path that is important, but how you have dealt with it. Ensure that you obey the rule on honesty: be sure to express every aspect of your experience, but as positively as you can. The CV is an opportunity to show yourself in the best possible light – while still being honest.

If you were sacked from a job because you and your manager had a fearsome row, do not be tempted to put: 'I left my last job because my manager and I had a disagreement/could not get on.' Anything that is particularly negative is best left until the interview, when you can explain yourself properly and you have the recruiter's full attention. This strategy can help you overcome the first hurdle: when there are 400 CVs on someone's desk your chances of getting the job are 1 in 400. If the potential employer reads something negative like that, your CV will immediately join the PTD pile. If you get through to a first interview your chances are now probably more like one in ten. You are being seen because you already look like a good fit for the job.

In addition to potentially negative details about your career – which you could go into at the interview stage – you must omit certain other features from your CV, as discussed below.

Photograph

Unless you are applying for a job in which your looks would play an important part, it is best to not send a photograph of yourself. The reason for this is practical. For one thing, it is not relevant to the recruiter what you look like, and for another, you may in fact put him or her off you because many people do, unfortunately, make judgements based on physical appearance.

Some advertisements or agencies may ask for a photograph. If you are forced to send one, it is worth investing some time and money in a studio shot, rather than using the local passport photo booth. See what the photographs of the people in the trade journals of the industry are like and perhaps take them along to brief the photographer. You could also tell the photographer your 'thought bubble' description. An 'experienced works manager, friendly, competent' for example, conjures up a very different picture from a 'captain of industry, brooks no nonsense, dynamic'.

Salary

When in an advertisement the recruiters ask you to 'write, stating your current salary, to . . .', it is likely that they are using the figure you cite as one of the ways of judging whether your current level of seniority and job responsibility fits with the post they are trying to fill. If they give an indication of salary on the advertisement, then it is easy for you to see whether your current salary is within that band, or either side of it. If it is above, then you need to explain that you are prepared to take a salary drop (see below). If it is below, this is often taken as an indication that you are not sufficiently senior to fill the role. If you are applying to a new industry or job function which pays more than your previous one, then you need to explain this: 'I am a senior manager in a not-for-profit organisation, and my current salary is £XX,000. I know this seems low in comparison with your industry. My salary is considered fair in my sector for my level of seniority and experience, and I hope you will read my application with this in mind.'

If you are applying for a job after having been self-employed, it is difficult to answer the question accurately. You could say, 'As you will see, I am currently self-employed, so I cannot give a salary, but my annual turnover is £XX,000. My salary expectations for this job are in the range £XX,000—£YY,000.' (Notice that a range, rather than an absolute figure, is quoted. This allows some room for manoeuvre; with an absolute figure you can only depart from it – usually down!) If you are returning to work following a career break, you could state your finishing salary (with date), *and* say 'my salary expectations for this role are . . . ', after you have done your research on what is a fair rate for the job. If you know the organisation, you may know how they stand on this.

If the advertisement does not specify a salary but asks you to state what yours is, you run the risk of your CV joining the PTD pile because you may be too expensive. It may be that you would be pleased to take the job for all sorts of valid, but personal, reasons despite a lower salary, but you may not have the chance to put that across effectively, so if at all possible it would be better to omit your salary at the application stage. If, on the other hand, you are applying for a post which you *know* is going to pay less than you currently earn, you could say in the covering letter, 'I am being paid £XX,000 in my current job, but I know that if I wish to change industry to xxx which pays lower salaries, I will need to take a salary drop. I understand this, and would like you to read my application with this in mind.'

If they did not give an indication of salary but asked you to, and you fail to do so, it may or may not count against you. Opinion really does seem to be divided on this. It could appear that you have something to hide. Some recruiters consider that if you omit the salary when you have been asked to give it, you have failed one of the basic requests in the advertisement, and they will put your application straight into the PTD pile. Others are more lenient, believing that salary is only one of a number of factors that should be considered when reviewing the applications.

In general, it is better to avoid giving your current salary if they fail to give a salary range, unless expressly asked to. If you must give your salary, then do so. If you receive any bonuses, make that clear. If you have any perks such as company pension, car, or private health insurance, list those as well.

Try to satisfy the employer on the three key questions (see 'Show, don't tell', above) first. If you succeed in doing that with your CV, the chances are that you will be invited to an interview and you will be in a much stronger bargaining position at that stage.

It is a different matter if you are sending your CV to an agency. Agencies are paid on commission, usually a percentage – sometimes as high as 30 per cent – of the candidate's first-year salary for placing you in a permanent job. So it is in your, and the agency's, interest if it knows what you earn at present, including all the fringe benefits, and what you would like to be earning.

References

Never send copies of references unsolicited. It is also usually a bad tactic to name referees on your CV. This is because until you get to the interview, and have a chance to see clearly what the job is about, it may be difficult to judge who could give you the best and most appropriate reference. It would look rather odd if you changed your mind about your referees after attending an interview. To avoid this situation, many people simply say in their CVs, 'names of referees available on request'.

If recruiters like what they see in you, they will ask for referees at the first or second interview. The exceptions to this are some public-sector, government and academic jobs, for which recruiters take up references before the first interview. It is usual in these cases for detailed job descriptions to be available so you can make an informed choice about who would be best. If in doubt, take the time to make a telephone call to the employer. If the organisation has not specified the number or sort of referee it requires, someone involved in the recruitment should be able to give you helpful guidance.

Choose your referees carefully, and brief them about the job, the competencies required, the organisation and the industry. Armed with this information, they can give a reference which could help you get the job. Do them the courtesy of giving them a copy of your application, and keeping them posted on progress with the different jobs you have applied for. In this way, they will feel you are being professional about your job search, and this can only help you. Most organisations will not appoint without writing and/or speaking to referees, so these people are important to you – take the time to manage them well.

Gimmicks

Gimmicks can backfire, and are therefore best avoided. They include using coloured paper or fancy bindings, being flippant in the covering letter and saying something like 'Hey, have I got an offer for you!', or re-writing the advertisement in plain English or to describe you and your qualities (tempting, but do not).

Spurious leisure interests

List only those leisure interests which are genuine, and which you can talk about in a knowledgeable and enthusiastic way. Even here, make them work well for you. If you play badminton make something of it: for example, saying 'I play badminton in our local league' or 'I have just started badminton lessons to get fit' sounds much better than just the word 'badminton' in a long list of other interests. If you are involved in school activities, saying 'I was elected chair of our Parent/Teachers Association' sounds better than 'school activities'. This shows that you were elected from among your peer group, and so works positively for you. Use your hobbies to illustrate your abilities to work in a team or be a leader (generic skills again!).

A special note to returners

Whatever sort of career break you are returning from, it is especially important for you to show you have been doing interesting and relevant things in your absence from the workplace. This is because, unfortunately, being at home or travelling for a while are not valued in the same way as a 9 to 5 job is.

Like any career changer, you will also need to demonstrate your worth to a prospective employer. In your CV, talk about achievements (either paid or unpaid) which you are proud of, not duties carried out. Show your potential: do not simply tell people about it. Link what you have done with how it would benefit an employer. Many people who take a career break do things that help their local community, which can be an advantage when they return to work. Occasionally, what started off as a leisure or voluntary pursuit can turn into a new career.

Margaret and Will, for example, moved from the city to a small village with their four children. There, the pace of life was more relaxed, and the children could play freely. However, as the children grew up, they missed out on some of the advantages of urban life, such as easy access to organised youth activities. So Margaret found out about how to start a youth club and find and equip suitable premises, raised funds and joined the Youth Club Association. Her own children benefited, as did all the other children in the village. When they were older she continued to use her knowledge and experience of community affairs as a parish councillor. This led to an interest in local politics, and she now works for a political agent in her parliamentary constituency.

Paul, on the other hand, was a solicitor in central London. In his early thirties, with no family ties, he decided to go on an overland trip by truck with 20 like-minded companions to Nepal. He took his laptop computer along, which he plugged into the engine of the truck to re-charge overnight. Paul had intended to write up a journal simply as his own record, but as the trip progressed he found that he was more fascinated by his companions than by the sights. He began to write his journal with the intention of finding a publisher on his return. Although he was not successful in finding one, and had to return to his job as a solicitor, his experiences led him to start thinking laterally about various options. He started investigating a change of career to literary agent, for which a legal background and empathy with what writers are trying to achieve are very useful prerequisites, so he is in a good position to make a smooth transition, should he choose to do so.

CVs that work

As recruiters are unlikely to have much time in which to read each CV, they need to be able to extract the salient details quickly and easily, and to use these to judge whether to see you or not. So, keep your CV short, at a maximum of two pages, with the most important information on the first page. CVs in the USA, usually called resumés, are usually only one page long. This is worth knowing if you are applying to an American-owned company.

A 'traditional' CV

A traditional structure is:

- name
- address
- telephone/fax number
- date of birth
- marital status and children
- interests/health
- secondary education
- tertiary education
- professional qualifications
- employment history in chronological order (i.e. most recent experience last).

Unfortunately, if you follow this order, you will find that the first page is taken up with information which does not help the recruiter decide whether to see you or not. If he or she carries on reading – and there is no guarantee of that – he or she will have to go all the way to the end to find the interesting and relevant information about you.

CURRICULUM VITAE

Name:	Christopher John Candidate
Address:	27 Northway Road, West Illsley, Northampton NN1 1DD
Telephone:	(01629) 678234
Date of birth:	18 August 1950
Place of birth:	Solihull, West Midlands
Nationality:	British
Marital status:	Divorced
Children:	One boy, aged 21, at university
Health:	Good
Interests:	Modern drama and mime, mountain biking, Thai cookery
Other:	UK passport holder, clean driving licence

Qualifications:

1966	GCE O-levels in English Language, English Literature, Maths, French, Physics, Art, Drama
1968	GCE A-levels in Art (grade B), English Literature (grade C)
1971	Diploma in Stage Design (Croydon Art College)
1976	Advanced Diploma in Technical Management (Johnson Institute of Dramatic Arts)
1984	Member of Technical Dramatic Arts Institute (MTDAI)
1989	Fellow of Technical Dramatic Arts Institute (FTDAI)

Experience:

1971–3	Lighting Engineer, Brighton Repertory Company, East Sussex – did lighting for a variety of shows, such as light musicals, modern drama

- learnt about sound effects
- designed new lighting system
- assisted with set construction

1973–6   Leading Technician, Birmingham City Opera
- designed and built lighting and sound system for new stage
- some experience of stage management
- designed lighting effects for *Aïda* and *The Beggar's Opera*

1977–85   Technical Manager, Stirling Festival Hall
- staff responsibility (six people)
- member of technical management team of 12
- assisted with stage management of some drama and musical productions
- some community outreach work with Arts Council funding
- experience of set design (light musical)

1985–92   Head of Technical Services, Birmingham City Hall
- responsible for technical aspects of multi-functional 1,000-seat hall
- head of technical management team
- team of supervisors with 50 staff reporting
- advised other local venues on lighting, set and sound effects design

1992–   Technical Director, Edinburgh Festival
- full budgetary control of all technical aspects of Festival
- team of 200 permanent staff
- responsible for all main venues (25 locations)
- responsible for 15 technical temporary sub-contracting companies
- seconded to Leicester Stage Company to advise on staging opera

Analysis of the 'traditional' CV

In fact, this person is very well qualified for the job for which he is applying (Director of Technical Services at the Barbican). But the recruiter has to wade through a lot of irrelevant details such as his divorce and ancient history about helping with set construction in the early 1970s to get there. The candidate has given information mainly about his duties, rather than about his achievements. He has been very concise, so his CV will fit the two-page rule, but perhaps it is too brief, making it difficult for the recruiter to see quickly and easily what he has done. Also, he does not give a clear idea of what he wants to do next.

A successful CV

The following structure produces a much more successful CV:

- name
- address
- telephone/fax number/email address
- profile/career statement
- career and achievements to date (in reverse chronological order)
- qualifications and education
- interests
- personal details.

Christopher Candidate
27 Northway Road, West Illsley
Northampton NN1 1DD

Tel: (01629) 678234
Fax: (01629) 567123
Email: CCandidate@xxx.co.uk

Profile
I am an experienced director of technical services for all the dramatic arts, with particular skills in managing large teams of technicians and sub-contractors, and managing high-profile venues. I have full budgetary control (£Xm) for all technical aspects of the annual Edinburgh Festival (XXX,000 visitors p.a.). In a seconded

post at the Leicester Stage Company, I was Technical Director of three new multi-functional large-capacity theatres. I am now seeking a board-level role in a venue of international reputation.

Career summary

Technical Director, Edinburgh Festival   1992–present
This senior role was created to support the Festival's growing international artistic reputation

- I created a new organisation to provide dedicated technical services to 25 main festival locations, varying from large outdoor venues to pub back rooms
- I recruited a new team of 12 specialist managers to provide stable leadership and management to our 200 permanent staff
- I have worked with artistic directors such as Trevor Nunn and Michael Bogdanov to stage innovative shows for audiences of 6,000+ people
- Because of increased visitor numbers, I selected and managed 15 sub-contracted companies to provide ancillary services to our own, ensuring quality is maintained and keeping costs under control
- I set and manage our annual technical budget of £Xm. Recently, costs have risen in line with increases in venues and audiences, but remain at X% of ticket price
- In 1997 I was seconded to the Leicester Stage Company for nine months to give technical direction for their three new large-capacity theatres. I was retained as Technical Director during their three-year start-up period

Head of Technical Services, Birmingham City Hall   1985–92
I lead the technical team at this high-profile multi-functional venue

- I ensured the technical team provided excellent technical management of three 1,000-seat multi-functional theatres/conference halls so that resident and visiting company needs were always met
- To make sure full cover was always available, I selected and managed a top technical management team of five

- I employed specialist sub-contractors for visiting shows and conferences, e.g. the Birmingham City Motor Show
- I managed our permanent staff of 50 people to provide a comprehensive service, and employed freelance staff in busy times
- During 1987–90, I was asked to lecture regularly to advanced diploma students at the Johnson Institute of Dramatic Arts. I learnt new skills and how to teach people with little or no technical or practical experience of dramatic arts

Technical Manager, Stirling Festival Hall   1977–85

This role provided much-needed technical management during a period of change

- I managed a team of six supervisors (overall staff of 40) to provide a quality service to house company and visiting companies – drama, opera, musicals, orchestras
- Whilst I was at Stirling, we received Arts Council funding to develop our community work, and to expand into new areas such as inviting internationally renowned orchestras. I initiated work placements for 20 young people on drama courses at local colleges, and community outreach programmes. The programme was very successful, with good audiences in remote country areas. I also gave free technical advice and provided technicians for local amateur and semi-professional companies. The orchestras presented a challenge with the acoustics and rehearsal space, which we solved satisfactorily
- I assisted with stage management of *Hedda Gabler*, *The Boyfriend*, *Macbeth* and *Peter Pan*. This gave me additional stage and people management experience

Leading Technician, Birmingham City Opera   1973–76

This role provided technical support to this growing opera company

- I had full responsibility for the design of a new stage lighting and sound system, with a budget of £250,000
- I provided maternity leave cover for the Assistant Stage Manager for one season. I learnt new skills and gained an understanding of an ASM's job and its challenges

- I was given full design and production responsibility for lighting shows such as *The Beggar's Opera, Turandot, Aïda*

Lighting Engineer, Brighton Repertory Company　　1971–73
This was my first job, where I practised the skills I had learnt at college, specialising in lighting and sound effects. I helped our Chief Technician to design the new lighting system, and the basic design is still in use 25 years on

Education and qualifications

Fellow of Technical Dramatic Arts Institute (FTDAI)　　**1989**

Member of Technical Dramatic Arts Institute (MTDAI)　　**1984**

Johnson Institute of Dramatic Arts　　**1976–77**
Advanced Diploma in Technical Management

Croydon Art College　　**1968–71**
Diploma in Stage Design (credit)

Bromley Grammar School　　**1961–68**
A-levels in Art and English Literature (1968)
O-levels in English Language, English Literature, Maths, French, Physics, Drama, Art 1966

Other information and interests

Date of birth: 18 August 1950
Interests: mountain biking at club level, committee member of Charnwood Orienteering Club, Thai cooking for friends
PC & software skills: daily use of Word 7 and Excel to prepare documents

Analysis of the successful CV

This CV too conforms to the maximum of two pages of A4 rule, but gives much more information to the recruiter than does the previous one. It may need to be edited to fit the specific job for which the person is applying more closely.

Plenty of hooks are provided:

- interesting details, such as, 'I worked with artistic directors such as Trevor Nunn', 'initiated work placements . . .'

- reflections on what he learnt, such as 'new skills and how to teach people with little or no technical or practical experience of dramatic arts'
- specific information on his achievements: 'created new organisation to provide dedicated technical services to 25 main festival locations . . .'; 'retained as Technical Director during three-year start-up period'; 'the basic design is still in use 25 years on'
- the limits of his authority/responsibility: 'set and manage our annual technical budget of £Xm'; 'selected and managed 15 sub-contracted companies . . .'
- showing *what* he did: 'I ensured the technical team provided excellent technical management of three 1,000-seat multi-functional theatres/conference halls', and *how* or *why*: 'so that resident and visiting company needs were always met' – showing he understands why his contribution counts
- after each job title, a single-line description of the job function is given before launching into specific achievements. This is helpful on two counts: sometimes job titles are not self-explanatory; and it shows an understanding of how the job fits into the overall organisation – again, 'showing not telling'. It also implies the generic skill of team-working, as well as clarity of thought
- some idea of his computer literacy: 'daily use of Word 7 and Excel'.

Moreover, the CV lists the jobs he has done in reverse order, so the recruiter sees the most recent, and most relevant, material first. His first job is described in just a few short lines, which is appropriate as it was such a long time ago. Quite rightly, his two most recent jobs are allocated plenty of space.

If Mr Candidate had decided he wanted to concentrate on his academic and teaching interests, the CV would change because the thought bubble would be different. The profile would be different too, and he would need to make much more of his involvement with in-company training, work placements, secondments with local drama students and lecturing at the Johnson Institute.

Mr Candidate's CV has comprehensively answered the first two of the three questions on his ability and motivation. Regarding the third question of cultural fit, some sense of him as a person does emerge: he is commercially minded, but tempers that with artistic excellence; he sees the value of passing on skills to the next generation; he is conscious of the need to balance quality of service with cost control. If Mr Candidate were called for interview, a recruiter could quickly double-check on the ability and motivation. He or she could then spend the majority of the interview on the cultural fit. This would be appropriate because the more senior the position, the more important the cultural fit becomes.

With appropriate modifications, this CV could be used successfully to apply for advertised posts, to send to agencies, to cold call, and to network.

Application forms

Despite the abundance of advice available on how to write a good CV, many are still badly written. Some are over-written and/or dishonest, with applicants claiming job titles, responsibilities and interests which are simply untrue or inflated.

CVs give candidates a golden opportunity to tell the recruiter their story in their way. Potential employers find out only what the candidate chooses to tell them, not necessarily what they need to know.

Supplying application forms solves this problem, as long as they are well-designed and sensibly written. All candidates are required to supply the same information, thus making it easier for recruiters to judge their suitability. The selection process can be shown to be more transparent because recruiters can prove that they gave everyone a level playing field, thus meeting some of the criteria of the equal opportunity legislation.

The role of application forms

Organisations which use application forms have to ensure that they are clear and well designed. Having one form for use in the recruitment of all levels of job – from a new graduate to a senior executive – and all job functions – from working on reception to working in sales – can lead to an inflexible format. Some organisations overcome this by having different forms for different levels of job. Because of the resources needed to design (and post out) application forms, often only large organisations have them, including most government and public-sector employers.

To some degree, application forms are self-selecting, weeding out people and therefore reducing the number the recruiter needs to look through. Many people send off for forms and the accompanying information but decide when they receive them that they are too daunting to fill in (or indeed that they do not want the job), and forgo the chance of applying for the job.

Filling in application forms can be more of an effort than sending off a CV, so how can you make them easier to complete? The short answer to this is the same as for compiling your CV or writing your letter of application (see next section): you should match what the organisation wants with what you have done, show not tell; be focused on what you want next and talk about achievements, not just duties.

Sometimes the organisation gives you a clear steer. For example, the form may have a note along the following lines:

> Please complete these sections carefully after reading any supplementary information regarding the post, particularly the job description and list of job competencies. The decision to invite you for interview will be based on the information you provide on this form and how closely you meet the specified competencies. Continue on an extra sheet if necessary.

There may also be a section on 'achievements, personal qualities and skills' – perhaps just a blank space with an instruction saying, for example:

> Please use this section to indicate how far you meet each of the competencies required for the post. List experience, achievements, personal qualities and skills which you feel are relevant, against each competency. You may include paid and unpaid work, work within the home and leisure interests. Continue on an extra sheet if necessary.

Some application forms have main headings such as personal details, employment record, professional qualifications/training, supporting evidence and references. The introductory blurb to the 'supporting evidence' section might say something like:

> Using the job description provided, please use this section to outline where your knowledge, skills, experience and abilities are specifically relevant to this post. These may have been gained outside the workplace through activities and interests.

The Overseas Development Agency (ODA) takes the trouble to send a very full information pack, with detailed information on the job, the posting, the country the job is based in, its culture, living conditions, the likely hardships and other key considerations. The applicant gets a real sense of what the job would be like, and many people realise it would be impractical for them for all manner of reasons. The ODA knows this is likely to happen, but finds that this approach saves everyone a lot of effort and time.

Filling in application forms

Although you could, in theory, pick up a pen and start filling in an application form off the top of your head and with very little preparation, you should resist the urge to do. Doing it systematically will help you submit a form that captures your achievements and skills effectively and in a way that is specific to the job and organisation to which you are applying.

(1) Go through the job description highlighting all the key competencies and experience the organisation needs. Be honest with yourself: does your experience match what it wants? If not, is it worth spending your time on the application form for a job for which you are unlikely even to be interviewed?

(2) Take each highlighted item and draft on some blank paper something that you feel does you justice. Remember the 'show, don't tell' advice, make everything achievement-based, and quantify those achievements. Take a look at the form. How much space do you have? Should you write in note form rather than complete sentences? Some forms invite you to use extra pieces of paper, but do not be tempted to have so many that the form begins to look like a scrapbook.

(3) If possible, get someone else's opinion about what you have written. A second pair of eyes will usually spot something you have missed, or expressed badly.

(4) Photocopy the form, and do a draft. Put it aside for a while, and have another read through the job description. Does the draft form fulfil the job criteria? Does it sound like you?

(5) When you are happy with the draft version, fill in the original form. Unless you have access to an electronic version of the

form, it may be difficult to avoid filling in the form by hand, because forms do not lend themselves to being used in a computer printer. Ensure that you do so neatly and legibly. Another option is to type up the answers on a computer, print them out and stick them on to the form before photocopying the form, so you have a neat version.

Letters of application

Whether you are sending off your CV or an application form to an organisation, you will have to write a strong covering letter to go with it. The letter should be quite short (3-4 key paragraphs on a single sheet of A4), and attract the reader enough to want to turn the page and read the CV.

There is an art to writing a good letter of application, as there is for compiling a CV. Some recruiters place as much importance on the letter as they do on the CV.

If you are replying to an advertisement, take a highlighter pen and mark all the points on the organisation's 'wish list', and then match each major one in your letter. Letters to agencies need to be well-researched and then followed up. With cold call and networking letters, you need to discover the 'wish list' first, and then write an appropriate letter.

- Match what the organisation wants with what you have done.
- Try to answer the three questions (Will you be able to do the job? Will you actually do the job? Will you fit in?) in the letter, so the reader is persuaded to find out more by reading the CV.
- Show, rather than tell, the recruiter that you are able and motivated, and capable of fitting in.

In response to an advertisement

Letters of application should show, above all else, that you can meet the criteria in the advertisement. This is true whether you are applying directly to the organisation or to an agency which is handling the recruitment on its behalf. In the past, many letters of application were little more than a covering note along the following lines:

Contact details

Date

Dear Sir

I saw your advertisement in last week's *XXX Advertiser* for a Works Manager. I enclose my CV.

I look forward to hearing from you.

Yours sincerely

Joanna Stephens

What is wrong with this? In the new, and tougher, job market we are now in, this letter is failing Joanna Stephens in a number of ways.

- Ideally, she should address it to the recruiting manager or the person mentioned by name in the ad.
- She should summarise the most attractive points from her CV as related to the job vacancy, to encourage the recipient to turn the page and read it.
- She must address the three issues of whether she can do the job, is enthusiastic about it and will fit in.
- It is a small point, but letters which start 'Dear Sir' ought to end 'Yours faithfully'. Those beginning 'Dear Mr/Ms/Mrs _____' should end 'Yours sincerely'. She has not applied these simple points of etiquette, and is thereby signalling that she is an outsider trying to get in.

If you are applying for an advertised vacancy, it is better to send in your application as soon as you can, because the first applications received – while people are really keen to evaluate the response – are usually given more attention. Such a reaction may not be very professional, but it is human nature. It is possible that applications received late which are just as good as the first few may be given less attention. It goes without saying that if a closing date is given, you must respect this. Most organisations will give you either two or three weeks from the date of the ad's appearance.

Personnel and Training Officer
Salary range £XX,OOO–£YY,OOO

We are one of the largest estate agencies in southern England with xxx offices in xx towns and cities. We are known for our innovative and professional approach. We need an additional Personnel Officer to play a key role in our expansion. You will join a friendly team at our Head Office in XXX, who provide a professional personnel service to over 400 staff in our Southern Region. You will have two main responsibilities: (1) the implementation of our new training and development plans, and (2) recruitment throughout the region.

You will need sound experience in sourcing suitable external suppliers of training, and of briefing our internal training team. You will also have proven experience in all aspects of recruitment including interviewing. You are likely to be professionally qualified with at least three years' experience, together with excellent interpersonal and communication skills.

In return we offer a 37-hour week, 5 weeks' annual leave and non-contributory pension scheme.

Please send your CV with a covering letter setting out why you are suitable for this post to Mrs Janice Wallace, Personnel Manager, . . . The closing date for applications is _____.

Contact details

Date

Dear Mrs Wallace

I would like to apply for the post of Personnel Officer as advertised in the *XXX* on [date], and I enclose my CV.

Since 1993 I have been recruitment officer with the XYZ Partnership, and have been wholly responsible for the past two years for the recruitment of approximately 50 people at all grades. Because we have ten regional offices it has sometimes been hard to ensure a uniform approach in equal opportunity interviewing. So we reviewed our interview training for our 20 senior managers, and I gave extra coaching.

For the last eight months I have been briefing our six external training providers. I recently sourced a new provider for our negotiating skills course. I have worked in a variety of personnel and HR functions since graduating in 1989, and been a Member of the Chartered Institute of Personnel Development (MCIPD) since 1993.

I read about your new training plans in *People Management.* The core team mentoring scheme sounds similar to the XYZ Partnership scheme which I recently piloted in Marlborough. It has been a great success. I am keen to apply my learning in the larger context of your team across the southern England region.

I am keen to be considered for this interesting position, and look forward to hearing from you soon.

Yours sincerely

John Michaels

Analysis of the letter in response to an advertisement

John Michaels's letter would interest the reader to carry on and read the CV. He has drawn attention to his skills and achievements and matched them to what the organisation wants. In doing this, he has answered the first two questions well. The third question is more intangible, but there are some clues:

- 'because we have ten regional offices it has sometimes been hard to...' shows that he understands about the difficulties of being in Head Office and the vital need to communicate well with people away from the centre. This would be an issue in the new position because it is also a Head Office job
- 'I am keen to apply my learning...' shows he is motivated to try new things which fits well with the employer's point about innovation.

Application letters from people returning to work

In the section on how to write a CV it was pointed out that you should include your voluntary and unpaid work to show you had not stagnated during your career break. If you are returning from travelling, you should point out that you have reflected on those experiences and linked them to what you want to do next, showing their relevance to the advertised vacancy. The same is true of letters of application: you must show that although you have been out of the job market, your skills are still relevant and transferable.

Your approach will depend on how long you have been absent from paid employment and what you have done with yourself in the meantime. Let us imagine you were at a similar level to that of the personnel and training officer post advertised above, before you took a career break two years ago to care for your elderly father. If you wish to apply for it you could say in your letter:

> From 1996 to 1999 I was Recruitment and Training Officer at the IT consultancy XYZ Associates. I was responsible for a staff of four administrators, split evenly between recruitment and training. We ran between 40 and 50 training events annually, using either our own network of staff trainers or externally sourced consultants. I was responsible for both the choice and selection of who was most suitable, their briefing, etc. We also recruited staff at all grades in their four regional offices in the Midlands.

> My father became seriously ill in late 1999 and I took an extended career break to nurse him. I am now ready to return to full-time work. During the break I kept up to date with the latest news by subscribing to the trade journals and attending CIPD branch meetings. When I could, I took occasional work as a sales negotiator in my local estate agency, Hubble & Hill.

> I recognise that I have been out of the job market for two years. However, one of my reasons for replying to your advertisement is that I have some estate agency experience, so I would understand both the recruitment and training and development issues.

Is this candidate worth seeing? The answer is a definite 'yes'.

Speculative letters to agencies

If your industry tends, at least for your job function, to use agencies a good deal, they will be a vital part of your job search. Before you decide whether or not to approach agencies, make sure you have fully researched the use made of them in your field. Bear in mind that as many management and supervisory posts are filled by the use of agencies as by advertisements.

If John Michaels decides to use an agency in his job search, he should start by researching them as described in Chapter 4. Once he has found a number of agencies that he thinks will suit him, he should telephone and talk to a consultant. For advice on talking to an agency, see Chapter 4.

He could follow up his telephone call by sending the following letter:

Contact details

Date

Dear Mr/Ms [name]

I was very pleased to have a chance to talk to you yesterday and, as discussed, I enclose [or attach, if the note is being sent by email] my CV. It is written to reflect my career aim of combining training and development with recruitment in a more senior head office role in a service industry. I firmly believe that these two combine well – the right people have to be recruited in the first place before any organisation can begin to develop its staff's potential, to the benefit of both the business and the individual employees.

As agreed, I have summarised my most recent achievements. Since 1993 I have been recruitment officer with the XYZ Partnership, which specialises in outsourced payroll. I was wholly responsible for the past two years for the recruitment of approximately 50 people at all grades. For the last eight months, I have briefed our six external training providers. I recently sourced a new provider for our negotiating skills course.

I have experience of working in a head office with a regional structure. Because we have ten regional offices it has sometimes been hard to ensure a uniform approach in equal opportunity interviewing. Therefore, we reviewed our interview training for our 20 senior managers, and I gave extra coaching to them. I have worked in a variety of personnel and HR functions since graduating in 1989, and have been a member of the Chartered Institute of Personnel & Development (MCIPD) since 1993.

XYZ Partnership's business is expanding, and opportunities do exist, but not to do anything particularly new or challenging. So I am investigating more senior roles in my local area of Reading and Basingstoke. My current package is a salary of £XX,000 plus profit-related pay, which is usually in the range of X–Y per cent of salary, with five weeks' holiday and a non-contributory pension. As agreed, I will telephone you in the next two weeks so we can arrange to meet at your offices in Slough.

Yours sincerely

John Michaels

Analysis of the letter to an agency

John has clearly made a good contact, and had a useful and friendly conversation. He is deliberately providing the consultant with the information he needs to place him in a suitable job:

* a clear career aim
* a targeted CV
* information about himself and what he believes to be important: 'I firmly believe that these two . . .'
* some sense of his interpersonal skills, which the consultant would have already gleaned from the telephone call. The tone of the letter reinforces this: 'I was very pleased to have a chance to talk to you yesterday . . .'
* his recent experience and achievements
* a clear brief on where he is looking for work: 'in my local area of Reading and Basingstoke . . .'
* a reason why he is looking for a move
* his current remuneration package (agencies are paid on commission, so this information will translate immediately into potential revenue for the consultant).

Speculative letters to organisations

If you are targeting a particular industry or organisation, do some research (see Chapter 4) on it first. This will help you find out how to match what you have done with what the organisation needs, and will also reveal its buzzwords or culture – all of which are very important when you are not applying for a specific, advertised vacancy.

181

Then amend or re-write your CV accordingly, and write a letter which focuses on what you have discovered in your research. For example, you may have found out about a recently awarded contract, planning permission granted for a new site, etc. This information should be woven into the letter as it shows why you are interested in the organisation and demonstrates that you have sufficient interest to devote some of your time to research it. Most potential employers would be flattered by this attention, which increases your chances of getting a favourable reply.

The networking letter

If you use networking – which fills up to 50 per cent of management and supervisory posts in the UK – it is really a two-step process. The first step is to approach your contact and talk to him or her, either on the telephone or face to face. During this conversation, you can establish the current trends, present preoccupations, and so on. The second step is to amend your CV, write a suitable accompanying letter, and wait for a positive response.

A networking letter could look like this:

Contact details

Date

Dear Anne

It was a pleasure to meet you at Catherine's party. As promised, I'm dropping you a line to summarise my experience, and to suggest how it might fit with your organisation.

As you described it to me, your print production and design business in Basingstoke, which you started with Stephen about ten years ago, has grown to almost 40 people. You now feel you need a dedicated HR and training person, but not on a full-time basis. I have in the past worked in a small consultancy, so I have a good understanding of these issues in smaller organisations.

Since 1993 I have been recruitment officer with the XYZ Partnership, and wholly responsible for the past two years for the recruitment of all staff at all grades. For the last eight months I have briefed our six external training providers. I recently sourced a new provider for our negotiating skills course. So you can see I am well used to finding good staff and good suppliers – the key to any thriving consultancy.

We have had problems in ensuring a uniform approach in equal opportunity interviewing in all our offices. So we reviewed the interview training of our top managers and I gave them extra coaching. If you thought coaching on this or similar topics might be appropriate for your staff, I would be happy to do it. I have worked in a variety of personnel and HR functions since graduating in 1989, and been a Member of the Chartered Institute of Personnel & Development (MCIPD) since 1993.

The XYZ Partnership specialises in outsourced payroll. The business is expanding, and opportunities do exist, but mostly to do more of the same. So I am investigating other ideas, either in employment or in self-employment, in my local area of Reading/ Basingstoke.

It is a coincidence that we both know Jack Williams from Design Engineering Associates. He has been talking to me about doing similar work for him, and, as he is in Fleet, that might fit in well with my plans. If I were to work as a contractor for you and Jack, both organisations could benefit from my HR skills without making a full-time commitment. So I would be pleased to take the ideas we cooked up in Catherine's kitchen further. I will talk to Jack this weekend, and telephone you next week for a chat.

Yours sincerely

John Michaels

Analysis of the networking letter
As you might expect, this is a rather different sort of letter from others John Michaels has written.

- Because of how they met, the style can be more informal – 'the ideas we cooked up in Catherine's kitchen . . .'.
- John clearly made the most of the opportunity when meeting Anne at the party, and has established a good rapport with her – 'It is a coincidence that we both know Jack . . .'.
- He has tailored his letter to present his work experience in a way that matches with what Anne needs. So instead of talking about head office and regional branch difficulties, which are clearly of little interest to Anne, he has highlighted previous

relevant experience – 'I have in the past worked in a small consultancy, so I have a good understanding of these issues in smaller organisations.'

- He is trying to anticipate Anne's company's needs and show how he could be useful – 'If you thought coaching on this or similar topics might be appropriate for your staff, I would be happy to do it.'
- He is showing flexibility in linking one of Jack's ideas with Anne's business in much the same area, which could be of mutual benefit to everyone. So Jack and Anne get their part-time HR/training person, and John can stay in his preferred geographical area.
- He is also showing that he is taking the initiative – 'I will talk to Jack this weekend, and telephone you next week for a chat.'
- Importantly, John is showing (rather than telling) many of the attributes and attitudes which are vital to a small business, such as flexibility, creativity, linking chance meetings and seeing opportunities.
- He has been honest and said why he wants to move. He is unlikely to be jeopardising his current job by doing this, and it helps Anne to understand his motivation.
- He puts a good case for the benefits of having a part-time person – 'both organisations could benefit from my HR skills without making a full-time commitment'.
- He is putting himself in Anne's position, and showing he understands how important people are, especially in a small consultancy – 'I am well used to finding good staff and good suppliers – the key to any thriving consultancy'.

The cold-call letter

A sample of a cold-call letter that is completely speculative and written without the benefit of networking is:

Contact details

Date

Dear [name]

I am writing to you as the . . . . [job function] of . . . . [organisation]. I read in . . . . [trade press/newspaper] that you have recently been awarded the XYZ contract. As I gained a good deal of experience in that process/product/etc. in my previous job at . . . ., I thought it could be useful for you to know about me. During my time at ABC Limited, we worked with XYZ for many years, and were particularly pleased with its . . . . [a feature or benefit]. It enabled us to make our moulding process 10 per cent more productive because of the speed of melt. My particular role was as Quality Manager, so I understand the product very well. Over the years, the account manager [name] at XYZ and I worked together well and developed a good working relationship.

I would be keen to discuss with you in greater detail how my experience could be useful to you with your new contract. If you would like a chat on the phone, please call me at the contact number at the head of this letter. If I do not hear from you, I will telephone you in a couple of weeks.

Yours sincerely

Jean McCann

Analysis of the cold-call letter
The success rate for cold-call letters varies. As Jean McCann has done, you can boost your chances of getting a positive response by:

- making sure you write to the correct person
- showing your interest in the company by researching it so you have a news item to which you can relate your approach
- directly linking your experience with what the company is likely to want and/or need
- being gently assertive about wanting to keep in touch with the person.

Pre-interview hurdles

Sometimes organisations take the trouble to interview candidates only to find that they are either not technically competent or not motivated enough to do the job. In order to avoid wasting precious time, many companies now try to assess the applicants' competence, motivation or cultural fit by asking them to do tests, the results of which determine whether or not they will be shortlisted for interview.

Tests

Tests to assess job applicants come in a variety of forms. Psychometric tests check whether a candidate is motivated and shares the aims of the organisation, mental acuity tests determine how good you are at verbal or numerical reasoning, and tests of technical competence check your ability to do something that is technically important and an integral part of the job: for example, that someone applying for the post of an experienced forklift truck driver can in fact drive a forklift truck.

Psychometric tests

Psychometric tests are used to judge an applicant's motivation and possible cultural fit – they are meant to give the recruiters some sense of 'what makes you tick'. They should be administered by trained and qualified people, who will usually be from the organisation's HR department. In many cases, you are meant to receive feedback on your performance in a report and/or get a chance to discuss that report.

These tests are not designed to trip you up but to check for genuine job/organisational fit. They will be paper-based or computer-based, often forcing you to choose between a limited range of options. For example, you may be asked to answer 'always', 'usually', 'sometimes', 'occasionally' or 'never' to a question about whether you prefer to work on your own. If you were applying for a job which relied heavily on a team effort for success, then answering 'always' or 'usually' to this question will severely hamper your chances of success. The thinking behind this line of questioning is transparent, and so you have a choice here. If you genuinely would answer 'sometimes', 'occasionally' or 'never' then you have nothing to fear from this question.

On the other hand, if you really would like to reply 'always' or 'usually', you can choose to be honest or dishonest about what you actually put down as your answer. The honest approach is to mark your preferred choice, and accept that as a consequence you may not get through to the interview. This is probably in everyone's long-term interest. The less honest approach is to give the answer you think the recruiter wants. This can store up problems for everyone later on, because you are not giving a true portrayal of yourself, and the interviewers may feel short-changed.

Other psychometric tests are less transparent, so you will not have the moral dilemma outlined above. It is best to regard them as a hurdle you have to overcome. The organisation may be looking for a certain sort of person, which you either are or are not. So just relax, follow the instructions and be yourself. You cannot influence the outcome so nothing you do will make any difference.

How important are these tests in determining whether you will be asked for interview? Staff at most organisations view them as providing interesting additional information, which may be raised at interview along the lines of, 'I note from your XXX profile that you like . . . . Can you give me some examples of that from your work experience?' Few recruiters will view them as the fount of all knowledge, and will apply their judgement too.

Mental acuity tests

These tests, many of which check a candidate's verbal or numerical reasoning, are different from psychometric tests in that you can practise for them. If the job calls for good numeracy skills – for example, one which requires the analysis of figures – the employing organisation would be justified in asking you to do such a test. They are likely to be problem-solving questions, along the lines of, 'If one man walks across the desert at a rate of x km per hour, and a car travels in the opposite direction at y km per hour, when . . .?' Alternatively, you could be asked to analyse some figures and answer questions on what you have done. If the organisation is large, it will have asked enough people to do the test to have its own 'norm group' against which your results will be measured, usually on a centile scale. If not, you will be measured against an appropriate centile scale from the organisation which devised the test.

Practising beforehand can boost your result, because you can work out the drift of the questions, and see the sorts of problems that are likely to come up. Copies of the most common tests should be available in your local public library: ask the reference librarian for help. Your local Jobcentre or Learning Skills Council (in England and Wales) or Local Enterprise Company (in Scotland) are also good places to ask.

How important the results of these tests are depends on the organisation. Some set great store by them, and want everyone they recruit to fall into the XX centile against their norm group. Others view them as a source of useful extra information. Of course, if the tests are judging skills that are central to the job you have applied for, the results will count for a lot more. For example, if the job is to do with analysing figures, a poor score in a numerical test will introduce considerable doubt about your technical competence. A spectacularly low score will mean that you will certainly not get called for an interview. Again, this is probably just as well – these tests are accurate in what they measure, and are unlikely to mislead the recruiters about your skills.

Technical competence tests

Depending on the kind of job you are applying for, this sort of test could take the form of writing, checking, presenting, solving or completing something, often under a time constraint. For example, if the job were as a journalist you might be asked to write a short piece in the style of the newspaper, journal or magazine on a pre-selected topic. If you fail such a test you are unlikely to get through to interview.

Assessment centres

Another form of test, which lasts much longer, is the kind you have to do at an assessment centre. You will usually be there for most or all of a day. A wide range of organisations use them: for example, the armed forces will ask job applicants to attend a specialist centre for a few days to test their physical and mental fitness. At such centres you are likely to be asked to do all or some of the tests referred to above.

You may also be asked to participate in a group discussion or group activity, in which you and the other candidates will be asked to talk about a particular issue or solve some problem together. During the test the group will be watched by trained assessors, who will record the exchanges and the contributions made by individuals. To get any score at all, despite your nerves and reservations about the falseness of the situation, you must say or do something. Some simple and straightforward things you must do are: listen to instructions and record them, learn everyone's names and use them, search for common ground, listen to people and summarise contributions, be co-operative, be aware of time and remind others, give credit to others, stand back from the activity and re-state any objectives you have been given, look for solutions, and build group consensus. Some fairly obvious things will count against you: being crassly competitive or aggressive, interrupting people and not listening, taking credit for something you did not do, being unkind or unfair, staying silent or not participating, standing aloof and not 'playing the game'.

Depending on the job you have applied for, in addition to the group exercise described – which is very common – you could be asked to do any or all of the following.

- An in-depth technical interview. For example, if the job were as a client director in a consultancy, you may well have an interview with the sales and marketing director to check on your knowledge and experience of their market. This would supplement any technical test you may have done.

- An interview with a senior person or panel, who has the final decision-making authority. Although this can be nerve-racking, it is also your chance to put questions to them as well. This is especially important if you have any misgivings about the job, as they should be able to answer them, whereas a junior person would have to refer your questions to someone else.

- A presentation on a topic relevant to the job and/or the organisation's activities. Many jobs now call for the ability to give a talk, make a presentation, make your case in a meeting of colleagues, or present the latest figures, so this test is commonly used. For example, an important part of the client director's job above would be to do presentations to clients, so the recruiters will want to check out these skills in a live situation.

- A situation that replicates as far as possible some other aspect of the job you are being interviewed for. For example, Steve is a charity worker, and applying for a posting as an overseas emergency co-ordinator, responsible for on-the-ground logistics, people and project management in war-torn situations. His weekend assessment was held in Kent – which nobody would regard as a war zone – but it was very outdoors-based, with outside activities interspersed with intense planning sessions and crisis meetings indoors. This was a good design, as it was clearly intended to see Steve perform under what could be his usual working conditions, and because Steve could see why they were asking him to do these things, he was able to enter into the spirit of things and just be himself. He got the job.

Ask yourself why the organisation is going to all this effort. Training assessors and setting up these sorts of exercise is expensive, so it will not be done just for fun. These activities are used as a test because in today's world the success of organisations is to a large extent dependent on employees co-operating on projects, working together in ad-hoc teams and coming to a consensus. Also, with many staff having increased autonomy, needing a broad and flexible range of skills, and being able to set and meet their own objectives, organisations will often want to assess your skills in these areas before they appoint. Look again at the job description and consider what you know so far about the job and the organisation's culture. What competencies is it looking for in suitable candidates? Can you list some core skills that are likely to make the recruiters feel confident in and comfortable about someone? When you can write that list, you will know how to behave in this sort of artificial situation. You will be briefed before and/or during the assessment.

Being selected for interview

A good CV and letter of application will increase your chances of selection for a first interview, especially if you are changing job function or industry. Clearing this first hurdle of being invited to an interview can be hard and you may be demoralised till you do, so allow yourself a small treat when you do get selected.

How organisations select people for interviews

With equal opportunity legislation in place, organisations must take care to recruit in a non-discriminatory way. Ignorance is no defence. Organisations that take their recruitment seriously observe good practice and follow some version of the procedure given in this section. Some are lax and may operate in a discriminatory way. Most fall somewhere in between, and may use some but not all of these policies. During your job search you are likely to encounter all three sorts of organisation. Use your experience of them as another way of judging whether you want to work for them. Recruitment is a two-way process, after all.

Unless organisations can demonstrate a clearly legitimate business justification for doing so, they are required by law not to discriminate against job applicants (at any stage of the recruiting process) on the grounds of:

- race, colour, sex and sexual orientation, national origin, religion, age, citizenship
- marital status, pregnancy, future childbearing plans, children's details, childcare arrangements
- disability, handicap, medical conditions, previous illnesses
- height or weight
- English-language skills
- friends/relations working for employer
- arrest records, spent conviction records, military service discharge
- credit rating.

If an applicant feels he or she has suffered discrimination, redress can be achieved via an industrial tribunal. It is the applicant's responsibility to demonstrate that discrimination has taken place. The employer, on the other hand, must show that the decision was made for sound and justifiable reasons. If the tribunal upholds the complaint, the employer will be ordered to pay compensation, which is set by the tribunal and is not subject to any financial limit. The Equal Opportunities Commission★ and the Commission for Racial Equality (CRE)★ sometimes offer assistance to individuals in such cases. While discrimination against job applicants is notoriously difficult to prove, because the burden of proof is on the individual, it can be costly for the employer – not just in money terms, but also in respect of damage to the firm's image.

Increasingly, organisations are moving away from a job description which only lists responsibilities and duties, and are teasing out the underlying competencies people need to fulfil these responsibilities and do the duties outlined. This is known as a competence-based approach. So the competencies will be listed, either as an extra part of the job description or on a separate sheet. If you apply for a job with an organisation that uses this approach, you will probably be asked in your application to provide evidence of each competence. If you have an achievement-based CV, this should be straightforward as you can extract examples of what you have done as 'evidence'. Sometimes, the organisation will state whether a competence is 'essential' or 'desirable', which is helpful as it shows you the relative importance given to each. At interview a structured approach is used, where standard questions are asked, with supplementary questions when extra information is needed. This process may seem complex, but research shows it to be more successful at finding suitably skilled and versatile people – particularly when combined with assessment at an assessment centre.

Professional recruiters do not compare candidates against each other. Instead, they assess each person against the criteria and competencies specified in the advertisement, person specification and job description. They then place his or her CV into one of three piles – 'Must see', 'Possible' or 'Polite turn-down'. The recruiters may then go through the CVs in the 'Must see' pile and try to differentiate between those competencies that are necessary and those that are desirable, using a matrix (see example below) to analyse the applications. At the first and second interviews, this information will be transferred to a second matrix so the recruiters can summarise and record impressions and extra evidence that crops up during the interview(s).

If a competence-based approach were being used, the matrix would comprise the competencies that are required. Alternatively, a seven-point scheme is used by many recruiters to record the data about the candidates, as follows:

- physical make-up: health, appearance, bearing, speech
- attainments: education, qualifications, experience
- general intelligence: intellectual capacity
- special aptitudes: mechanical, manual dexterity, facility in use of words and figures
- interests: intellectual, practical, constructional, social, artistic
- disposition: influence over others, steadiness, dependability, self-reliance
- circumstances: any special demands of the job, such as willingness to work unsocial hours, travel in UK or abroad, etc.

The following example demonstrates this process.

Charity Shop Manager, based in Winchester

XYZ charity runs 500 shops, which are at the front line of our campaigning and fund-raising activities. We are launching 30 new-look stores to sell the full range of XYZ trading goods and donated merchandise to fund our work with disadvantaged people.

As you will be responsible for the merchandising, promotions, security and day-to-day running of an XYZ shop, it is essential that you have solid retail management experience. Our success relies on your ability to manage and recruit a hardworking team of volunteers, plan ahead, exercise budgetary control and meet your sales targets.

Stock is very varied, so a flexible approach is important to maintain and operate a suitable stock-control system. Good communication skills are necessary, too, because you will be training and developing volunteers' skills and team spirit. You will be competing with other local traders in an attractive part of town so the shop should attract the highest level of customers. Some Saturday working is required.

From this advertisement it is clear that the following skills and qualities are being sought: experience of retail management, involving merchandising, promotions, security, managing and recruiting staff (volunteers), budgeting and planning, meeting sales targets, maintaining and operating a stock-control system; good communication skills, training and developing volunteers' skills; engendering team spirit; setting up an attractive shop; willingness to work occasional Saturdays.

The recruiter will use these criteria to decide which CVs go into the 'Must see' pile. This pile will then be systematically analysed as follows.

First analysis of candidates

	Jonathan Evans	Christine Bamford	Philip Castle
Physical make-up health appearance speech	to be seen	to be seen	to be seen
Attainments			
GCSEs/A levels	8/2	9/3	8/0
HND/degree/ professional qual.	–	Business studies, Univ. E. Anglia	GNVQ in retail management
General intelligence	sounds bright	sounds good	sounds very keen
Special skills and experience			
1. retail management	M&S 18+ entry, Section Manager, 10 years' retail experience	Top Shop, graduate entry, now Deputy Shop Manager, 5 years' experience	W.H.Smith, Section Manager, started as Sat worker, 15 years' experience
2. merchandising	yes	yes	yes
3. promotions	?not much	yes	no
4. security	yes	?some	yes
5. recruitment	no	yes, Sat staff	no
6. managing staff	yes, up to 6	yes, up to 12	yes, up to 10
7. training staff	yes, plenty	yes, plenty	yes, ?plenty
8. budgeting & planning	?some	?any	yes
9. sales targets	?	yes	?
10. stock control	?limited	yes	yes
Team spirit?	should be good	sounds OK	OK
Communication skills?	- ditto -	- ditto -	- ditto -
Can set up attractive shop?	?little experience	?not much	?some
Saturday working	yes	yes	yes
Disposition			
Confident	check	yes?/check	check
Enthusiastic	letter sounds good	sounds keen	keen
Responsible	well used to it!	yes	?
Security-conscious	very	seems to be, check	yes
Self-reliant	?check	?check	?check
Organised	seems to be	highly!	yes
Proactive	check	check	check
Focused	?what next	clear about goals	?what next
Interests	swims, badminton	motor bikes, mountain biking	French cookery, modern French cinema
Circumstances	wants to return to Winchester (mother ill). Family in Far East in 1970s	keen to move to area. Travel in India	strong interest in working with the developing world
Notice period	6 weeks	4 weeks	4 weeks
Salary expectations	check	check	check
Overall impression	to be seen	to be seen	to be seen

A number of people may need to see your CV and letter of application, so these summary sheets can be passed around with the file of 'Must see' candidates. People can add their own comments and questions. In preparation for the interview, all the information will be transferred to a second sheet which is dedicated to an individual.

Name: Jonathan Evans
Date of interview:_____

	Application	Interview	Comments
Physical make-up	to be seen		)
health			) check
appearance			)
speech			)
Attainments			
GCSEs/A levels	8/2		check on in-house
HND/degree/	–		qualifications
professional qual.			
General intelligence	sounds bright		question to check
Special skills and			need more info
experience			
1. retail management	M&S 18+ entry,		check breadth of
	Section Manager,		experience
	10 years' retail		
	experience		
2. merchandising	yes		get examples
3. promotions	?not much		clarify
4. security	yes		run through his
			system
5. recruitment	no		
6. managing staff	yes, up to 6		enough experience?
7. training staff	yes, plenty		systematic approach?
8. budgeting & planning	?some		enough experience?
9. sales targets	?		)
10. stock control	?limited		) check
Team spirit?	should be good		)
Communication skills?	should be good		) check
Can set up attractive shop?	?little experience		more info needed
Saturday working	yes		discuss
Disposition			
Confident			check
Enthusiastic	letter sounds good		
Responsible	well used to it!		
Security-conscious	very		
Self-reliant			?check
Organised	seems to be		
Proactive			check
Focused			what next?
Interests	swims, badminton		

Circumstances	wants to return to Winchester (mother ill). Family in Far East in 1970s	why not internal transfer within M&S? Check interest in trading with the developing world
Notice period	6 weeks	
Salary expectations		check
Second interview?		
Overall impression	to be seen	

The 'Comments' column is used both as a reminder of questions to ask or points to clarify, and as a place to record extra information.

Organisations which take recruitment seriously will train their interviewers, whether they are in the personnel/HR department or are line managers. This training will cover communication skills such as the use of open questions, listening and reading body language. It will, as has been pointed out, also deal with equal opportunity issues, so that any bias is avoided during the recruiting process.

Some organisations use a panel of interviewers. This is particularly common in the public sector, charity, teaching and academic fields. If the employing organisation is professional about recruitment, the panel will have decided on which of its members will handle the different aspects of the interview. This usually extends to who will ask each question. This preparation is done to avoid interviewers tripping each other up, or repeating themselves, so that they give candidates a good impression of their organisation and make sure all their questions are answered.

In other organisations candidates may be interviewed by either only one person, or a few people but one at a time. They may, for instance, be seen by someone from personnel/HR, who will give them information about the organisation, may administer any tests (see above), etc. They will then be passed on to their prospective line manager, who will interview them in depth.

Knowing how organisations select candidates for interviews can help you pitch your CV and letter accordingly. The next step is to prepare for the interview itself.

Preparing for interviews

For a variety of reasons, interviews can be a poor way to judge whether someone can and will do a job, and whether he or she will fit in with the organisation. This could be because both interviewee and interviewer are poorly prepared and, in the case of the interviewer, untrained as well. The consequence of this is that none of the three questions (about competence, motivation and cultural fit) is fully probed and answered, so the company could end up with a poor or reasonable – not a good – fit.

Despite the fact that some interviews are not effective in what they set out to do, nearly all organisations use them to recruit staff. Some augment the interview(s) with tests of technical competence, psychometric tests and the use of assessment centres (see above). Interviews are, therefore, a hurdle every jobseeker has to learn to take in his or her stride. The competence-based approach described earlier is improving the effectiveness of interviewing as a way of selecting the best candidate. It has clear benefits to the candidate, as it is based on evidence about what you have actually done, so you are more likely to be able to relax, talk naturally and be yourself. Theoretical or hypothetical questions, in contrast, are difficult to answer in a genuine way because they are about what you might do, and so most people sound a bit wooden when answering them.

Organisations which try to recruit as professionally as possible are more likely to help themselves by:

- using a standardised procedure for selection (see above)
- having two rounds of interviews: at the first the candidate is screened by a 'gatekeeper', i.e. someone from the personnel department and/or a line manager; at the second he or she is seen by the line manager and a more senior manager
- being aware of the latest legislation on matters such as equal opportunity interviewing
- paying candidates' interview expenses
- using tests of ability, psychometric tests, group exercises, assessment centres, etc.

An interview is the best opportunity for you as a jobseeker to impress your suitability upon the recruiter. It is vital, therefore, that you prepare well for the occasion.

You could start by asking yourself why you are going to the interview. This is not as silly as it sounds. The answer(s) could be: to get through to the second interview to learn more about the company to help you decide whether you would like to work for it or not, to show the recruiter how well you fit the job, to get interview practice. Make sure you know what you want from the interview so you can prepare for it accordingly.

Depending on the type of organisation, it may be possible to make a visit to the company before your interview. This will help with your preparation in lots of practical ways, especially if you are returning to work after a career break or are changing industry.

You will be able to check the route to the offices and any travel hold-ups. If you time your visit to coincide with lunch-time, you could check what employees in the organisation wear: you may not want to be a company clone, but you might as well fit with the culture, rather than clash with it. During your visit you could take the opportunity to pick up some company brochures from the reception area if none were sent to you in an information pack. These are enormously revealing documents, and will be a big help in your preparation because you can find out both hard facts (product information, sales patterns, etc.) and softer, more company-cultural facts (possibly revealed in the language and pictures – if any – in the brochures).

The most important element of your preparation should be anticipating the questions you are likely to be asked at the interview and rehearsing the answers. Again, it cannot be emphasised too strongly that what employers need to be convinced of at every stage of the recruiting process is whether you can do the job (which tests your competence and ability), whether you will actually do it (your motivation) and whether you will fit in (cultural fit).

The first of these questions ('Can you do the job?') probes your competence, including your skills and achievements. The interviewers know from your CV what qualifications you have and what your previous or current job description is, so they are unlikely to approach the issue directly by asking for a summary of what you have been doing. Instead, the kind of questions they may ask to establish your abilities are: 'What is the greatest challenge you have faced in your current job?', 'How did you handle it?', 'What did you learn from the experience?', 'Can you describe one difficult situation you had to deal with recently, and how you handled it?', 'Looking back over your career, what has been the achievement you are most proud of, and why?', 'What do you enjoy most about your present job and why?', 'What do you enjoy least and why?' You may even be asked what makes you special – in other words, why the organisation should employ you in preference to the other candidates. This probing could take the form of: 'Why should we give you the job?', 'How do you think you could get the best from your team/colleagues/manager?'

The second question ('Will you do the job?') aims at uncovering your motivation levels. The sort of questions asked for this purpose are: 'What are you looking for in a job now?', 'Why would you like to work for our organisation?', 'What aspects of this position interested you most when you applied/heard about it?', 'What do you bring to the teams you work with?'

The third main issue recruiters will want to satisfy themselves about is cultural fit. They will not be so crude as to ask 'Will you fit in?', but will try to ascertain the answer to the question by asking, for example: 'How do you like to manage your staff?', 'How do you deal with any disciplinary problems?', 'How would your staff/manager describe your management style?', 'Looking back over your career, where have you been most happy, and why?', 'What do you know about us as an organisation, and what do you like about what you know or hear?'

Remember that in addition to answering the three sorts of questions above, you are also trying to build a rapport with the people opposite, as this could be the start of a new relationship. When you answer the questions, try to tailor or relate them to the job and organisation. This helps the interviewer see that you have thought yourself into the job already, and proves once again your ability, motivation and 'fit'. For example, when answering the question, 'How would your manager describe your management style?', you could answer, 'They usually describe me as fair and involving, which I think would fit with your organisation because . . .'

Do not forget that the interview should be two-way. The interviewers will be trying to see whether you can do the job, want to do the job and would fit into their organisation. At the same time you should be thinking about the answers to these about the position and the company.

- Can I do this job? Is it just within or beyond my competence and therefore a good challenge? Or it is very much beyond my competence, and would I struggle? Is it too easy, and would I get bored quickly?

- Do I want to do the job? What is the challenge in the job for me? Which of my strengths is this job playing to? Which of my weaknesses will I struggle most with? What would my prospective boss be like to work for? What are the prospects like here? How does this job fit with my long-term career plans?
- Will I fit in? How would I describe the atmosphere? If I were to prepare a 'thought bubble' for this organisation, what would it be? Does it fit well enough with mine for us to be compatible? What are the people like? Are they 'my' sort of people? What is 'success' in this organisation? How are people rewarded? What is the structure like? Do I like all these things?

Having all these questions to answer for yourself may help to remove the feeling that an interview is a test you pass or fail, and enables you to see that you must also use it to make a judgement.

Interview checklists

Before attending an interview you need to focus yourself in a number of ways: on the company, on yourself, and on what you want by the close of the interview. The checklists below will help with your preparation.

The company and the position

- What do you know about the company (including its culture)? What gaps can you fill before the interview? How?
- What do you know about the job? Do you have a job description? If so, become familiar with the job and the required competencies. What do you think is the greatest challenge in the job? How would you handle the first six months? Is there anything that strikes you as odd, or out of place? If you do not have a job description, can you obtain one before the interview? It may be available, and perhaps all you have to do is to ask for it. If for some reason there is not a job description, at least by asking for one you have shown how keen you are.
- What do you know about the interviewer(s) and the selection process? Do you know the names and the job titles of the people who will be interviewing you? If so, can you anticipate who is likely to ask which question? Will there be only one round of interviews, or two? Are there any supplementary tests or procedures?

- Do you know where the organisation is and how to get there? This is an obvious question, but you must make sure you do not arrive late – it sends a message that you are at worst unenthusiastic and at best disorganised. Arriving early signals that you are keen. It also gives you a chance to calm down and absorb the atmosphere of the place.

Yourself

- What is your 'thought bubble' for this job?
- How does that translate into a pithy and memorable career statement?
- What are your major achievements/what makes you special?
- How do you prove you can do the job?
- What is your career goal/your motivation? How does this job move you towards that goal?
- How well does your career goal relate to this particular organisation and this job?
- Are there any tricky/difficult/problem areas in your CV/application form/letter of application, and how will you deal with them positively?
- What will you wear? Have you checked the industry/company norm?
- Have you got all the paperwork together?
- Have you got everything you need in your briefcase (paperwork, money, tissues, newspaper or book, hairbrush, umbrella)?

During the interview

Aim to leave a lasting impression of yourself, and before the interview ends:

- be sure you have understood what the job entails, especially in terms of the competencies and the duties listed in the job description
- satisfy yourself that you have the right impression of the cultural fit between you and the organisation
- find out what the next stage is, and the timing
- try to come to a view about whether you could/would want to do the job, or whether it might be better to pull out at this stage
- decide who would be the most appropriate referee(s).

Dealing with nerves

It is only human to be nervous before you start something that is important to you. However, you could take a number of steps to calm yourself down and feel more confident.

Look natural

Do not be tempted to go out and buy a new outfit just for the interview. If you are not working, it will be money you can probably ill afford to spend. If you are working, it is still not a wise investment. This is because you show yourself in the best light when your nerves are under control, and you are being as much like yourself as the artificial situation of an interview allows you to be. If you have just bought a new outfit, it will still feel new and you will be unused to it and may not know how to sit comfortably in it. It is both cheaper, and a better interview tactic, if you can wear something smart and appropriate which feels 'like you'. In other words, you can put it on and then simply forget about it. This leaves you free to concentrate on more important things, such as what you are going to say.

Nevertheless, what you wear matters. There are three things to consider. Apart from being something you feel comfortable in, it should be an outfit which says clearly what you are, and what people would expect you to wear. For example, if the interview were for a job as a junior designer at a small co-operative theatre company, a city suit would look incongruous. Conversely, if you were going for a job in the City, anything other than a dark suit would look very out of place. The cultural fit factor comes into play here, so it is worth finding out what people in that organisation and industry sector wear. This includes colours, styles, formal *vs* informal, etc.

You may or may not want to reflect the style of the people already working in the organisation. It may be entirely appropriate for a consultant, for example, to look like an outsider – indeed, looking different could even add credibility. However, if you want to be an employee, you need to signal that you can be an insider. Many organisations are quite tribal, and clothing is a highly visible sign of membership – can you/do you want to join their tribe?

Last-minute preparations

Arriving early for an interview helps with nerves and therefore improves your chances of success. First, you have to find the right entrance to the premises and sign in and/or get your security badge; you may find it useful to visit the toilet and tidy yourself up. All this can take some time and usually longer than you think. Most reception areas have somewhere you can leave your coat, get a coffee and leave the paraphernalia you needed for the journey but not for the interview itself. Being laden with possessions could give the impression that you attract clutter. Also, if you are nervous, the fewer things you have to drop, fumble or fiddle with the better. So get rid of that coat with the awkward buttons and leave the recalcitrant umbrella and crumpled newspaper in reception.

What *should* you take in to the interview room? A clear plastic folder looks neat and efficient. In it you could put all the correspondence relevant to the interview. This includes the job description, the job advertisement, your letter of application and a copy of the CV you sent to the organisation. You could add any company information you have such as the accounts or brochures, and a list of dates when you could attend a second interview. In case you are worried that you may get muddled and lose your thread during the interview, you may want to carry with you a small piece of paper on which you have written your thought bubble, plus your unique selling points and major achievements. You could also add a list of questions you have for them.

While in the toilet, you might like to calm your nerves with a few tricks used by actors and singers such as:

- yawning, which relaxes the lower jaw, and gets extra oxygen into the system
- smiling, which again relaxes the lower jaw, and releases endorphins (proteins which act as natural painkillers) into the body
- practising 'affirmations'. These are short statements in the present tense about what you want to be. For example, 'I am a skilled trainer who works well with groups'; 'I am good at managing projects, and always finish on time and within budget'
- running cool water over pulse points to lower the heart rate. The most accessible pulse points are in the wrist and at your temples
- urinating. Nerves are a diuretic, so pre-empt this physiological reaction
- tensing up your upper body muscles while breathing in, and then relaxing them while breathing out (the latter should take longer than the former)

- breathing in deeply through your nose (on the count of five seconds), right down into your diaphragm, holding the breath for five seconds, and then breathing out through your mouth (for ten seconds)
- visualising something peaceful (such as a bubbling stream or a serene garden) or repeating a particular word (like 'calm', 'quiet', 'peace') to soothe yourself.

If you are an extrovert, talking to other people while waiting to be called in may help you relax. You could, for example, engage the receptionist or other people in the reception area in conversation about something general. On the other hand, if you are an introvert, this sort of inconsequential talk would probably make you feel worse. In that case, your best tactic would be to save your energy for the interview, and do something which relaxes you such as reading the newspaper or thinking about world events, the weather, or last night's sport.

Keep researching

Once you are settled in reception, sit quietly and absorb the atmosphere. What does it feel like? Are people dashing about with an air of barely controlled panic, or is there a sense of calm purposefulness? Does the atmosphere feel very quiet, friendly or leaden? Whatever it feels like, does it appeal to you?

The reception area is an organisation's most public area, and says a lot about it. Some companies display their products, samples and awards; others have lots of plants, or pictures of past luminaries; some may have a scale model of planned building works; or just a few dead plants or plastic flowers and uncomfortable chairs. The receptionist is the first person everyone meets, and his or her demeanour also reveals a great deal about an organisation. If you are an observant jobseeker you should be able to draw some inferences about the culture of the company. Not only can you find out a lot by simply sitting in reception, you may find topics that you can weave into the interview. You could enquire about or discuss some of the things on display such as the scale model, the products, or the awards, which will indicate to the interviewers your enthusiasm and powers of observation.

It is not just formal tests that organisations use to judge you. Sometimes, your attitude when being shown – often by the departmental secretary or assistant – to the interview room is also part of the selection procedure, as the interviewers may ask such people for their opinion of you. Many people reveal aspects of themselves in this short period that they would not dream of doing in the interview room, such as being patronising, making disparaging remarks about the organisation, or ignoring the staff member who is showing them the way to the interview room. Sometimes your interviewer will guide you back to reception. Just because you are no longer in the interview room, do not lower your guard – being shown around the office and meeting prospective colleagues are also tests, and should be regarded as part of the interview.

The interview itself

Who does what and when in an interview will vary from one interviewer to another, and from one organisation to another. If you are changing industry or job function, the new one may be different from the old, so check. For example, financial jobs are often dealt with by agencies, many of which will do an initial interview and then pass on the best few candidates to the organisation for either one or two further interviews. For jobs in teaching, schools advertise in the press themselves. The interested candidates often visit the school, which is a form of informal interview, and are then seen by a panel, which includes governors and sometimes a representative of the Local Education Authority. A further interview is rare, and the appointment is usually made on the day of the interview. Generally, for mid-level and senior appointments, you can expect two rounds of interviews.

It is important to remember that every question asked in an interview is asked for a reason. In organisations that follow best practice and ensure equal opportunity interviewing, all candidates will be asked the same set of questions. None the less, a good interview should be a conversation rather than a question-and-answer session, so recruiters will be flexible and ask supplementary questions depending on the replies given by candidates. This may be because they want to pursue something which sounds odd, or is poorly expressed, or to get extra information about a skill or an achievement.

Even in organisations that do not follow best practice, the structure of the interview is likely to be along the following lines:

- introduction to interviewer(s)/panel
- introduction to the organisation (structure, organisation's objectives and so on)
- (possibly) summary of job and required competencies – simply a reference to the job description
- discussion with you about your experience, skills and achievements (probably CV-based). This is used mainly to check competence and motivation
- more general discussion that is aimed, either overtly or not, at checking the cultural fit. This could be on your interests, what you like about your current job, etc.
- an opportunity for you to ask the interviewers any questions. Do not be tempted to ask 'pay and rations' questions that can make you look self-seeking, and therefore give a poor impression. It is probably safest to say something along the lines of how much you have enjoyed the discussion/finding out more, repeat how interested you are in the job, and finish with your short career statement as it relates to the organisation. If you have any questions about the organisation, select the most important one(s) now
- outline of what happens next in the process and when. You may be asked for names of referees at this point.

In common with many interactive situations between people, interviewing has its own set of rituals. However odd they may appear to be, you cannot change them while you are on the side of the desk seeking work. Remember that the vast majority of interviewers do not set out to trip people up intentionally, or to humiliate them. On the contrary, a well-trained interviewer will be adept at putting candidates at their ease, therefore enabling each one to show him- or herself in a favourable and natural way. Of course, you may be unlucky enough to come across untrained and inexperienced interviewers who view the interview as a chance for them to monopolise the conversation or put the candidate down. Again, it is vital to remember that interviews are a two-way process, as you and the organisation are each checking out the other. The way the interview is handled is probably indicative of other aspects of the organisation. If you are left with the impression that the company does not realise the importance of handling recruitment in a professional way, do you think it is likely to be any more committed to induction, training and development, giving feedback, and so on? As a prospective new employee, all these things will be very important to you, particularly in the first year or so in the new job.

This will be especially true if you are changing job function or industry, and therefore have a steep learning curve to deal with in your early days. An organisation which is either unable or unwilling to support its new employees may not be the best choice for someone making a major career change. So make sure that you feel as confident about the organisation as you want the recruiters to feel about you.

Making a good entrance

There is conflicting evidence about this, but it does seem that people are inclined to make up their minds about someone very early on in an interview, possibly within the first two or three minutes. So making a good entrance and beginning matter. So does your body language. Some people believe that interviews are in fact poor indicators of someone's ability to do the job. Perhaps that is because recruiters take so much notice of body language, what someone is wearing, the handshake, amount of eye contact, and similar factors.

Because the entrance and those first few minutes are so significant, remember to do three things: make eye contact, smile and give a firm handshake. When you are introduced to the interviewer(s), remember their names and try to use them in your replies because in combination with the eye contact and smile, you are showing your interest. Be alert to how members of the panel address you: if they call you by your title, make sure you do the same too.

Discovering the sub-text of the questions

Questions asked in an interview usually have, as described earlier, a sub-text that relates to one of three issues: competence, motivation and cultural fit. If you are changing career or are returning to work, you will be unfamiliar with, or out of practice at, working out the sub-text to questions, for which a good and positive reply needs to be framed. Trained interviewers are taught to ask searching and open questions. If they perceive that you sound vague or uncertain about something, it is their job to find out why by probing deeper.

One golden rule to remember is to match what they want with what you have. Crucially, this means that you must be very alert to what they want, and couch your experience, skills and achievements in terms which fit with them. Therefore, be prepared to ask for clarification if you do not understand a question, watch their reactions to your replies, and 'read' them to see whether their confidence in you is increasing. Many people make the mistake of thinking that standard replies are the way to respond to standard interview questions. This makes for a stilted and unnatural conversation because interviewer and interviewee keep missing each others' cues.

Below are some questions you may face in an interview. Taking the three-question approach of competence (C), motivation (M) and cultural fit (CF), can you sort each question into the appropriate category? Some may fit two, so you would need to circle both, such as C, M.

Question	C	M	CF
(1) How would your team describe you?	C	M	CF
(2) What is your greatest challenge in your present job?	C	M	CF
(3) What attracts you most about this job?	C	M	CF
(4) Could you describe a successful day?	C	M	CF
(5) What are you looking for in a job now?	C	M	CF
(6) Looking back over your career, where have you been most happy and why?	C	M	CF
(7) Now you have seen the job description, what do you think is the greatest challenge in this job?	C	M	CF
(8) Can you suggest three things you would do to meet that challenge in your first six months?	C	M	CF
(9) What do you admire most about your present organisation and why?	C	M	CF
(10) What skills do you bring to the teams you work in?	C	M	CF
(11) Can you describe a time when things went especially well?	C	M	CF
(12) What was your particular contribution to that success?	C	M	CF

(13) How does this job fit in with your longer-term career?	C	M	CF
(14) Can you tell me about when you successfully managed a difficult situation at work?	C	M	CF
(15) What did you learn about your management style from that experience?	C	M	CF
(16) Why would you like to work for us?	C	M	CF
(17) Who or what has influenced you most in your career?	C	M	CF
(18) How would your staff describe you?	C	M	CF
(19) What are your strengths?	C	M	CF
(20) What are your weaknesses?	C	M	CF
(21) What do you know about our organisation?	C	M	CF
(22) Which manager have you most enjoyed working for and why?	C	M	CF
(23) As your manager, how should I manage you so you can perform well?	C	M	CF
(24) What is in your guilt pile at work?	C	M	CF
(25) What do you think is the greatest threat to our industry at the moment?	C	M	CF
(26) Why should we employ you?	C	M	CF
(27) What have been the high and low points in your career?	C	M	CF
(28) Why did you choose those?	C	M	CF
(29) What training have you done recently, and how did it help you do your job differently/better?	C	M	CF
(30) What can you say about your leisure interests?	C	M	CF
(31) This job requires a lot of . . . . How does your experience relate to that?	C	M	CF

Once you have spotted which category the questions fall into, can you also think up succinct and positive replies to them? People who can be fluent, extrovert and personable usually score highly in interviews. Such skills transfer from industry to industry, job function to job function, and from interview into performance on the job. Any fool can over-complicate to obscure, confuse and hide his or her ignorance, but it takes real ability to be clear, focused and concise. Therefore, it is in your interest to practise these and similar questions so that you will be able to demonstrate these desirable qualities. You could team up with another jobseeker and the two of you could help each other.

Evaluating replies

In the exercise below, read each question and choose the reply you think gives the most positive impression, and decide why. Then choose the one you think would be least helpful or even damaging, and could lead you into even deeper difficulties, and, again, decide why. While evaluating each of the responses, try to anticipate the follow-up questions.

The post being interviewed for is a legal executive for a medium-sized firm of solicitors. The firm requires the jobholder to be competent in the following ways: have a steady and reliable approach to work, possess an ability to get on with people, be able to work to agreed client guidelines, have legal and management experience, be accurate, and be able to maintain confidentiality. The smartest candidates will select aspects of their current job which match well to what this organisation seems to want, at least according to the job description. Note: additional information to what is written in the job description may emerge during the interview, so the interviewee needs to remain alert to pick up on that and weave it into his or her responses.

Question: What do you like most about your present job?

Reply 1: I really enjoy the variety of my job. Each day is different. I meet or talk to new people all the time. As I know the job well, my boss is quite hands-off and I pretty much do my own thing these days. (Candidate's assumption: 'They want to know how sociable I am. Also I am proud that my boss trusts me enough to let me act independently because I am good at my job.')

Reply 2: I enjoy my job because our legal aid centre is very busy, and we have new people coming in all the time. Each person's worries are individual, and need to be treated confidentially. We have excellent guidelines on this, which everyone is trained in. (Candidate's assumption: 'They want to know I can work with people in a confidential manner and in a certain way.')

Reply 3: At Victim Support, we meet all sorts of people. They can be very distressed and sometimes frightened. They are often young so I can be like an older brother or sister to them. I really enjoy that caring side of my job. (Candidate's assumption: 'I have some legal experience, and am very good with people, and I have always been praised for my caring nature.')

Reply 4: At Elgin & Summerfields we have a broad range of clients, all of whom need to be treated confidentially and in 'the E&S way', as our senior partner, Mr Elgin, would say. I enjoy being part of a small, busy office where I feel my contribution really matters. (Candidate's assumption: 'I am proud to work for an established firm of solicitors with a distinguished reputation. Standards and people matter at E&S, I hope they do at this place too.')

Reply 5: At Anderson & Roberts, we have clear guidelines for our work with clients, which ensures confidentiality. I enjoy seeing our new and established clients regularly. It has also been a good experience for me to manage our new junior, who joined nine months ago. In a funny way, it has taught me a lot about my job. (Candidate's assumption: 'Clear guidelines are important, but so is the client relationship. They want management experience, and supervising the junior may not be much, but I can at least talk about it.')

Commentary on the replies

As a general guideline, you need to relate a fact about yourself to what the organisation needs or wants. Bearing this in mind, here is an analysis of the responses given above.

Reply 1: This is a worrying reply, making the candidate sound a bit like a social butterfly. Also, given that the job requires the ability to work to agreed client guidelines in a steady methodical way, an interviewer would be concerned as to whether this person could willingly work in this way, because he or she had a lot of freedom in his or her last position. The interviewer would want to ask three supplementary questions. The first would be about the sociability. The second would probe whether the candidate works to guidelines or not. The third would be aimed at finding out more about whether he or she is too used to having the freedom to act independently without much supervision. The sub-text to these would be 'I am beginning to think that we do not have a good fit here: I'd better check this out.' Depending on the replies to these extra questions, the interviewer may probe still further, or move on to another line of questioning. The original disquiet may remain.

Reply 2: This reply would make an interviewer feel much more confident. The candidate seems to have read the job description, has legal experience, although not in a practice, and has been trained to deal with clients in an appropriate way. Any supplementary questions asked would only be fact-finding, to enquire about the nature of the guidelines and the training. If satisfied, the interviewer would then move on to other areas.

Reply 3: It does not appear that this candidate has read the job description. The interviewer may wonder how the person got through to the stage of the first interview and whether it would be a complete waste of time to carry on. Although a caring nature is better than an uncaring one, this job is not about being an agony aunt or uncle to clients. Despite feelings of gloom, a trained interviewer would look for contrary evidence, i.e. not for evidence that will confirm his or her unease, but for some that will disprove it. So he or she will ask a probing question along these lines: 'We do need to be supportive when clients are distressed, but a legal executive needs other skills as well. You have a copy of the job description: can you tell me about your experience of other aspects of the job?'

Reply 4: This person sounds professional and well trained, and obviously has legal practice experience. Is he or she perhaps too much in the E&S mould to fit in here? Some obvious supplementary questions that may be asked here are: 'That sounds very professional, what do you think are the strengths of your client guidelines?'; 'Is there anything you would change?'; 'What sort of contribution do you feel you have made at E&S?'

Reply 5: This reply, which shows that the candidate has read the job description, will make an interviewer confident about his or her ability. Although the person does not have much experience of managing people, he or she has obviously reflected on what he or she has learnt, which is always a good sign. Supplementary questions are likely to be: 'What do you think it has taught you about your own job?'; 'What have you learnt about managing people?'; 'Could you tell me more about Anderson & Roberts' client guidelines?'

Replying to awkward questions

You may find in an interview that you are asked questions that seem particularly nasty and searching. They may be tricky to give a positive reply to and may relate, for example, to redundancy and career breaks. Comfort yourself with the fact that you are at the interview because someone thinks you can probably do the job, and however horrible the questions, the interviewer is asking them only to be convinced of your competence, motivation and cultural fit.

You seem rather over-qualified for this job. Why do you want it?

Is this a competence, a motivation or a cultural fit question? It is most likely to be a motivation question with a little competence added in. The sub-text to this question is probably something like this: 'You will get bored and leave us quickly, and then I shall have to start all over again.' Your job is to make the interviewer feel confident and comfortable, so what would be the best reply?

Reply 1: I have always wanted to work here, and this job will get me in so I can look around the organisation. Of course, I would give you six months or so . . .

Reply 2: I have been in the xxx division [of the same organisation] for some years, but my new boss is driving me crazy, and I have heard on the grapevine that yours is a good department to work for.

Reply 3: I have been made redundant, and I am going slowly batty at home, so I need a job to get me out of the house.

Reply 4: I do have lots of relevant experience, but that would benefit you because I know all the relevant people, and could be fully effective really quickly.

Reply 5: I am well qualified, but I want the job because I see the greatest challenge to be . . ., and with my experience I could tackle that well.

Reply 6: As you know, I am returning from a two-year break, and I need to build up my confidence in a job which does not stretch me too much.

Reply 7: As you know, I am returning from a three-year break, and I want an undemanding job which I can do 9–5, so I can then go home, forget all about work and spend time doing other things.

Reply 8: As you know, I have travelled for a year or so in the Far East, and this has given me some unique experience of . . ., which would be directly relevant to this job because you need . . .

Reply 9: No, I am not over-qualified. I think I have just the right experience for the job.

Reply 10: I am well qualified, and I worked hard to get those qualifications. I cannot believe you are counting my hard work against me.

Commentary on the replies

Although some of these answers are really poor, most interviewers have heard them – or similar ones – at one time or another. If you were faced with this question yourself, what would you say? In short, the smart candidates will acknowledge the questioner's concern by saying 'yes, I am well qualified', and then follow that up with a positive statement related to the organisation and/or the job. For example, 'but I think that would be to your advantage because I understand all the processes very well and can suggest some modifications' would set the interviewer's mind at rest. However, just saying the words will not give a favourable impression of you – they are only part of the message. You need to make sure that you sound positive and firm, and look the interviewer in the eye to reinforce the verbal message. You will ruin the effect of the good words if you speak in a quavering voice, wring your hands and look at your feet.

Here is an analysis of the replies and a re-wording of some of them to make them more positive.

Reply 1: Why is this so bad? It is an entirely selfish reply, and makes the candidate sound very calculating. Perhaps he or she genuinely has a long-held ambition to work in the organisation and wishes to convey that. How can it be said in a less damaging and more positive way? He or she could try, 'I have wanted to work for you for some time because I think your products are very innovative. My experience would be good for the organisation because I . . .' This reply is likely to lead the interviewer off the subject of over-qualification, and on to firmer ground in the two directions the candidate has signalled. One is the match between his or her experience and the organisation's needs in more depth, and the other is the innovative nature of the products.

Reply 2: This is obviously a response from an internal candidate, and is sycophantic. To complain about one manager in front of another is a foolish thing to do, whether you are an internal or an external candidate. Although both statements may be true, the interviewee is not helping him- or herself by stating them. An alternative could be, 'I have been in my present job for some years, and it is time to do something new. My experience would be good in this job because I . . .' A smart interviewer would pick up on the reason for making a move, and probe deeper, asking a supplementary question along the lines of 'Why do you want to move if you are settled?'

Reply 3: Again, this is probably true, but very negative. It needs to – and can – be expressed much more positively: 'As you know, I was made redundant from XYZ. My experience there has taught me the importance of customer satisfaction, and I know how crucial that is in a business like yours.' Once again, the candidate is showing how beneficial his or her experience will be to the organisation. He or she will be asked further about the redundancy (see below).

Reply 4: At last, a positive reply. The interviewer could probe the interviewee's knowledge more, or acknowledge how important it is to be fully effective quickly, and ask a follow-on question such as: 'How much notice do you need to give?'; 'Yes, you are right: in our business you cannot afford any down-time. What would be your first priority in the job?'

Reply 5: Another positive reply. The interviewer can either discuss the comment about X being the greatest challenge in the job, or explore how X would be tackled.

Reply 6: This may be true, but a damaging remark to make in an interview, especially since the question is aimed at uncovering the candidate's motivation level. A better response would be: 'I am well qualified, which I think would benefit you because . . .' The candidate may well need to update his or her skills and gain confidence (see Chapter 3). Some organisations have a deliberate policy of recruiting returners to the job market, and may have special training available. The candidate is right to be concerned about his or her lack of confidence, and would want to explore the organisation's policies on training, and whether there is a supportive culture.

Reply 7: How this is received will depend on the sort of job on offer. If the organisation is looking for someone who will be committed to working beyond 9–5, this is a dreadful reply. If it needs a person to do just a 9–5 job, for example, to work with sales reps, this reply is disarmingly honest. Assuming the latter to be the case, a re-worded reply might be: 'I am well-qualified for the job of making appointments for the sales reps as I did this for two years before I had the break with the twins.' The interviewer is being invited to explore the job the candidate had before the career break. He or she might follow up with a supplementary question: 'If it is so similar, why do you want this job?' An honest reply here may be: 'The twins are still quite small, and so I need a job with definite hours so I can organise childcare. I have the skills and experience you need, and I want to get back to the world of work.' Interviewers must not ask about childcare but candidates can offer information, especially if they think it may allay an employer's concerns.

Reply 8: Extended travel breaks make many interviewers uneasy: they worry that the candidate will get itchy feet and go off again or they wonder whether he or she will be able to acclimatise to the structure of work after being free of tight schedules for a long period. However, this is a good reply because it has linked the travel experience back to the world of work. This sends two messages, one direct, one indirect. The direct message is 'I have reflected upon my experience, and see how helpful it would be in your job because . . .' The indirect message is, 'I am ready to settle again because I have taken the time and imagination to relate my travelling to this job and your organisation.' The interviewer is being invited to ask: 'In what ways would your experience be directly relevant . . .?'

Reply 9: The candidate should never argue with the interviewer. Instead, he or she should smile, and say firmly: 'On the contrary, I think my experience would be very useful to you because of . . .'

Reply 10: Getting aggressive and aggrieved are probably as bad as arguing. No matter how cross the interviewee is, he or she must not let that anger show. This would be a better response: 'Yes, I am proud I went to university as a mature student. Being older meant that I could directly relate the theory to my earlier work experience, which I think would be beneficial to you because . . .'

'Why were you made redundant from your job at . . .?'

Redundancy, whether forced or voluntary, is a change from the established order of someone's life and recruiters need to be sure that the person has recovered from the experience sufficiently to start again, with vigour and self-confidence.

Reply 1: My boss and I had never got on, so when we lost the XYZ contract, he used it as an excuse to get rid of me.

Reply 2: I was the last of the old guard, so when orders dropped off, my face did not fit any more.

Reply 3: It's an occupational hazard for most people nowadays, isn't it? I applied because I know you have just got that contract for XYZ, and we worked as one of its suppliers for some years, so I thought my experience would be useful to you.

Reply 4: I volunteered, actually. I was fed up with the new management, who were always obsessed about costs and never bothered about quality.

Reply 5: With so much foreign competition, orders had dropped off and I was one of many to go. It's been like a breath of fresh air to me, and I thought my experience of working with some of your products would come in handy, so I applied.

Commentary on the replies

Some of these replies show that the candidates are still suffering from the trauma which so often accompanies redundancy. This is not to say that the hurt and anger are not justified; it is simply not appropriate to display these emotions at an interview. A candidate making a very negative response might as well stop wasting the time of all involved in the interview and leave right away. Although it would amount to stepping outside the role, the interviewer might take the time to suggest counselling. If the candidate is at all observant he or she will notice the latter's reactions to his or her comment, and try to rescue the situation.

Beware of volunteering very negative information about why you left a job. Of course, you should be honest, but also be positive. As mentioned earlier, inexperienced interviewers do not look for what is called 'contrary evidence', which would balance up the positive or negative impressions they are forming about someone. For example, if a candidate has given the impression that he or she lacks experience in a particular aspect of the job, an untrained interviewer would continue to look for more evidence to support the bad news, rather than look for something positive to counter-balance the negative. Once you realise what he or she is doing, you can turn things around to the positive by giving a strong lead.

An analysis of the responses above reveals a lot about the candidates making them.

Reply 1: An interviewee providing this answer is offering his or her own interpretation of events, not a statement of fact. It is aggressive, negative and very damaging to his or her chances. The interviewer, especially if he or she is the prospective manager, will hear lots of alarm bells ringing. He or she, if skilled, will recognise that the candidate still harbours so much resentment that it will be carried over into the next job. It is his or her job to find out how deep it is, and make an assessment based on that. How could this response be made more positive? 'When we lost the XYZ contract, our costs were too high, so redundancies were inevitable. I would like to work for you because my experience fits well with your need for a . . .'

Reply 2: Much the same analysis as for the first response applies here. Instead of being aggressive, this answer is a self-pitying one. A skilled interviewer would probably say, 'And why do you think your face suddenly did not fit any more after all those years?', so the candidate finds him- or herself in a deeper hole. A better response would be: 'Because of stiff foreign competition we could not invest as much as we should have in new machinery, so redundancies became inevitable. I was interested in this vacancy because you said you needed . . . As foreman, I have plenty of experience of this . . .'

Reply 3: If this first sentence were said with a rueful smile, the candidate would probably get away with it. The follow-on comments are very positive, and show that he or she has not been idle, but has kept up with local news. Most importantly, he or she has matched his or her experience with the needs of the organisation. The supplementary question will move off the dangerous ground of redundancy, and deal with the new contract instead.

Reply 4: This reply is even worse than numbers 1 and 2. This time the resentment is palpable, and all an interviewer needs to say is, 'Tell me more about it', and the floodgates will open. Some recruiters may regard those who take voluntary redundancy as gold-diggers, who do not need to work full-time again because they got so much in redundancy pay, so a candidate should beware of saying he or she volunteered. This response needs to be re-worded: 'As you probably know, we were bought out last year by XYZ Limited, who applied stringent cost controls. It became apparent that we were over-staffed, so redundancies were inevitable. I was interested in this job because you need . . ., and I have worked with that system for some years.'

Reply 5: This is a quick acknowledgement of the reasons, then moves on to more positive things. A supplementary question might delve into the 'breath of fresh air' comment, so the interviewee should be prepared with a positive reply to that. No matter how old a candidate is, organisations want him or her to have vigour and enthusiasm. If a person's redundancy has genuinely revitalised him or her, he or she could say so in a positive way: 'It was a shock, but now I feel like a new man/woman. It's been good for me to think again about what I can offer employers, and I think my main strengths are . . .'

After the interview

Just as interviewing procedures vary across organisations and industries, what happens afterwards does too. You may be told within a few minutes or hours of the interview whether you have been successful (either in getting the job or making it to the next round of the selection process), or it may take much longer for the organisation to make its decision. If the latter is the case, you can do several things while you wait to hear from the company.

- Analyse your performance as objectively as you can. Review how you thought it went and decide what you will do differently next time you are interviewed. This self-review is especially helpful if you are not in work at present, and are therefore missing out on the process of peer review that many people take for granted at work.
- Follow up with a short letter. Sometimes you come away from an interview and suddenly remember on the journey home that you did not say something which now seems important. Also, perhaps the more you think about it, the more you are convinced that you and the organisation are a good mutual match and you feel very enthusiastic about the job. Either way, you have nothing to lose by writing a short letter to those who interviewed you, saying just that. It is best to time its arrival just before they make a decision on the second interview or the final decision, perhaps two or three days after the interview. Writing such a letter is unlikely to boost you from being sixth out of six candidates to

being first, but it might move you from, say, being the fourth to the third. This improvement may get you a second interview, as many recruiters like to see a maximum of three people for a second round. It will be most useful when recruiters perceive the candidates to be of fairly equal merit, and then it may just make the difference. Of course, you have absolutely no way of knowing this – so you might as well try anyway. You could make three main points in such a letter: say how much you enjoyed the interview and why, point out how enthusiastic you are about the job, and give any extra information which may help the interviewers with their decision.

- Ask for feedback. That can help you with your job search because it gives you vital information about how you are coming across, helps you become more practised at interviews, and gives you added accuracy in your self-review. If you were unsuccessful, never ask why you did not get the job, because you will not get a reply. You can, however, ask for feedback on your interview. A short, polite telephone call along these lines can get you useful information: 'As you know I am changing careers from X to Y, so it would help me a lot to have your feedback on where I came over well, and what I need to improve.' Listen, probe – just a little – if you do not understand something, thank the person and finish the call. Do not argue or try to convince him or her that you would have been the best choice: the decision has been made, that job is history. Your purpose in ringing is to do better in the future with other interviews for other jobs. If approached in this neutral but friendly way, many recruiters are happy to help.

- Keep in touch with the organisation that turned you down. If you are very keen to work for a particular organisation, then it will help if you keep in regular contact, say every two months or so. Watch for job advertisements, and keep an eye on the trade press for interesting snippets of information about it. Many temporary jobs will turn into permanent jobs, because organisations like to recruit people they have got to know, and got the measure of. So if your circumstances allow and you can do the job on offer, try to get temporary work at your chosen organisation. Once you are working there, keep an eye on the noticeboards, get to know people, show how keen you are, and so on. Working somewhere as a temp is a very good networking opportunity.

Second interviews

Second interviews give both recruiters and candidates a chance to reflect upon the information gained during the first interview, and to ask questions prompted by this reflection. They are often an opportunity for more senior managers to see the candidates and give their approval to the final selection. A maximum of three candidates for a second round is usual. Second interviews can be used by potential employers to probe deeper into something that you tripped up on or sounded unsure about first time around, which is why it is important for you to analyse your performance after an interview and think of ways of improving on it.

For a second interview, candidates are often asked to participate in a test that acts as a tie-breaker. This varies depending on the industry, but you could, for example, be asked to make a presentation on some aspect of the organisation's business, or to suggest how you could contribute to the business, or to outline the challenges facing the industry. You may have to do this in front of an individual or a panel of senior managers, and may be expected to use visual aids such as overhead projectors. These tie-breakers are, of necessity and by intention, quite tough, because the organisation is faced with a difficult decision. It is more than likely that all the candidates in the second round are judged able to do the job, but the recruiters want to find the absolute best. They will be uncompromising in that search.

If you have got to the stage of a second interview, you have done very well. How can you improve your chances even more? Intelligent research is never wasted. By now you will have a lot of information on the organisation, its products, its customers, its suppliers, its hopes and plans. If you are – as is usual – given advance notice of the test you have to perform, put a lot of time and effort into perfecting it, and use your network to help you. Some people in the network may be good for inside knowledge of the industry or the organisation. Others may be able to help you by casting a professional eye over your material and suggesting changes.

If you do not have to take part in a test, but have simply been asked to attend a second interview, you could improve your chances and sharpen up your research skills by preparing as if you had been. At a second interview you are likely to be asked questions such as:

'How would you tackle the first six months in the new job?', 'What do you consider to be the main objectives in this job?', 'How would you develop this post after the first year or so?' Be prepared to show competence and motivation, but above all your cultural fit. You can demonstrate this by your choice of language, such as using 'we' rather than 'you' to show you have already thought yourself into the organisation. You can also continue to relate how well you fit with what they want, and how you now understand their priorities, for example: 'I think this would work well with your plans for ...'; 'I know you prefer to . . ., so I would . . .'; 'I understand you value your reputation as . . ., so it would be important to . . .'; and so on.

If you are offered the job

Often the candidates for a post are fairly evenly matched, and organisations agonise over the final decision. Sometimes, the needs of the business overcome strictly fair recruitment practices, and a person may be chosen because, for example, he or she is immediately available, which means the organisation will not have to wait for the notice period to elapse; or because he or she lives very close by, so no removal expenses will be incurred. If the decision is made for such seemingly arbitrary reasons, there was clearly nothing between the candidates. As suggested above, you could tip the balance with an enthusiastic follow-up letter, so make sure you keep up your momentum.

If you are offered the job, you have to decide whether you want it. If you are out of work, or are desperately unhappy where you are, your answer is likely to be, 'Of course, I want it, I need a job.' Before you say 'yes', make sure that your checklist of questions has been answered (see also 'Preparing for interviews', above). These could include the following.

- Do I have a clear idea of what the job entails? Is there a good balance of the known and the unknown to challenge me?
- Do I have a job description? Does it cover everything that was discussed at the interview(s)?
- Would I be happy there? What are the people like? Is the cultural fit OK?
- What about training and development?
- Are there opportunities for a good career there?

- Do I want this job? Am I motivated by the organisation's vision and plans? Can I work for that manager?
- Is the package OK?
- Does this job fit in with my longer-term career plans?

Just like your interviewer, you should consider not just your competence, but your motivation, and whether the cultural fit is good enough. Of course, the salary and package are important, but other considerations may be more relevant, especially if the job gives you the chance to change industries or job functions, or gets you out of the unemployment queue. Being out of work for a long period of time can be very damaging to relationships and to your self-esteem, so do not allow pride to get in the way of a good decision. It may be wiser to accept the job on offer than to hold out for better prospects, but only you can make that judgment.

Do not feel you have to make an instant decision – ask the organisation for time if you need it and are being pressed for an immediate answer. You may need to think about issues such as moving home, uprooting the family, leaving an area you know well, and so on. Allow yourself a couple of days to consider the offer, and ask a few people whose opinion you value.

The offer may be made verbally over the phone, or more commonly by letter. Sometimes, two copies of the contract will be included, so that you can sign them both, retaining one for your information and returning the other to the organisation. You should have discussed the terms of employment – such as basic salary, any profit-related pay, bonuses, salary reviews, holidays, pensions and so on – at the interview. If you did not, you will have to rely on the contract to give you the details. You are likely to have some margin for negotiation, especially if you know that the job has been hard to fill. If you are already in employment, do not resign until you have received the offer in writing and find that the terms in the contract are acceptable to you.

If you turn down the offer, you need to be clear both for yourself and in your communication back to the organisation of your reasons for doing so. If it is for a reason that is non-negotiable – such as wanting to work at home two days a week – and that was not brought up in the interview, the organisation would be quite justified as regarding you as a time-waster, so any application you make to it in the future is likely to join the PTD pile immediately. On the other hand, if your circumstances suddenly change, and you are unable to relocate for perfectly justifiable and understandable reasons, the organisation may not dismiss any future applications from you.

Starting work

Starting a new job is exciting and challenging. It is also tiring because you will have a lot to learn. Make sure you remain as focused as you were during your job search. To be successful, especially if you have changed job or industry or have returned following a break, you will need good training, support and feedback, so make sure you get it. The vigour and enthusiasm you demonstrated during recruitment will now be tested with the new challenge.

You will also be part of a new network of people, and now you will be sought out by career changers wanting to tap into your knowledge of the industry and learn the latest jargon and industry gossip. Be prepared to help others in the same way that people in your network had helped you. Just because you have got over the drawbridge successfully, do not raise it against others who are also eager to cross.

Chapter 6 looks at self-employment. This may be an option you are considering, in addition to salaried employment, as you take the time to think about your next move. It may be that you take a part-time salaried position, and become self-employed as well. Whatever your situation, the next chapter will provide you with plenty of information as well as food for thought.

Chapter 6

Running your own business

- To survive and thrive in self-employment you need determination, business skills, self-discipline and flexibility.
- If at all possible, the best way to establish your own business is to do it gradually so you can minimise the risks of failure on a big scale.
- Researching your potential clients, your product or service, the competition, pricing and the market is essential before drawing up a business plan.

Whether you are about to be or have been made redundant by your company, are returning to the job market after a long break, have reached the end of a contract and need to find a new career; or simply got to a point in your life where you feel you want a change of direction, you may be considering starting your own business.

This is an option that appeals to many: over 2.3 million of the estimated 3.7 million enterprises in the UK – that is, 62 per cent – are classified as 'size class zero'. This odd term means that they operate as 'one-man/woman bands' – self-employed people or owner-managers of companies – on a relatively small scale, and with no employees. In fact the vast majority of UK businesses are small: only 1 per cent have more than 50 employees. At present the self-employed comprise 13 per cent of the working population. By 2007 this figure is expected to rise to 15.2 per cent, which is more than 4 million workers. So if you are considering self-employment, you could be joining a sizeable, and growing, band of people.

The difference between running a large business for someone else and running a small one for yourself is substantial. You will lack, among other things, the support and infrastructure that being in a large organisation brings with it. On the other hand self-employment has its rewards in that you can – in theory at least – make a reasonable living, and enjoy the satisfaction of being independent and doing work you have chosen for yourself. To achieve this, you must be committed, choose a business which is right for you, and prepare yourself as thoroughly as you can beforehand.

Much of this chapter is written assuming that you are starting your own business, as opposed to taking over an existing one. However, many sections would also be relevant were you to take over an established enterprise. For example, you would want to review most aspects of the business. Some may have to alter because of legislation (e.g. regulatory requirements or insurance). Others you may choose to alter, such as pricing and patents; you might want to review the basic business idea, or check assumptions about the market, product, customers, and so on. Some considerations may be more personal: you could need more training, or help to decide whether self-employment is for you. All these aspects of running a business are covered here.

If running your own business appeals to you, this chapter will help you decide whether you have what it takes. It shows you how to check whether you have a viable enterprise, where to get finance and what the best structure for your business may be. It considers the taxes you might have to pay and the legal constraints which might apply. Then, if you are ready to take the plunge, it will guide you through the initial stages of making your business a reality. Sources of information and advice are also provided. For more detailed advice on working for yourself, see *The Which? Guide to Starting Your Own Business,* published by Which? Books.

Statistics on self-employment

For those considering moving from employment to self-employment it may be instructive, and perhaps a little sobering, to consider a few facts and figures. The rather dramatic statistics in this section are not intended to put you off setting up in business. They are merely a pointer to the realities of starting up – and successfully running – a small or medium-sized firm.

Start-ups and closures

Figures for business start-ups and closures are hard to come by. One way of estimating them is to look at HM Customs and Excise statistics for the number of businesses registering and de-registering for Value Added Tax (VAT). The data are not comprehensive because the smallest firms do not have to register, but the changes in the figures are a good guide to the pattern of start-ups and failures. The most recent figures, for 1999, show that there were 178,500 new registrations and 172,000 de-registrations throughout the year – a net increase of 6,500.

A rather different picture is given by data from Barclays Bank, which provides banking services to small businesses. It estimates 438,000 start-ups in 1999 (a decline of 4 per cent from the previous year), and 387,000 closures (almost unchanged from the previous year).

Survival rates

The same bank also issues figures for how many businesses make it through their early years. At the March 2000 survey the figures are as follows:

Time from start-up	Percentage of businesses survived
6 months	90%
12 months	79%
24 months	58%
36 months	45%
48 months	37%
60 months	30%

These statistics are chilling: four-fifths of businesses survive to celebrate their first birthday, but one-fifth do not, and the majority of businesses close before their third birthday. The rate of attrition is not constant, and businesses are very vulnerable to closure in the first 6–24 months of life. Obviously, no figures are available for how much money individual entrepreneurs lost, how they felt about such early business death, or how badly their confidence was knocked.

Of course, not all closures are indicative of business failure; the reasons may not be related to financial problems or difficulties. A general improvement in the economy or changes in personal circumstances may persuade some business owners to go back to paid employment or to retire early.

Common difficulties faced by small businesses

In research conducted in 1996 for the same bank it was found that many of the challenges businesses face when they first start up are different from those they encounter after they have been operating for up to a year.

Some 70 per cent of the businesses surveyed had had difficulties when starting up. The three main problem areas for the entrepreneurs involved were: organising start-up finance, identifying potential customers and setting the right prices. Once they were in business, however, the main difficulties were: a lack of business, cash flow/late payment and competition. Two-fifths of businesses looked for help to overcome their difficulties, and over a third first contacted their bank for assistance, and then business support organisations such as Business Link* (or regional equivalent) and Enterprise Agencies. (See 'General help for small businesses', later in this chapter.)

Is self-employment for you?

Those employed in organisations may envy the lot of the self-employed: the lack of bosses, no hierarchy (or at any rate, only one in which you are at the top), the absence of office politics and few restrictions on decision-making. However, there are many enviable aspects of employment too, which are noticeably absent when you work for yourself, such as paid holidays, a sickness scheme, an employer's pension scheme, maternity/paternity leave, health insurance cover, a job description, an annual appraisal, feedback, colleagues, career progression, staff restaurant and a (reasonably) secure income and future. You need, therefore, to be absolutely sure that the goals you seek are worth the hard work and sacrifice and that you have the determination to achieve them.

Why do you want to be self-employed?

By its very nature, starting a business is a step into the unknown, and it may be difficult for you to gauge how you will react to unforeseen circumstances that could crucially affect your future. If you are strongly motivated, you have a good chance of overcoming the sorts of problems that running a business will inevitably bring. Look closely at your motives. Be honest with yourself: why are you keen on starting a business?

- Is it for money? In the early stages, you may run at a loss, or be able to draw only a small salary from the business. It may take some time before you can afford to pay yourself a reasonable salary. You will need to plan ahead, too: don't underestimate the amount you'll need to finance even a modest retirement pension for yourself. This is likely to be at least £2,000 a year and often more. Be very realistic in your business plan about how much you expect the business to make in the short, medium and long term. How will you react if it makes less than you expect and plan for? Will your motivation sustain you through disappointment and difficulty?
- Is it for the job satisfaction? Many people become disgruntled with their existing organisation, and yearn to work for themselves because they want to do what *they* want when they want to do it. If you are one of them, you will need a deep and passionate interest in your business idea, experience and knowledge, and real ideas about how to sell it, market it, price it, alter it, adapt it, and so on.
- Do you hunger for independence? The advantage of being independent is that you are free to make the decisions and take the risks, with no one to block you or pour cold water on your brilliant ideas. The downside is that because no one knows the business as well as you do, you may find that you do not have anyone to turn to for support with decision-making or to stop you making a bad decision. If you employ people, you will have to show leadership even when you are feeling low and uncertain – which will inevitably happen at some time.
- Do you want to be a success/achieve your full potential? Other people are often impressed if you run your own business. Are you doing it for yourself or to prove to someone else who did not have faith in you (boss, relative, friend, partner) that you can do

it? As we have seen, not all businesses are successful; and apart from the risk of failure, what if you find it is drudgery, not joy?

- Is it to achieve a better balance between work and other aspects of your life? For example, do you need more time to give to children or elderly relatives? Or perhaps you want to escape from a seemingly endless daily routine or hours lost commuting. However, bear in mind that although being self-employed may give you choice over where and when you work, you may still have to work long hours. A survey by a well-known corporate magazine and a large firm of accountants found that half the people running their own businesses worked over 60 hours a week and more than a quarter took less than two weeks' holiday a year.

When you work for an organisation the criteria that determine whether it is a success may or may not be up to you, but when you run your own business you have to decide how you will judge success – and then achieve it. Your motives for starting in business will dictate your yardstick of success. Your personal concept of 'success' will colour many of the decisions you make about your business but may also place constraints upon you. For example, a decision about how much income you want to take can affect how much profit you want or need to make, how much time you want to devote to the business and whether you do the work yourself or pay someone else to do it. If your priority is working from home, your business opportunities are necessarily limited – it would after all be difficult to run a manufacturing plant from your garage or to employ any staff if they have to be accommodated in your back bedroom.

A frank self-assessment

Answering the questionnaire below will give you some idea of the sort of personality that is likely to thrive in self-employment: obviously, it is not for everyone. Use the questionnaire to reflect on fundamental issues such as your motives for self-employment, degree of dependence (emotional, financial or both) on a regular salary and ability to stand up to the inevitable pressures. As you go through it, it will be fairly obvious what your answers indicate.

(1) How do you feel about having a manager? (A) It helps me to set clear goals. (B) It inhibits my freedom to act and often gets in the way.

(2) How do you feel about colleagues? (A) I like the companion-ship of others. (B) I am fairly self-sufficient.

(3) How do you react to the thought of always being on the look-out for work? (A) It appals me. (B) It excites me. (C) It's inevitable but acceptable.

(4) Do you like to have a job description? (A) Yes, I like to know what I should be doing. (B) I'm not particularly bothered.

(5) Do you like to receive a regular income which arrives on the same day each month? (A) Yes, very much. (B) Yes, it is nice but that security is not crucial to me.

(6) Do you like to receive regular feedback? (A) Yes, it helps me a lot to know how I am doing. (B) It helps, but I can review my work for myself.

(7) Do you like the security of an organisation around you? (A) Yes. (B) No. (C) I'm not fussed.

(8) Can you set your own vision/career goals/work objectives? (A) Not on my own; I like and expect input from my organisation. (B) Yes, pretty much so. Having other people's input may be useful, but not really necessary.

(9) Do you like to have a working environment where someone is on hand to clean the toilets, mend the copier, fix your PC, empty the waste paper bins, etc.? (A) Yes, of course I do. (B) It is nice, but I can do those jobs for myself.

If you answered all or mostly As, you are probably not suited to self-employment; if your answers were mostly Bs (or the two Cs), per-haps running your own business is for you. To survive and thrive in self-employment, you need particular attitudes, skills and knowl-edge, some of which would not be required, encouraged or even greatly valued by an employer:

- a dogged determination and commitment
- a very broad range of business skills
- the ability to be customer-focused so you meet their wants, not just what you like or find convenient to give them
- a single-minded dedication to your business idea and the stamina to pursue it day after day, for months and years, often on your own. But to prevent this dedication becoming obsessive, it must be linked to an ability to listen to others, to learn from your mis-takes and to take advice

- a willingness to take calculated risks and be opportunistic
- fluent communication skills and powers of persuasion
- a willingness to be an individual, perhaps even a maverick
- enormous flexibility: many people start in business with one idea, but find over time that the market needs something different – perhaps wildly different – and that to survive they have to adapt and make quite radical changes to their business
- innovation and imagination
- the ability to sell and market your product or service constantly
- self-discipline
- the strength to stand or fall by your own decisions.

In addition to these personal qualities you will need technical competence, no matter what you do. You must have, or acquire, business skills. Organisational skills to manage yourself, the business, processes and procedures, and staff (if you have them) are essential. Selling skills will also be required, because even if you do not plan to do the selling of the product or service yourself, you may have to start off doing so, and you will also have to sell your idea to those financing you.

Running your own business does not necessarily mean working alone, but you may have to at first because you cannot afford to pay someone else. Being a 'one-man/woman band' may seem to make great business sense – there will no PAYE to sort out, no employees' liability insurance, you can control the costs very closely, and so on – however, working alone can be an isolated and isolating experience. You need to consider your temperament, and, if you need a fair amount of people contact, think about how you will build that into your business. You may be fine if your work entails going out and meeting clients and customers, or being in daily contact with suppliers or customers. Another consideration is that, for example, while you are busy in the 'sales department', making a phone call to a supplier, all the other 'departments' are 'shut'. There is no-one staffing the front office, doing a mailing, designing a new product, chasing up late payments, etc. Furthermore, do you actually want to be doing all these things? Is it making the best use of your abilities and time?

Catherine started out on her own, and was very busy in the first few months. So busy, in fact, that after nine months she was in chaos: invoices unissued, materials over the floor, late with the VAT, etc. It was true that she was busy, but being only human, she was also making time for what she was good at (designing, writing, selling) rather than what needed to be done (chasing late payments, issuing invoices, doing the VAT). So be honest with yourself. Would you be like Catherine, and put off what you consider to be the 'boring bits'? Might it be a good idea to consider some part-time help – perhaps from an agency – to make sure you keep on top of everything? Catherine did take on someone, and although it has cost her in terms of profit, it has probably saved her sanity – and prevented her business from failing, because the cash flow has been properly managed and Customs and Excise (VAT) paid on time.

Last, but not least, you will need support from your family and possibly friends too. Even if they are not giving direct financial support (and many do), you are likely to be heavily dependent on the patience and goodwill of a husband, wife, partner and children who may all have to cope with the pressure of your long hours, non-existent holidays, financial worries, and so on. If you do not actively enlist this support and keep communicating on progress, the inevitable ups and downs, and so on, you could put an unacceptable strain on your family relationships, your chances of business success, or both.

Your business idea

If you wish to become self-employed, you have three business options: (a) to produce something – for example, an invention, a manufactured good or something you grow or make, (b) to distribute something, either as a wholesaler or a retailer, or (c) to provide a service. You may want to set up a dotcom company, either as a distribution channel for one of your ideas or as the business itself. Dotcom business is a new and exciting phenomenon and may have enormous potential, but as with any enterprise, the business idea and its execution must be good to survive. At present dotcom is a turbulent market and expensive to enter, with most companies failing to make a profit for some years.

Whichever option you choose, there are three further choices:

* sticking to something you already know
* trying something which is new but not completely unfamiliar
* trying something completely different.

In general, these options are in ascending order of risk: your chances of success are likely to be greater if you have some prior experience of the business area you are entering. There is, however, an exception: franchising (see below). You should benefit from the experience of the franchise owners, which – in theory at least – should reduce your risks.

Sticking to what you know

Think carefully about what you already know. Your knowledge and experience could be very extensive, gained from years in an industry or job function. Look around you: in your local area, in your industry where you are already known and with which you are comfortable. If you can come up with an idea that exploits what is already familiar to you, you are likely to be in safe territory.

You do not have to continue in exactly the same line of work as you are in or have just left. Take an objective, lateral and considered look at your existing skills. Could they be adapted? For example, an electrician could specialise in theatre and conference work instead of competing against local electricians who already dominate the domestic market.

To succeed, you need to be confident and comfortable with your skills, experience and knowledge. You would still need to learn about running a business, but the subject of the business would be known to you, so you should be facing few surprises. You would know your market well, what people are prepared to pay, what they want, when and how they pay, and what their needs are. Above all, part of the market would know you – your reputation, your skills, your experience. So in the start-up situation you would not have to spend as much money, time and effort in telling your potential clients about yourself, because they probably already know.

You could choose to stay in the field you know well but offer a new product or service. For example, John moved from a job as a commercial accountant in the auto-parts industry into providing a commercial consultancy for that same industry. He needed to learn about running a business and being a consultant, but his potential clients already knew him and felt confident and comfortable with him and his skills. He made a flying start.

In such a case your market would know you but, because you are offering something slightly different, you will need to convince customers that you can deliver the goods (or services). You cannot afford to risk your reputation by making a bad presentation or delivering a poor service or product. You should be a quick learner and a good listener to be successful with the new venture.

Trying something new but familiar

If you already make or do something in your spare time, this could provide your business opportunity. However, there is a big gap between a hobby which makes pin-money and a business idea with broader appeal for a product or service which can be realistically priced and professionally marketed and sold. A hobby is often done for love, not money, and can be very labour-intensive. If you plan to turn it into a business, you may not be producing the goods or carrying out the service yourself any more, but paying someone else to. If you were to price your labour at a realistic level, you might find that the selling price would be more than your market would stand.

Jennifer had been in the car-hire business in a variety of line-management roles, and was well known within the industry because she had worked in a number of different companies, done some industry training and given talks. She left to become a management development trainer, specialising in the car-hire industry. She was offering a new product to an existing market. Being extremely familiar with her market, she could offer a specialised service. She already had some of the skills for her new job, and learnt the ones she lacked as quickly as she could. In the early days, her deep knowledge of the industry complemented her presentation skills.

Another potential drawback is that, having never used these skills or experience before in a commercial capacity, you could be trying to sell your product or service to a market of which you have scant or no knowledge: you would not know what potential clients want, what price they are willing to pay, what the trends and problems are, where they buy from already, what their buying patterns are, or how and when they pay. You are an unknown quantity to them, too. So you will have to spend more time, money and effort to tell them, and make them feel confident and comfortable that you will be better than their existing supplier.

Melanie had been a traffic manager for a well-known firm of national and international hauliers. When she was made redundant, she decided to set up her own business. She could not enter her former employer's market, because not only was it saturated, but it was dominated by big players with whom she could not compete. Knowing from her experience in the business that fragile tableware and ornaments were some of the hardest items to transport successfully, she decided to set up a company which would move such delicate items to department stores and specialist shops in the UK from continental Europe. Her familiarity with the business of packing, importing, suppliers and traffic management were all vital here. She made contact with the suppliers, the stores and their third-party hauliers. Her experience, skills and knowledge bought her entry into her new market.

Trying something completely different

The most risky course is to start a business providing a product or a service you know nothing about to a market that is completely new to you. If you choose to do something as radical as this, make sure you do your research thoroughly (see below) before you embark upon it.

You might already have come across a promising business idea. If not, your local area might provide inspiration. Consider what goods and services are needed there. Keep yourself well informed by reading the local press. Have you had difficulty getting things done at home or at work? Do people need to go outside the area (at a greater cost to themselves) to get a service which you could provide locally? Ask around your neighbours and friends. What goods or services do local companies require? If a new business park has recently opened, what do the small, medium and large businesses need? Do they need sandwiches and beverages delivered at lunch-time, local deliveries made, odd jobs done, newspapers and magazines delivered, a travel agency, a photocopy and photo processing shop?

Peter was a book-keeper-cum-accounts assistant in a builder's merchants. As part of his research into business ideas he identified an under-exploited market: offering hairdressing and hair colouring to people in their own homes. He was aware that in making the switch he would be moving from a business-to-business operation to a very personalised customer operation. He could not bring to his new venture skills, knowledge or experience of the industry or its suppliers, nor was he sure what facilities he would need. He did not know much about the market either, or how to make contact with potential customers, how much they would be prepared to pay, which service(s) would be most popular, and so on. The hair-dressing/hair-colouring business may have been a good idea, but he had to think carefully about whether he was the best person to be doing it. Perhaps he could have considered financing someone else to do it, taking a share of the profits, or have teamed up with a hair-dresser while providing the necessary business skills.

Franchising

A franchise is a business concept or system which someone (the franchiser) has already developed and is willing to sell to other people (the franchisees). Examples of franchises abound in, for example, the fast-food industry, restaurants/coffee shops and print shops. Buying a franchise should ideally be a lower risk and faster route to establishing a business, because:

- the broad market research should already be done (although you will still need to research how the product or service relates to your local market)
- the product or service should already be established
- the product or service might already have or will soon acquire a strong brand image
- there may be on-going marketing by the franchiser, perhaps at a national level
- raw materials or stocks may be supplied
- prices may already be set
- detailed guidance and training on how to operate the business may be available
- help in finding suitable premises, fitting them out and so on may be offered.

Does this sound like a recipe for success? It can be. Some very successful household names are franchise organisations. However, you must be wary of the pitfalls. A franchise is not usually a cheap option, so you need to do some very serious homework before you put any money on the line. If the franchiser fails to be completely candid with you, this should set off some alarm bells. For example, are the company accounts of the franchisees available from Companies House★? Franchisers make money *because* you, the

237

franchisee, make money, and ought not to be making money *from* you. Everything they do should be targeted at helping the franchisees. There are certain basic questions that need to be answered, as follows.

- Are they running one or more of the outlets themselves? This is important for two reasons. Firstly, if they are not, how can they understand the realities of running the business faced on a daily basis by the franchisees? Secondly, if not, why not? Could it be because the business idea is not really viable?
- Have other franchises in the particular business been sold? Are they successful? Can you talk to some of the existing franchisees without the franchiser being present?
- What is the product or service like? Is there a market for it in your area?
- Is there any protection from competition – for example, has the product been patented; does it have an established and well-respected brand image?
- Will you have sole rights to sell the product or service in your particular area?
- How sound is the franchiser? Its continuing existence will generally be important to your business success
- Does the franchiser belong to the British Franchise Association (BFA)*? Its members are bound by a code of ethics which should offer you some protection
- What on-going marketing does the franchiser contract to do?
- How much does the franchise cost? Look for an up-front fee and a percentage paid from your profits. An arrangement whereby the bulk of the cost comes from profit is preferable because the franchiser then has a greater interest in your on-going success
- Are there hidden charges? For example, are you obliged to buy materials and/or stocks from the franchiser? Are the prices higher than you would pay elsewhere?
- How long does the franchise last? Can you renew at the end of that term? What happens if you want to sell early?
- How much back-up will you get from the franchiser?

Be wary of cowboy franchisers. Harry was made redundant from his job in the City and after many months of unemployment and job rejections he was tempted by an advertisement promising a high income from selling small electronic alarms. For an up-front fee, Harry was supplied with printed brochures and a manual. In addition, he bought a minimum quantity of stock for £900. The franchiser promised that a national TV and newspaper advertising campaign was about to be launched, after which customers would be beating a path to Harry's door. No advertising campaign followed and, despite Harry's best efforts, he sold only a handful of the devices. He received no reply to his calls to the franchiser, who after a while vanished completely, leaving Harry hundreds of pounds out of pocket.

Always get your solicitor and accountant to check out the franchise deal before you commit yourself. You can buy a useful guide to franchises from the British Franchise Association. Visit its web site or the Small Business Service (SBS)* web site.

The informal business start-up

If possible, the best way to establish your own business is to do it gradually. Making an 'informal' start-up means setting yourself up in a small way to see whether a market for your product or service exists out there, what prices people will accept, whether it might suit you, and so on, so you can reduce the risk of failure on a large scale. If it works out, you will be able to build up a client list and contacts with suppliers before you move into business full-time. You could test the water in various different ways.

Joe was art director of an advertising agency which specialised in the motor industry. For some time he had wanted to be self-employed, but was uneasy about making the change. He managed to negotiate an arrangement which benefited both his company and himself whereby he was employed for three days a week for a guaranteed period of nine months with the option of extending for a further six months. With this as security, he was free to pursue his own work for the remainder of the week.

When he was in his early twenties David dropped out of horticultural college and started work in a garden centre. As he was very knowledgeable about plants, regular customers would often ask for his advice about planting, diseases, pruning, and so on. After a while, some of them asked whether he could visit their gardens to have a look at a sickly plant, prune a wisteria that had never flowered, or whatever. He would visit in the evenings and at weekends.

Both jobs were physically very demanding, but after about 18 months he had just enough clients to be able to give up the job at the garden centre. He remained on good terms with his former employers and became a valued customer of theirs. Twenty years on, he has a successful business, a prestigious client list, and has added landscaping and garden design to his business.

Michael's passion was rock music. When his amateur band broke up and he became bored with his day job, he wanted a change of direction. He started organising local rock bands to play in pubs and clubs, working on the business only in the evenings and at weekends. After about a year, he had built up enough business to give up his job and become a music promoter full-time.

Market research

Whatever business idea you decide upon, your next step should be to research your potential market extensively. Obviously you cannot research every business possibility, so you need to refine your ideas down to one or two on which you can focus in depth. In doing market research you must look carefully at five different aspects: your potential customers, the characteristics of your product or service, your competitors, pricing the product and accessing the market.

You will need to tap into various sources of information to build up a picture of the market and the openings available. The Internet will be a very valuable resource, giving you quick and easy access to information on how to research and implement your business idea, and the opportunity to communicate with individuals, groups and organisations who could be helpful to you. Some organisations have publications available to download directly from their web sites, and the main clearing banks also have advice available on-line. See 'General help for small businesses' later in this chapter, and the addresses section in the back of this book.

Primary information is what you get from your own investigations. Small businesses tend to have very specialised markets in which first-hand knowledge is vital, so it would be foolish to ignore this source. Primary information might come from:

- interviewing people already in the business – for example, existing colleagues, suppliers or customers, people running similar businesses, perhaps in a neighbouring town, or people running complementary businesses who might be able to tell you something about the customers

- asking people to complete questionnaires – for example, about where they shop now for the product or service you have in mind, how often they buy, whether they switch brands, and so on
- asking friends and family for their reactions to your business proposition
- inviting people to test your product or service, if you are able to offer it on a small scale. For example, if you have created a specialist cheese, can you make up a small batch to be tasted? If you are going into interior design, could you draw up a detailed plan for a friend's home?
- taking or sending brochures or samples to potential customers, or offering them free sessions of your service, in order to invite feedback and gauge their interest
- going to meetings of a relevant professional body or institute, and asking people there about their assessment of the market and its prospects. This might be especially useful in helping you to judge the level of competition
- going to conferences and talking to delegates.

You should also look for secondary information – i.e. information that other people have already obtained from their investigations. Secondary information can be a rich source of statistics about the size of the market, the major players, potential customers, pitfalls to be wary of, and tried-and-tested techniques. Sources might be books, journals, newspapers, reports, articles, or sites on the Internet. Your local reference libraries – including those in universities and Enterprise Agencies – are a vital resource. Your local Business Link may be able to help. The Department of Trade and Industry (DTI) web site and/or library in London could also be useful.

The customers

When you think of and research a product or service you must have a clear idea of who your clients are likely to be. Using categories and profiles of people provides a way of focusing on your target customers.

The customers for consumer products and services can be categorised in a number of ways: for example, by socio-economic group (A, B, C1, etc.), disposable income; gender, age, development of the family (young single people, young couples with no children, young couples with the youngest child under 6, couples with older dependent children, older couples with no children at home, older single people). Customers for business-to-business enterprises can be categorised by, for example, industry sector (agriculture, fishing, etc.), region, number of employees, turnover, research budget, need or business problem.

Government statistics, population censuses and local and national surveys may help you to assess whether the area in which you intend to operate has a sufficiently large segment of your target customers.

Having identified your potential customers, you need to know whether their needs for your type of product or service are presently being met and, if so, from where and on what they base their decision to use a particular supplier. If you can identify your customers individually – for example, you are targeting people in a given geographical area, or only those in large houses or with large gardens, a written or verbal questionnaire might be a good way of collecting this information. Questions could include some or all of the following: What problem is solved by their purchase of this product or service? How often do they buy? Who supplies them now? What price are they paying? What discounts and credit terms apply? What especially do they like about the product or service? How is it used? How satisfied are they? What improvements or additional products or services would they like to see?

How will you find new customers? The nature of the business will determine this to a significant extent. Retail businesses will greatly depend on 'walk-in' business. This may be generated from various sources: advertising, loss-leader promotions (offering an item at a specially low price, even if you lose money on it, because it will encourage customers to buy other things from you as well), word-of-mouth recommendations or just being in the right place. Business-to-business enterprises will rely on a variety of ways to find new 'prospects': some small consultancies may get as much as 80 to 90 per cent of their prospects from personal recommendation, with a small percentage coming from entries in directories and listings in other relevant publications. Others may rely on direct mail promotions, telesales operations, and so on.

Two other factors to consider are the rate of 'churn' and the conversion rate. 'Churn' is a term used to describe customer retention or the rate at which established clients are lost and new clients acquired. 'Conversion rate' describes what percentage of prospects turns into new contracts or sales. Both of these will depend to some extent on particular industry norms which you should be aware of. But the greatest determinant of churn is how well you meet the needs of customers (in every aspect: speed of delivery, how complaints are handled and discounts given, and customer satisfaction). Bear in mind that it is reckoned to be six times more expensive to recruit a new customer than to service an existing one, so ideally you should have a low churn rate.

The biggest factor in conversion rate is the quality of your sales and marketing: your presentation, price, how you compare with the competition, your knowledge of the industry, ability to meet their needs, responsiveness to requests for changes to specifications, and credit terms.

The product

Although this may seem obvious, it is worth emphasising that product research is inextricably linked with customers. A fundamental mistake that many UK companies continued to make until well into the 1980s was to try to sell what they could make rather than to make what people wanted to buy. In other words, their product development was internally driven by what they excelled at, rather than being externally driven by what their customers actually wanted. The only way to avoid this costly mistake is to be demand-led.

Inevitably, you will start by considering the fields where you believe you have some skill or opportunity. But you should then step back and define in broad terms what need or want you think you can satisfy. There may be more than one way to meet the identified need, but you should hone your thoughts down to the options to which you are best suited. The case study of Melanie, who started a haulage company specialising in transporting delicate artefacts (see 'Trying something new but familiar', above), shows how the process of narrowing down from an initial idea to a viable product or service might go. Melanie started off with quite general thoughts, and gradually became more focused, researching each step along the way.

When she left her employer she had her redundancy payment, her experience, contacts, industry knowledge and skills. She needed a business idea. Her first thoughts were: 'I know and like haulage, so I might as well stay in it, but I can't afford to compete with the big boys, so what could I do?'

She decided to focus on a niche area, looking first at light industrial (moving office furniture), domestic (moving house), specialist (moving IT equipment), and other specialist (exhibition or theatre work). She investigated what the current market was like in each. Light industrial and domestic were over-crowded, partly because they did not need specialist skills and knowledge. She decided that it would be hard to make a mark in either of those areas. This left her the two specialist areas. The second of those (exhibition and theatre work) meant a lot of heavy lifting, and staying away from home a good deal. Neither of these requirements appealed much, especially as she anticipated that in the early days she would have to do a good deal of the driving. This left her the other specialist area of moving sensitive or fragile equipment and goods, which seemed worthy of further investigation.

She used primary information and asked colleagues and contacts about the goods that were hard to haul, the rate of loss and breakages, who presently supplied the service at what price, the quality of service, etc. She also used secondary information on how much of that sort of trade came from outside the UK and, if so, from where; and who were the main customers needing the equipment or goods. Her business idea was becoming more and more focused: hauling sensitive or fragile equipment or goods from outside the UK would play to her strengths, and appeared to be an under-developed area. The question was: what particular equipment or goods?

She decided to use three criteria to make her choice. The goods she wanted to transport had to be: something that people in the haulage industry regarded as 'tricky' and which would therefore deter most competitors, subject to a delivery gap that her business could plug, and of interest to her. 'Should it be equipment or goods? Equipment such as IT seems fairly well covered with a number of well-organised, efficient operators, so perhaps not that.

Fragile or sensitive goods, which everyone struggles with, looks hopeful – china, glass, ornaments, crockery, sculptures and lamps, especially from places in continental Europe such as Portugal, France, Poland, Romania, Italy.'

You can see how Melanie ended up finalising her business idea. It was based on her existing expertise, but was refined by potential customers, their needs, an understanding of the market and an assessment of what service she could best provide.

You do not have to settle on just one product or service. You could offer several versions, with varying functions or aimed at different types of consumer, displaying different qualities and sold at different price levels. But always you must keep your eye on the target: what the consumer wants. If your product is more sophisticated than the prospective buyers are likely to demand, or too expensive for the ultimate consumer, you must simplify it or decide to find another market for it.

Unless you have complete control over the product and any materials needed to make it, you must also consider the availability of supplies before deciding definitely on one product or another. For example, if the product requires the skills of several craftsmen – cabinet-makers or precision engineers, say – make sure from the start that you have a supply of skilled labour to depend on. It is no use building up a market for a product if you cannot maintain the supply at a competitive price. It might be better to settle on a product that can be made by less skilled labour.

The competition

Unless you have come up with a completely new product or service, you will be competing with established businesses, run by people who are familiar with every aspect of their business: products, distribution channels, clients, pricing, and so on. You will need to know all about them and also think about how you will differentiate yourself from them. There are certain key questions to which you need answers.

- Who are your rivals?
- Where are they?
- What are their strengths and weaknesses?
- What do you know about their quality and range of products?
- What do they charge/what are their credit terms/discount structure?

- Why do people buy from them?
- How do they make contact with their prospective customers, i.e. how do they market/sell themselves?
- If, as far as you know, no competitors exist, why is this? Is it because there is no market, or because you are genuinely the first to notice the gap?

The price

The price you charge for a product or service will generally be one of the most important factors influencing your potential customers' decision about whether or not to buy from you. This will depend, to a greater or lesser extent, on whether your product is price-sensitive or not – that is, whether the customer's decision to buy is based solely or principally on price. Dictionaries are a good example, where the pricing is very competitive and there is little variation in the product: sometimes the 4 pence difference between £4.99 and £4.95 will greatly influence the buying decision. If your product or service *is* highly price-sensitive, you may struggle to compete, as your rivals will have probably taken out all the possible costs already, and as a new entrant to the market, you may not have achieved those efficiencies yet. If a price war develops while you are in this early stage, and you have to reduce your selling price, the reduction can come only from your profit margin. This leaves you vulnerable.

Of course, even in a price-sensitive market, you can still compete on different criteria. These could include:

- speed of delivery
- high discounts for volume sales
- discounts for very prompt payment
- high responsiveness to customers (e.g. a tailored, individual service of some kind)
- specialist knowledge and skills in short supply
- a 'personal' touch that other suppliers lack
- an 'inclusive' service where others charge piecemeal.

As a general rule, smaller enterprises can compete most easily on the service they offer to customers, and this can set them apart from their larger, and/or more established competitors.

The price you charge for your product or service can be determined in different ways: the cost-plus, competition-based, or going rate/demand-led methods. In reality, for most small businesses, the distinction between these methods will be slightly blurred.

Cost-plus pricing

The basic principle of this mode of pricing is that you estimate your costs, and then add a mark-up for your own profit. This approach has a number of problems. Firstly, your costs might be low, but this does not necessarily mean that the price of the final product should be low. Secondly, although in theory cost-plus should guarantee you some element of profit, it will not if the price arrived at is more than customers are willing to pay. Thirdly, although your costs may be low when you start out, they could rise – for all sorts of reasons over which you have no control, such as the price of raw materials or transport – and when that happens the only squeeze can be on your profit margin.

In particular, if you are offering a service, you must avoid the common error of under-pricing.

It is all too easy to see how inexperienced people make this mistake. They may feel that they are just starting out, learning on the job, and are embarrassed about charging the full rate since they feel like trainees. Or they may really be unaware of what the competition is charging. Both reasons are dangerous – because if you start low, you stay low. In addition, perceptions about pricing must be taken into account. The cliché 'you get what you pay for' holds true for many buyers. There are plenty of examples of products being launched, at considerable cost, at a low or lower-middle price, and failing badly because consumers perceive the low price to mean a low-quality product or service. Often these products are withdrawn and then re-launched with different packaging at a higher price.

A common approach to arriving at a price is for people to take their desired income, divide it by the number of days worked, approximately 230 per year, add a bit and fix that as their day rate. This ignores some important factors:

- selling/marketing: many business advisers suggest that if you are self-employed you should spend 40 per cent of your time, i.e. two days in five, selling and marketing your business. This means that you need to make your money in three days per week, which is an average of 12–14 days per month, totalling 144–168 days per year, not 230. So, for example, if you provide a service at a day rate of £250, multiplying this by 230 days gives a healthy annual turnover of £57,500. But, if in fact you are productive on only 144 days, your turnover will be reduced by £21,500 to £36,000, which is significantly less

- energy: depending on your business, you may not be able to sustain your energy to do the work all day, every day without exhausting yourself. This is especially true of intense work with people or physically demanding work. You would not be able to do, for example, personal counselling for seven hours continuously a day. You should, therefore, bear in mind that you cannot necessarily base your calculation on working a full day every day

- travelling time: if you have to travel to the place of work, for example, as a contract cleaner, that travelling time between clients is not chargeable and has to be seen as down-time. You could perhaps work from 8am to 8pm, in, say, two-hour blocks, but you would not be doing chargeable work for 12 hours each day

- seasonality: your business may be seasonal. For example, if you run training courses, you would have to bear in mind that training tends to be concentrated in two seasons, one running from mid-January to mid-July and the other from mid-September to early December. So you would have to make a full 12 months' salary in about nine months. If your business were literally seasonal (for example, if you were in gardening) you would need alternative or related work to sustain you during the low season of winter. Business would tail off in October and not pick up again until March or April

- type of business attracted: if your prices are very low, you may be attracting 'bad' business, i.e. customers who pay late, default, complain constantly, demand a lot of free extras on top of the basic price, or haggle all the time. Such customers actually cost you a lot of time, which translates into money, but that could be very difficult to quantify. Of course, you could get bad business even with higher prices, but they tend to put off the time-wasters. 'Bad' business and poor credit control account for many business failures, because the business owner simply runs out of cash

- over-demand: if your prices are very low, you may get more business than you can handle. This could be a fatal mistake – you take on the business because you are reluctant to turn it down, then you find you are unable to deliver to your previous standards, for whatever reason, and your reputation suffers as a result

- raising the price to sensible levels: if you start with prices that are too low, you might find that it is extremely difficult to raise them to realistic levels without losing customers.

Competition-based pricing

Basing your price on what the competition is charging is less disastrous. How an organisation pitches its pricing depends on a number of factors: the perceived value for money of the product, and the image and quality of service; being able to offer something out of the ordinary, such as being on call at all hours, or having a tailored service; or particular industry knowledge which benefits the customer in some way(s). So make sure that you study the competition well before you fix your price. However, basing your prices on those of your rivals risks certain pitfalls:

- too little information: you may have an unrepresentative sample of competitors, so your assumptions may be false, causing you to price either too high or too low
- biased information: the people you rely on may give you biased data, for whatever reason(s) of their own, so once again, your assumptions will be based on poor or wrong information
- pricing too low: perhaps the competition is also priced too low, which your sources are unlikely to tell you. They may be suffering from any of the symptoms listed under 'Cost-plus pricing', such as 'bad' business or difficulty in raising their prices to realistic levels; or they may not be aware that people are willing to pay more for the product or service
- wrong comparisons: it is quite feasible that what the competition is offering is not really comparable with what you are offering. Some element (that you are unaware of) of the rival business may be different from yours, such as credit terms or method of delivery. This may mean that it is not truly your competitor, so for you to use similar pricing would be misguided
- inferior service: it is possible that even though you have rivals dealing in the same product or service, the quality provided is different. You may, for example, have deeper knowledge of the industry or offer a customised service at no extra cost. Customers are usually prepared to pay extra for a premium service

- missed opportunities: basing your prices on what the competition charges smacks rather of a 'me too' attitude. It does not allow for changing business or economic circumstances and the new opportunities they can bring.

Demand-led pricing

This method of pricing is based on what customers are prepared to pay. If you are in a new or rapidly growing industry, you may be able to charge relatively high prices. If your product or industry is mature (i.e. well established), your venture will face considerable competition, and you will need to differentiate your product or service from that of the competition. If your product or industry is in decline, you will find, as a small and new player, that the costs of entry to that market are very high and it is likely to be extremely difficult to compete in it, which may force you to set your prices at a very low level indeed. Being in a mature market could work well if you bought a franchise for a well-known or household name, product or service, for example in fast food, plumbing or photocopying. Franchisees usually have no latitude in fixing the prices of their products, because the franchiser will want, among other things, uniformity of pricing across the brand.

Pricing based on demand is the norm in service industries. You need to be constantly checking what the clients will tolerate in terms of price and be prepared to negotiate. You must also keep an eye on your competitors and use their prices as a yardstick for your own negotiations (see above). Demand-led pricing has advantages:

- profitability: if you can charge more than some of your competitors because you offer something extra for which your clients are prepared to pay a premium, you can work fewer days to make as much as your rivals do over a longer period. This means you can take on more work than they can
- demand matching supply: if pricing is at the correct level, you will not be swamped with 'bad' business, but have enough to match supply, i.e. what you can happily handle. This saves your sanity and keeps the customers happy too
- satisfied customers: if customers know they are paying too little for a service, they worry that corners are being cut in ways they cannot see, such as expenses. So paying the going rate will make most customers feel comfortable. Also, the majority of people

like to feel they are being fair, so paying the going rate will satisfy them in that way too

- getting big-company business: large organisations like to deal with others of a similar size and are prepared to pay high prices to do so. This may be linked to ego, and the security of a large player talking to an equal and understanding each other's language. If you as a smaller player want to join this circle, your prices need to reflect those aspirations
- research: if your pricing is demand-led, by definition you will be in touch with your market, its fluctuations and trends, and therefore reap the rewards of this market knowledge.

Other pricing factors

Many products fit into specific price ranges, and manufacturers deliberately tailor their goods to fit into one of these. Some manufacturers produce similar product ranges, each one for a different category. Cosmetics, for instance, tend to be cheap and cheerful for the young, medium-priced for the average user, and extremely expensive for the richer consumer. If your business is going to be in manufacturing, you should decide at an early stage into which price category your product will slot. If you cannot fit into the lower and middle range, because your costs are high, you will have to aim at the higher category; but then you will have to make sure that the prices reflect some special and unique quality of your goods, and demonstrate very clearly to the customer that this is so. Alternatively, you could look again at your costs and try to reduce those.

You may eventually arrive at different rates, based on different clients' ability and willingness to pay. For example, if you are in a service industry, you may charge a lower rate for charities and the education sector, because you know their ability to pay high rates is severely constrained. Conversely, you may charge a higher rate for international companies because their ability to pay is not restricted. This is fine, and makes for a mixed business. The flexibility may also protect you from any changes in one area of your market having too much impact on your business.

Access to the market

Access is about getting your product or service to the customer. How you do this will depend on whether you are manufacturing or marketing a product, or delivering a service. If you intend to manufacture a product you will need to consider how you will sell and distribute it. Will you use wholesalers or sell by direct mail to your customers? Will you use agents or retail outlets?

If you are intending to market a product, access is all about where to sell – in a retail outlet, by telesales, by direct mail catalogue, or on the Internet. What will be the ambience of the retail outlet or image of that operation? If you intend to sell someone else's products, whether as a wholesaler or retailer, will you do so using a catalogue with telephone ordering and next-day delivery by a third party, like many stationery suppliers? Or will you use direct mail or act as an agent (like Avon Cosmetics) or open a shop? Some organisations use a mixture of direct mail using catalogues and retail outlets – examples of this approach include IKEA and Past Times.

If your business is to deliver a service or act as a consultant, you still need to consider how and where you will do that. If you are a gardener or window cleaner, you will go to your clients' homes. It will not matter where your office is based (except that being too far away from potential clients would be inconvenient and possibly expensive), nor what it looks like because no one is ever likely to visit you. But you will still need to consider your equipment, how you dress, any vehicles used for business purposes, and so on, because they say a good deal about the business.

Your business plan

Most businesses that fail do so because those running them do not have a structured business plan and/or sound business skills. A business plan could be seen as a route map which defines the roads you will take from where you are now to where you wish to be. When planning a journey you would have to work out where you are going, whom you will travel with, what you need to take with you and how much money you will need. You would also need to research the place you are going to: whether you need to learn any new languages, and whether there are any special requirements such as visas and injections. You should apply the same principles to a business plan.

Business plans are used for a variety of purposes: as a selling document to help you raise finance, as a plan against which you measure your actual performance, and as a way of seeing whether what you are proposing is feasible and viable.

Having researched your market and decided that you do have a viable business idea, this is your next step. Do not assume that if you do not need outside finance you can skip drawing up a business plan. It is an essential discipline which forces you to clarify your ideas and helps you to spot potential problem areas in advance; later on it will help to alert you if your business drifts off track.

You can get help in drawing up your business plan from, for example, your bank, your local Enterprise Agency or Business Link (or regional equivalent). See 'General help for small businesses', below. If you find it difficult to draw up the financial projections (see below) seek the help of an accountant.

The nature of your business

Your plan should start with a concise outline of your proposed business. Assuming yours is a relatively small business, this part of the plan should probably run to two or three pages. If you are envisaging a large venture, you would need to give more information. The plan should include details of:

- what the business is being set up to do
- the market for it, including size of market, competitors, the gap you have identified and intend to fill
- your product and/or service – give a brief description, highlighting its key features and customer benefits, anything which makes it different from what is already available, and intended pricing
- how the business will be managed – if by you, your relevant skills and how you intend to fill gaps in your skills. If you will be working with others, similar details for them
- operational details – for example, where you will be based, how many employees you will have, equipment required, supply lines, legal constraints, cost of premises, and licences required
- your proposed marketing and selling techniques
- a summary of the financial position – forecast profits for the first five years, expected cash flow, finance required. Do not get bogged down in details here: your financial statements will provide them
- if you are seeking outside backers, the prospects for them as investors.

The financial details

You need to draw up financial statements giving three types of information:

- expected profits or losses over the first few (normally five) years of your business. For the first year or two, you should give a monthly breakdown; for the later years, annual projections will be enough. The profit and loss statement shows where your income will come from, what expenses will have to be met and what surplus, if any, remains
- expected cash flow over the same period. This should show where the income will come from and when, also what expenses will have to be met and when. Knowledge of your cash flow is extremely important. Even if you have a profitable business, if your customers are not paying you in time to meet your bills from suppliers you could go bankrupt. Looking at the timing of your financial flows tells you how much working capital (the money you need to keep you going during the interval between paying for your outgoings and receiving your income) you will need to act as a buffer. If you cannot provide this amount of working capital yourself, you will have to add it to the amount to be borrowed or raised from outside backers
- projected balance sheet at the end of say, the first two years. A balance sheet is a snapshot of the business at a point in time, showing what it owns (the assets) – for example, equipment, stocks, investments, cash – and how those assets have been financed (the liabilities) – whether by you, by loans or by money put into the business by outsiders.

If you are taking over an existing business, you should include the accounts for the last three years with some indication of whether they are a guide to the future prospects of the business and, if not, why there is to be a change.

Income

In projecting the expected income of your business you will need to think about the number of customers you expect to have, what you intend to charge them (net of any discounts and promotions) and what credit terms, if any, you are likely to offer. Depending on the nature of your business, you might build up your customer base rapidly or only slowly. For example, if you are selling something on the high street, you might expect to build up trade rapidly over the first 6 to 12 months. However, if you are selling a service for which recommendation is expected to play a large part in gaining new customers or where you need a proven track record in order to secure major contracts, the build-up could take two or three years.

The more slowly your revenue builds up, the greater your need for working capital is likely to be.

Costs

Costs you might incur before you even start to trade include:

- premises: buying or rebuilding, leasing, renting, converting or even building from scratch, installation of electricity, gas, telephone and any other services. You might be able to work from home, in which case these costs could be low
- plant and equipment, tools: for example, specialised machinery, computing equipment, fax, answering machine, office furniture, a van, etc.
- insurance: for equipment, premises, liability (public and employers')
- initial administrative costs: legal and other professional fees
- stationery: business cards, letterheads, envelopes, postcards and invoices all printed with your business name
- publicity: costs of the initial launch
- goodwill, if you are taking over an existing business. This is any excess of the price you pay over the value of the assets you have bought.

You should research this expenditure as accurately as possible and consider ways of reducing it if necessary. For example, you could lease or hire plant instead of buying; instead of buying a photocopier, you could use a local shop at first. The question of how to raise this start-up finance is covered in 'Sources of finance', later in this chapter. The start-up costs will have to be re-paid from your ongoing business activity, unless of course you are in a position to finance them from your own resources, such as redundancy money, savings or an inheritance.

When you begin to work out how much money you are going to need for your project, you must be sure to include not only the start-up costs but also the working capital.

Once you have got your business up and running, you will have to keep track of expenditure and income on a constant basis, aiming always to clear enough profit to keep the enterprise afloat. Costs fall into two types:

- variable costs: these will vary with the amount you produce (i.e. the number of units manufactured or jobs done). They include, for example, the cost of raw materials, power used to run machinery and petrol consumed in distributing finished goods
- fixed costs: these remain the same no matter how much you produce. They might include, for example, salaries and wages to staff, rent and rates, heating, lighting and other services associated with the premises, advertising and marketing, stationery and telephone, cost of maintaining vehicles, road tax, leasing and/or hire charges, insurance premiums, professional fees to accountant, solicitor, patent agent, etc., and interest on loans and depreciation for equipment, including vehicles, but not if leased. (Although you are not paying out hard cash for depreciation, the 'using up' of your capital items is still a cost to the business and you should include it in your accounts.)

Some costs are partly variable and partly fixed – for example, electricity bills will comprise the fixed costs of lighting your premises but could also cover the variable costs of running equipment.

The structure of your business

Your business structure needs to be clear. Your options are: sole trader, partnership, limited company, co-operative or franchise. Two common forms are sole trader and limited company, the pros and cons of which are given below.

	Sole trader	Limited company
Control	You have total control	You might share control with other directors
Getting started	You can start straight away	Various formalities need to be fulfilled

Bureaucracy	Minimal	Ongoing – for example, need to file annual accounts with Companies House. Accounts may need to be audited. Must hold Annual General Meeting
Protection of business name	None	Protected
Profits	All automatically to you	Profits accrue to company. Can be paid to you as salary or distributed to shareholders as dividends
Losses	Unlimited liability – your personal possessions can be used to meet business debts	Limited liability – company has separate legal identity. Normally your own possessions cannot be used to meet company debts
Access to finance	May be hard to raise loans without securing them against personal assets – for example, your home	May have better standing with banks and other lenders
Image with customers	May be less impressive	May give you better image
Trade credit from suppliers	May be harder to get – you might need to supply references	May be easier to get
Tax	For a small business, tax is likely to be lower if you are a sole trader. For a larger business, operating as a company is likely to be more tax-efficient	

National Insurance	Lower, but you are eligible for fewer state benefits	Higher
Retirement planning	Pension planning is more limited	Scope for making higher pension contributions
Selling part of business	Harder to do – means going into partnership	Easy – just sell shares
Death	Business ceases	Business continues

If you are going into business with other people, your choice is mainly between a partnership and a limited company. The details above for the sole trader apply largely to partners as well, with the following exceptions:

- control: you share control with your partners
- starting up: you will need to have a formal partnership agreement, setting out, among other things, who puts in what capital, how control and profits are shared, what happens when a partner leaves or dies, and so on. Getting the agreement right at the outset may save costly and acrimonious disputes later on
- sale of business and death: what happens depends on the terms of the partnership agreement.

Another option, if a group of you wish to set up or take over a business, is to form a co-operative. The essential feature of this form of business is that it is owned and controlled by a group of people – for example, the workers. There needs to be a voting system for making decisions. Any profits are shared between the members. A co-operative can be structured as a partnership (a minimum of seven partners are required for a co-operative), a limited company (minimum two members), a company limited by guarantee (minimum two members) or a co-operative society registered under the Industrial and Provident Societies Acts (minimum seven members). Bodies such as the Industrial Common Ownership Movement (ICOM),* (see 'General help for small businesses', below) publish model rules and can help you to register.

Franchises were covered in some depth earlier. From the point of view of business structure, you must have a contract with the franchiser, and legal advice is essential. You can get general advice from the British Franchise Association, and legal advice plus detailed help and guidance on the contract from a solicitor.

Tax, legal affairs and regulations

There are four main taxes which you may have to pay. A broad outline is given here. For more information see *Which? Way to Save Tax,* updated and published each year by Which? Books. Because you will generally pay less income tax and National Insurance (NI) if you are self-employed than as an employee (which includes being a director of a company), the tax authorities are fairly strict about whom they will class as self-employed. In general, you are on dangerous ground if all (or nearly all) of your income comes from just one source, and you are paid on a regular basis without having to send in an invoice. You are usually classified as self-employed if you can answer 'yes' to all the following questions.

- Do you have the final say about how your business is run (for example, where you work and the hours you work)?
- Do you put your money at risk?
- Do you bear any losses, as well as keep the profits?
- Do you provide the major equipment which you need for your work (for example, a van, machinery, computer)?
- Are you free to employ others, and, if so, do you set their terms of employment and pay them out of your own pocket?
- Do you have to correct unsatisfactory work in your own time and at your own expense?

If you answered 'no' to some of these questions, but you still think you are self-employed, see the Contributions Agency/Inland Revenue leaflet NI39/IR56 (*Employed or Self-employed?*), available from your local Contributions Agency or local tax office. You can ask for a decision from the tax office in writing on whether you count as self-employed.

Income tax

If you are self-employed as a sole trader or a partner, profits from the business, or your share of them, count as taxable. If your business is set up as a company, you might take money out either as a salary or as dividends. Both count as taxable income.

Tax is payable on profits from self-employment, salaries and dividends, if when added to all your other taxable income the total comes to more than your allowances and any other allowable expenses.

In the case of profits from self-employment, you will have to pay tax in instalments in January and July each year through the system of self-assessment. Salaries are taxed through the Pay-As-You-Earn (PAYE) system, which your company must by law operate if it makes payments above a given amount to the directors or other employees. Dividends are paid with a tax credit representing tax already deducted. The tax credit satisfies any tax due at the lower or basic rate, so only higher-rate tax, if applicable, needs to be paid.

Corporation tax

If you operate as a company, the company must pay corporation tax on all its profits. There is no equivalent to the personal allowances for individuals to be set against a company's taxable profits.

From 1 April 2000, companies with taxable profits of up to £10,000 pay corporation tax at the starting rate of 10 per cent. Companies with taxable profits over £10,000 pay tax that rises in stages until it reaches an average rate of 20 per cent at £50,000. Companies with taxable profits over £300,000 pay tax that rises in stages until it reaches 30 per cent at £1.5 million. 30 per cent is the top rate of corporation tax.

Small companies pay the tax nine months after the end of their accounting year. Larger companies, broadly those with profits over £1.5 million, have to pay in quarterly instalments.

National Insurance

If you are self-employed as a sole trader or a partner, you pay NI as follows:

- Class 2 contributions. These are paid at a flat rate as long as you are in business. If your profits are within a given limit, you can choose not to pay but you are then not building up the right to certain state benefits, such as basic retirement pension. You register for Class 2 contributions with the Inland Revenue

(NI Contributions) office, using form CWF1 (see 'Getting started', below). Leaflet CWL2 (*NI contributions for self-employed people – Class 2 and Class 4*) contains detailed information

• Class 4 contributions. These are paid along with your income tax and are a given percentage of your profits (or your share of the profits, if you are a partner) between a lower and upper limit.

As a director of a company, you count as an employee. You are liable for Class 1 NI contributions on your salary and any other earnings if you earn more than a certain amount. There is an upper limit above which these employee contributions are not payable. Your employer – i.e. the company – must also pay contributions on your earnings if you earn more than the lower amount. No upper limit on the employer contributions exists.

VAT

VAT is a purchase tax levied on most goods and services each time they are bought. If you are registered for VAT, you can claim back the VAT which you have paid on things you buy for your business, but you must also charge VAT on your own supplies to your customers. If you are not registered, you cannot claim back the VAT you pay, but you do not have to charge VAT either.

If your business turnover is above a certain level (£52,000 a year from 1 April 2000) you must register for VAT. Below that level, you can choose whether or not to register. Factors to consider are:

• the effect on your customers: VAT increases your prices. However, if all businesses in your line of work are VAT-registered, your prices will not be out of line. If your customers are also VAT-registered businesses, they can reclaim the VAT you charge

• the effect on you: can you cope with the extra work involved in keeping VAT records? Stiff penalties apply for failing to keep proper records and failing to pay VAT on time. You may get a visit from a VAT inspector at short notice and will need to have all your books up to date

• the effect on your business: if a lot of the things you buy for your business are exempt from VAT or zero-rated – for example, postage, journals and travel – you might not gain much from registration.

VAT returns have to be completed every three months and the tax has to be paid every three months. Once you have been registered for a year, you can apply to complete a VAT return just once a year if your yearly turnover is less than £350,000. In this case, you have to pay VAT monthly by direct debit based on an estimated figure. Contact your local Customs and Excise office for more information.

Legal affairs

Depending on your premises and the nature of your business, you might need to comply with certain planning requirements and building regulations (see below). Contact the planning department of your local authority to find out about these. However, on the whole, if you work on your own, relatively few legal requirements are likely to affect your business.

The position changes once you take on employees. This is a major step which exposes you to all sorts of additional legal requirements. Some exemptions are available – for example, if yours is a very small business – but you should check out your position regarding all of the following:

- health and safety procedures
- discrimination on the grounds of sex, race or disability
- the provision of written contracts and itemised pay statements
- the operation of PAYE to collect income tax and NI
- unfair dismissal
- maternity rights
- sick pay
- redundancy.

Regulatory requirements

There are six types of regulatory requirements to bear in mind and act upon if they apply to your business. These are: licences, intellectual property, premises, environmental issues, employees, and health and safety.

Licences

Type of business	What to do
• Cinemas and theatres	Apply to Local Authority
• Indoor sports venues	Licensing Department, Local
• Nightclubs	Authority Registration and

Type of business	What to do
• Public entertainment in any type of establishment • Residential care and nursing homes • Nurses' Agencies • Child-minding • Taxi and private hire vehicles • Pet shops and pet boarding kennels • Scrap metal dealing • Street trading	Inspection Unit (for residential care homes), or Local Health Authority (for nursing homes)
• Hotels (including guesthouses) • Restaurants • Mobile shops (food sales) • Other premises selling food • Abattoirs • Hairdressers • Massage • Skin piercing (including tattooing, acupuncture) • Work with asbestos	Apply to Local Authority Environmental Health Department
• Goods or Public Service Vehicle operators	Apply to the local Department of the Environment, Transport and the Regions (DETR) Traffic Area Office*
• Sale of alcohol in any establishment	Apply to local Magistrate; in Scotland to Local Authority Licensing Board
You may need a credit licence if your business involves: • Lending money • Issue of credit cards • Offering or arranging credit • Debt collecting • Offering debt adjusting or debt counselling services	Apply to the Office of Fair Trading (Consumer Credit Licensing Bureau)*

(continued overleaf)

263

Type of business	What to do
• Operating a credit reference agency	
• Hiring, leasing or renting out goods	

Data and intellectual property

If your business keeps information about people you must process it in accordance with the Data Protection Act 1998. If you keep such information on computer you may need to register. Apply to The Data Protection Commissioner.★

You should protect your company name and logo, any inventions, product designs or copyright. You should also avoid infringing the intellectual property rights of others. Booklets on intellectual property rights are available from the Central Enquiry Unit of the Patent Office.★

Premises

If a new building or change of use is involved, consult your Local Authority Planning Department. It can give you a useful leaflet, *A Step-by-Step Guide to Planning Permission for Small Businesses*. If the building you intend to use needs structural alterations, you should contact your Local Authority Planning or Building Regulations department.

Environmental issues

If you produce, import or export packaging, or if you have packaging at your back door for recycling, you are likely to be affected by the Producer Responsibility Obligations (Packaging Waste) Regulations. Contact the Environment and Energy Helpline.★

If your business uses refrigeration or air conditioning equipment, firefighting equipment or solvents for cleaning, check to see whether they contain ozone depleting substances, i.e. CFCs, HCFCs or halons. Your equipment supplier should be able to advise. If the answer is yes, you will be affected by legislation controlling or banning the use of these substances. A series of leaflets are available from the DTI Publications Orderline.★ Contact the Environment and Energy Helpline, or in Scotland, apply to the Scottish Environment Protection Agency (SEPA).★ General literature is also available from DETR Free Literature.★

Employees' rights

If you are taking over an existing business, the employees' existing terms and conditions of employment must be maintained. The DTI booklet *Employment Rights on the Transfer of an Undertaking* will be useful reading.

If you are setting up your own business, you might start off with no employees, but as the business expands need to take on someone to help you with aspects of it. Employees in a business have rights under employment protection legislation. The SBS produce a series of free Employment Rights Factsheets. Other booklets are available from your local Jobcentre or by phoning the DTI Publications Orderline. A useful handbook, *Employing People,* is available from the Arbitration, Conciliation and Advisory Service (ACAS) Publications.*

Health and safety

You have a statutory responsibility for the health and safety of employees and the public. If you have a factory or workshops you need to register your business with the Health and Safety Executive.* If you have an office, shop or business you need to contact your local authority. If your business involves the storage or preparation of food on the premises, you should contact your Local Authority Environmental Health Department.

Some businesses, such as guesthouses, hotels and residential nursing care homes may require a fire certificate, so check with your local fire authority. The Stationery Office* has a booklet *Fire Precautions in the Workplace – Information for Employers.*

Insurance

A useful introduction to buying business insurance is the free booklet *Insurance Advice for Small Businesses*, available from the Association of British Insurers.* Advice on business insurance is also included in *The Which? Guide to Insurance*, published by Which? Books. Business insurance is a complex area, so it is probably worth getting the advice of an insurance broker who specialises in commercial insurance. By becoming a member of the Federation of Small Businesses (FSB),* you are automatically entitled to legal and professional expenses insurance of up to £500,000 for each claim. This gives you some financial protection for various problems like Inland Revenue investigations, property disputes, jury service, personal injury and employment disputes, as well as 24-hour telephone legal advice. They also have an FSB insurance service, from which you can get other insurance. Individual membership costs £60 per year (plus a joining fee of £20).

Employer's liability insurance

The law requires that everyone on your payroll must be covered by a minimum of £5 million of this insurance, and that a current certificate of insurance be displayed at the place of work. However, family businesses with close relations as employees are exempt from the requirement to have insurance, unless they are trading as limited companies. Although you do not need to, you would be wise to include family members in your employer's liability insurance. Most insurance companies can give you a quote for this type of insurance.

Business property and equipment insurance

To protect your business, you must insure against the disasters that can overtake anyone. These include: fire, burglary, flood, subsidence, malicious damage, explosion, etc. In your policy you should make sure that the following are covered: the premises, contents, stock, goods in transit, and goods on a sub-contractor's premises. You may find that the trade association for your particular trade has a special insurance policy for its members.

Consequential loss insurance is a corollary to insuring against damage or theft as it covers further losses which would arise if your business were to come to a standstill following any of the disasters for which you have insurance.

Public liability insurance

This insurance covers you for claims by members of the public who have been injured as a result of your (or one of your employees') activities at work – for example, a brick dropping from scaffolding on passers-by.

Working from home

Your existing household insurance may cover your equipment and public liability if you work from home on a small scale. But you must tell your insurer that you work from home, or you may find that your insurance is invalid. Your insurer may insist on a special policy once your business equipment rises above a certain value, if your work involves people visiting your home, or if the risk of fire or theft is increased (because you store flammable or expensive materials, for example). Several companies offer policies for people who work from home.

Product liability insurance
This covers you for claims arising out of faults in something you or your employees have designed, manufactured or serviced.

Professional indemnity insurance
This covers professionals, or other people who provide a service, against liability claims resulting from negligent work.

Insurance for car and driver
Third-party insurance is compulsory on all your firm's vehicles. If your work involves a great deal of driving, you might consider insuring against the loss of your licence, which would otherwise mean the loss of your livelihood. It will provide you with the means to hire someone to drive for you.

Personal insurance
If you have dependants, your first priority should be adequate life insurance, with permanent health insurance a close second. 'Key person' insurance is something else to consider: this refers to any key partner or employee without whom the business would suffer.

Getting started

If you have decided to go ahead with your business, the steps you need to take now depend on the business structure you have chosen. You will need to inform the Inland Revenue (for tax purposes), Customs and Excise (for VAT) and the Contributions Agency (for your NI contributions) of your intention to become self-employed, and of the type of business (i.e. sole trader, partner, etc.).

Sole trader

Register for NI contributions using form CWF1 in the back of leaflet CWL1 (*Starting your own business*). The form will be forwarded automatically to your tax office, and if applicable, to Customs and

Excise for VAT registration. Either department (Inland Revenue or Customs and Excise) can supply leaflet CWL1, and their telephone numbers are in phone directories under those headings.

If you will be trading under a name other than your own, your stationery must carry your own name as well.

Partnership

Contact a solicitor to draw up a formal partnership agreement. Each partner will need to fill in form CWF1, as above, for the tax and NI authorities. If the partnership trades under a particular name, stationery must carry the names of the partners as well.

Limited company

The first thing you need to do is to register your company name at Companies House. You will then be issued with a registration number. The simplest way to do this is to buy a company off the shelf – this is a company which has already been registered but is not active. An accountant can help you do this. Alternatively, get help from an accountant and a solicitor to set up your own company. By law, you must appoint at least one director plus a company secretary.

Next, you must register for corporation tax, using the New Company Registration form CT41G, available from the Inland Revenue. Also contact the Inland Revenue and the Contributions Agency to arrange collection of income tax and NI contributions from employees (which includes company directors) through PAYE.

If the company is to be registered for VAT, complete form VAT1, available from your local Customs and Excise office.

You are required to display your company name at your business premises and on letterheads. You must also publicly display the Certificate of Incorporation and the registration date at your premises. Directors are responsible for filing statutory documents, e.g. accounts and annual returns.

General help for small businesses

Although self-employment is never an easy option, particularly for people who have always previously been employees, bear in mind that many others have done it – successfully – before you, and that plenty of advice and information is available to help you. Indeed, it might seem that the problem is not a lack of support, but rather a surfeit. Government policy in the UK has, for a long time, been to encourage businesses, and so a vast infrastructure has been set up to provide assistance and support.

Information and help for entrepreneurs

As the number of different agencies and organisations available can be daunting, the Business Link network has been developed as a first point of call – a one-stop shop where you can find out about financial and other support, and obtain advice.

Government help for Small and Medium Enterprises (SMEs) is largely decentralised and channelled through local agencies such as Business Link centres and Enterprise Agencies.

Business Link

Business Link centres are local business advice units which understand the special needs of new and existing small firms and can offer practical help and useful information.

You can get access to the help available from all the agencies operating nationally or in your area through your local Business Link centre or regional equivalent. Business Link centres are in England (call the Business Link Signpost number or use the web site★ for details of the nearest one to you), Small Business Gateway★ covers lowland Scotland, and Business Information Source★ the Highlands and Islands of Scotland. In Wales there is Business Connect (Wales),★ and in Northern Ireland, the Local Enterprise Development Unit (LEDU).★ Each centre is a partnership between Chambers of Commerce, local authorities, enterprise agencies and other bodies, such as commercial providers and local universities.

The support offered at these centres includes counselling, information, guidance and business skills training. Experienced business counsellors offer independent and confidential advice on a wide range of business-related matters. This can cover anything from preparing a business plan to finding premises, franchising, exporting, patents and tapping sources of finance. They are also a rich source of reference material, with various publications, free leaflets, access to the Internet, and so on.

Learning Skills Council

Subject to the passage of legislation, the Learning Skills Council will be formally established from April 2001. It will be responsible for strategic development, planning, funding, management and quality assurance of post-16 training and education (excluding higher education). The proposals are to have a network of 40–50 local Learning Skills Councils, which would be the local arms of the national body. According to the government's White Paper, *Learning to Succeed*, these will be responsible for 'raising standards and for securing provision to match local learning and skills needs'. At the time of writing, it is not clear how this local network will be run, and to what degree it will work with the SBS. The devolved administrations are working independently on how they will promote post-16 training and education.

Enterprise Agencies

Your local Enterprise Agency (local Enterprise Trust in Scotland) is another good source of support for new entrepreneurs. The address and telephone number of your nearest agency can be found through your local Business Link or equivalent, in *Yellow Pages* under 'Business Enterprise Agencies', in the phone book under 'Enterprise Agencies' via the National Federation of Enterprise Agencies,★ or by writing to Business in the Community.★

Local Enterprise Agencies, which are supported by partnerships between local industry and local and central government, are independent organisations, nearly all run by experienced business-people, offering confidential counselling, sometimes free, to people wishing to start a business. Their key purpose is to promote economic regeneration by providing help with the setting up and continued success of local SMEs. They offer business counselling, business training, consultancy and help with managed workspace.

They can also advise on problems relating to sources of finance, marketing, planning, training and finding premises, or refer you to other people. The agencies may run a number of other initiatives to support local small businesses, such as training sessions and seminars and small business clubs, and manage small workshop units.

Small Business Service

The Small Business Service (SBS) was set up in April 2000 as an executive agency of the DTI with two principal offices in London and Sheffield. It provides advice to small firms on financing, access to expertise, and ways in which to improve efficiency. It also has a remit to promote enterprise among disadvantaged groups in deprived areas. In England, from April 2001 there will be a number of local SBS outlets. At the time of writing – during the period of transition from Training and Enterprise Councils (TECs) to the LSC and SBS – it is not clear how the service in England nor the services in the devolved administrations will be provided. Business Link (or its equivalent) would be a good starting point for any queries, or call the general enquiry number for the SBS in Sheffield.

Several free booklets on all aspects of starting a new business, including regulatory requirements, start-up, sources of finance and information, are available from the SBS and also from Business Links, Local Enterprise Agencies or the DTI Publications Orderline. The SBS web site is very comprehensive and informative, with links to many related sites, and two of the above booklets, *A Guide to Help for Small Businesses* and *Buying a Franchise*, are available to download in PDF format.

Project North East

Project North East* (Newcastle's Enterprise Agency) publishes two excellent series, *Business Information Factsheets* (*BIF*s) and *Business Opportunity Profiles* (*BOP*s).

*BIF*s fall into 13 categories of information: pre-start, marketing, finance, management, staff, health and safety, legal, business services, premises, environment, information technology, international trade, and Europe.

There are over 300 *BIF*s and each factsheet is concise but detailed, informative and clear. They usually include sections of 'useful tips', 'further information', and 'useful addresses'. *Could You Run Your Own Business?*, for example, covers: assessing the risks, motives, pressures, age and experience, skills and qualifications, personality, family commitments, useful tips, further information and useful addresses. Up to ten free *BIF*s are available through the four high-street banks (HSBC, Lloyds TSB, Barclays and NatWest) and your local Business Link.

*BOP*s give detailed information on different business opportunities. Over 340 of them are now available, and they are regularly updated. Check whether there is one based on your business idea. Each one covers: market, customers, competition, promotion, start-up costs, training and qualifications, legal, further reading and useful addresses. Both *BIF*s and *BOP*s are updated at least every three to four years, some more frequently, depending on events such as legislative changes.

The *Complete Business Reference Adviser* (*COBRA*) was launched in 1997 as a one-stop information base for small (or potential) businesses and their advisers. It is available on CD-ROM and via the Complete Business Website (Cobweb). *COBRA* contains *BOP*s, *BIF*s, market synopses (brief reports on major market sectors), business support and finance, essential business contacts, sources of business information, events and exhibitions, the business legal library, market report listings, a list of small business books and a glossary.

Ideas, innovations and patents

The SBS has a scheme called Smart that provides grants to individuals and small or medium-sized businesses to make better use of technology and to develop technologically innovative products and processes. See 'Sources of finance' below for details of the grants available.

Business Link centres (and equivalent offices in Wales, Scotland and Northern Ireland, see above) have specialist innovation and technology counsellors available who can give you local advice and also help you to tap into European Research and Development initiatives.

The National Endowment for Science, Technology and the Arts (NESTA)* was set up with an endowment of £200 million from the National Lottery. It is intended to 'help creative individuals develop their full potential, while also helping to turn creativity and ideas into products and services and to enable these to be exploited effectively'. To this end, it provides both financial and other support. Its web site includes an on-line 'Inventor's Handbook'.

The Institute of Patentees and Inventors* is a non-profit-making organisation that offers advice on all aspects of inventing. Its web site includes an 'Inventor's Checklist', advice on how to protect your idea, and some good links to other web sites. The Patent Office★ helps small firms to protect their business ideas, inventions and logos by offering advice on patents, registered designs, trademarks and copyright, and has a range of free literature and a telephone help line.

If you are starting a business that is using new technology and you need assistance with premises and management, then a 'business incubator' might be for you. As the name implies, incubators provide assistance and support to entrepreneurs whose idea needs some extra help to get going. For a list of incubators in the UK, contact UK Business Incubation (UKBI).★ Science Parks, of which there are 50 across the UK, can also provide help to businesses. You can find the location of your nearest Science Park as well as get information on the sort of help they can offer by contacting the UK Science Park Association (UKSPA).★

Instant Muscle

Instant Muscle★ is a charity with 45 centres across England and Wales which specialises in helping unemployed people who are receiving Jobseeker's Allowance to return to work, including self-employment.

The charity can provide counselling and training and help with all aspects of business planning, and though it cannot give grants or loans, it can help with the drawing up of a sound business plan for submission to organisations that may have sources of funding.

Other sources of help and support

Many local schemes exist to help out-of-work residents to start new businesses. Contact your local Business Link or Enterprise Agency for details.

The DTI has set up a special web site called the Enterprise Zone★ where it intends to collate access to other sites which may be useful to small and growing businesses.

Information and help for co-operatives

Most new co-operatives register either as an Industrial and Provident Society (I&PS) or as a company limited by guarantee. They sometimes use the sets of model rules which are available from promoting bodies such as the Industrial Common Ownership Movement (ICOM) or Employee Ownership Scotland (EOS).* Model rules make registration easier, cheaper and quicker than having a constitution drawn up.

Industrial Common Ownership Movement
ICOM promotes and advises worker co-operatives and other forms of employee ownership, provides specialist registration and legal services for co-operatives and community enterprises, offers training and consultancy services, has an extensive mail-order catalogue of publications, can assist in raising money from Europe for co-operative training schemes, and provides legal, technical and practical services for its members. Membership is open to all co-operatives, support organisations and sympathisers. You do not have to be a member already to seek advice on starting up a co-operative. ICOM can also undertake promotional activities on behalf of its members.

Industrial Common Ownership Finance Limited
The Industrial Common Ownership Finance Limited (ICOF)* administers a revolving loan fund on a national basis for co-operative enterprises. It also has specific loan funds for particular areas of the UK. Loans range from £5,000 to £50,000 over five years at an interest rate of, typically, 10–12 per cent. Enterprises which apply for such loans must be able to demonstrate their co-operative status, and also their commercial viability.

Registry of Friendly Societies
The Registry of Friendly Societies* is the government department which gives information about rules and registrations and is responsible for registering Industrial and Provident Societies. The registry in London deals with England and Wales, while the one in Edinburgh deals with Scotland. Such societies in Northern Ireland come under the wing of the Department of Enterprise, Trade and Investment* in Belfast. During 2001 the work of the registry will be taken over by the Financial Services Authority for England, Wales and Scotland.

Employee Ownership Scotland
EOS offers guidance to groups of people wishing to form employee-owned businesses, including co-operatives. Such advice

covers all forms of business consultancy and a loan fund is available to provide capital requirements for new and existing co-operatives in Scotland.

Financial help

You may have the resources you need to start up your business. If not, you will need to obtain outside finance. Even once your business is up and running, you may find that you need extra resources – to finance expansion, for example.

Grants

Central and local government, the European Union, local authorities and certain other bodies make grants available to businesses. Grants are generally preferable to other forms of finance since there is no interest or dividend to be paid and they do not have to be repaid so long as the terms of the grant are met. However, there are often costs involved in complying with the conditions of the grant, which should be researched carefully. Whether or not grants are available to a particular business will depend on a number of factors particular to each grant. These include the purpose of the investment, whether it will or is likely to create jobs, the location of the business and the size of the business.

Advice on the grants available to individual businesses is available from Business Link centres in England, or the equivalent regional agencies (see above). Some of the grants available are listed below.

- **Smart** offers a package of support including grants to help businesses review and develop their use of technology. See below for more details.
- **Regional Selective Assistance** is a discretionary scheme aimed at attracting investment and creating and safeguarding jobs in assisted areas by making funding available for projects in most kinds of manufacturing industry and in some service industries.
- **Enterprise Grants** have been introduced specifically for smaller firms, typically for those projects that are too small to qualify for Regional Selective Assistance. The scheme operates in certain areas of England and is run by the Government Offices (these are the local outposts of central government, and are listed

in the phone book). Grants are normally either 7.5 per cent or 15 per cent of the project capital costs (up to a maximum grant of £75,000). You are advised to speak to either your regional Government Office or Business Link before submitting an application. There are similar schemes operated by the National Assembly for Wales, the Scottish Executive and the Northern Ireland Office. Businesses in Scotland will be able to apply for grants up to £100,000 towards manufacturing and some service projects based in Assisted Areas under a new streamlined service.

- **European Structural Funds** support a range of regionally based schemes aimed at new and small businesses, which can benefit small and medium-sized firms. The funds are administered by the Government Offices in the English regions, the National Assembly for Wales, the Scottish Executive, and the Northern Ireland Office.

Enterprise support in the devolved administrations

Wales

Under the 1998 Government of Wales Act, there is now one development body responsible for the whole geographical area, the Welsh Development Agency (WDA).* Its present remit is to help the regeneration of the economy and improve the environment in Wales. The Agency's main activities include providing premises, encouraging investment by the private sector, grant-aiding land reclamation, stimulating rural and urban development, and providing investment capital for industry. Its sponsoring department is the National Assembly for Wales. At present, the Training and Enterprise Councils (TECs) provide most training for self-employment and business start-ups throughout Wales. These will be replaced by Learning Skills Councils (LSCs) in April 2001, but as already noted, it is not yet clear how LSCs and the SBS will work together locally.

Scotland

As well as delivering local development and training, the Local Enterprise Companies (LECs) are responsible for advising and supporting people who wish to set up in business, and those already running a small business. They work in partnership with Small Business Gateway to offer a range of services, which vary from area to area.

These may include business counselling and advice, subsidised training and financial assistance through various enterprise schemes. The LECs are accountable to either Scottish Enterprise or the Highlands and Islands Enterprise (HIE),* depending on location.

Scottish Enterprise covers Grampian, Tayside, Central, Fife, Strathclyde, Dumfries & Galloway, Borders and Lothian, through a network of 13 Local Enterprise Companies. Their services include advice, training, financial and property assistance, environmental projects and business development advice.

Highlands and Islands Enterprise designs and delivers economic and community development, training, and environmental renewal. Its area covers Highland Region, Orkney, Shetland, Western Isles, the Argyll district of Strathclyde Region and the western Moray district of Grampian Region. Its services include financial assistance to businesses, the provision of factories and offices, training programmes, financial assistance to community and cultural projects, and various initiatives for environmental renewal. Ten LECs provide services on behalf of HIE.

Small Business Gateway has more than 60 outlets across lowland Scotland. The service combines the resources of LECs, Enterprise Trusts and other partners, such as local authorities. It provides impartial advice and assistance to new and growing companies, covering business start-up, business growth and general business information.

Northern Ireland

The Local Enterprise Development Unit (LEDU) is a company sponsored by the Department of Enterprise, Trade and Investment in Northern Ireland. It is the lead agency responsible for the promotion and expansion of small businesses in Northern Ireland that, in general, do not employ over 50 people. LEDU offers financial assistance, business advice and counselling on all aspects of business. Foundation grants of up to £500 are available to assist start-ups of community or co-operative businesses or social economy initiatives. The Social Economy Agency* can offer help from the earliest stages of development planning.

Banks

The main clearing banks (HSBC, Barclays, Lloyds TSB, NatWest) all have some form of business advisory service, free to customers. This help is intended mainly for established businesses. Increasingly, however, banks publish detailed booklets and packs for people who want to start a business, and welcome discussions prior to start-up. If you decide to raise finance through your bank, your bank manager will want to see your business plan. The bank might insist that any loan is secured – for example, against assets of the business or company, or your personal assets, such as your home. This means that if you failed to keep up the loan repayments the bank could seize those assets in order to get its money back.

Numerous merchant banks provide medium-term finance. Many banks have developed special schemes to help new businesses. They include unsecured loan schemes (i.e. not backed against the assets of the business or yourself, so the bank takes more risk and you may be able to borrow even if you do not at present have any substantial assets) and loans for which you pay only the interest for now, with the capital repayment deferred (these loans are cheaper at the outset, which can be handy if your business takes some time to build up, but you will end up paying more in the long term).

Other sources of finance

Smart

Smart is the SBS initiative to help individuals and small businesses make better use of technology and to develop technologically innovative products and processes, or buy external consultancy to improve their use and exploitation of technology. Smart replaced in 1997 the Small Firms Merit Award for Research and Technology (SMART) and Support for Products Under Research (SPUR) Awards. Scotland runs its own SMART and SPUR schemes, and Wales and Northern Ireland also have their own initiatives. Various different types of grant are available for projects which involve technological advances or novelty:

- **Technology reviews**. Up to £2,500 for firms with fewer than 250 employees towards the costs of an expert review.
- **Technology studies**. Up to £5,000 for firms with fewer than 250 employees to help identify opportunities to use technological advances.
- **Micro projects**. 50 per cent of eligible costs, up to a maximum of £10,000, for micro-firms (with fewer than 10 employees) to help develop low-cost prototypes of their new products.

- **Feasibility studies**. 75 per cent of eligible costs, up to a maximum of £45,000, awarded through competitions for firms with fewer than 50 employees for feasibility studies for new products.
- **Development projects**. 30 per cent of eligible costs, up to a maximum of £150,000, awarded through competitions for firms with fewer than 250 employees undertaking development projects.
- **Exceptional development projects**. Also for firms with fewer than 250 employees; up to £450,000 for a small number of exceptional high-cost development projects.

For more information about Technology Reviews, Technology Studies and Micro Projects, phone the DTI Publications Orderline. For information about feasibility studies or development projects, contact your local Business Link or your regional Government Office.

Shell LiveWIRE

Shell LiveWIRE★ operates throughout the UK, providing free local advice, information and business support to young people aged 16 to 30 who are considering self-employment. There is a free Essential Business Kit and one-to-one advice from a local business adviser. An annual competition, Young Business Start-up Awards, is held for new businesses.

The Prince's Trust

The Prince's Trust★ business start-up programme has helped over 37,000 people aged 18 to 30 to set up and run their own businesses. The Trust can provide advice and may give loans or bursaries to young people who have been unable to raise the finance they need elsewhere. Each business is allocated a business mentor, who offers help and advice for the first three years of trading. The Trust also offers new businesses ongoing business support and marketing opportunities.

BTG plc

BTG plc★ identifies commercially promising technologies from universities, research institutions and companies world-wide. It then protects this technology through patents, negotiates licences with industrial partners and shares the profits with the inventors. BTG holds over 8,500 patents and patent applications covering

250 technologies, and areas of activity include pharmaceuticals, agribusiness, medical technology, automotive engineering, electronics and telecommunications. It operates internationally and has offices in the UK, the USA and Japan.

British Venture Capital Association

The British Venture Capital Association (BVCA)★ is the representative body for companies that offer venture capital to finance new enterprises. Venture capital investors take a stake (generally a minority holding) in the business they invest in, their returns being entirely dependent on the growth and profitability of the business. They are unlikely to want a day-to-day involvement in the business, but may want representation on the board of directors. Venture capitalists tend to invest amounts over £100,000. Their names are listed in the Association's annual directory (available free from the BVCA).

Business angels

Business angels are private individuals who invest in new and developing businesses, usually in exchange for an equity share in the business. Generally they have owned or managed successful businesses themselves, and very often they will contribute to the management or strategy of the businesses in which they invest. Their contribution is usually between £10,000 and £250,000 but can be much larger.

The National Business Angels Network (NBAN)★ is a non-profit-making organisation which puts investors in touch with businesses looking for development capital and complementary management skills. It assesses business opportunities and matches them with suitable investors, using a computerised system and on a confidential basis. The market between private investors and developing businesses operates through experienced intermediaries, registered with NBAN. The organisation is backed by all the major high-street banks, the Corporation of London, the London Stock Exchange and the DTI.

3i plc

3i plc,★ a venture capital company (and a member of the BVCA) with 18 offices throughout the UK, invests in businesses across the whole spectrum, from family firms to high-technology enterprises. It helps them at all stages of change: at start-up, when risk capital may be required; during expansion; and later during phases of development such as diversification, acquisition, management buy-out and management buy-in. 3i is a long-term investor which takes a minority share in businesses. Its investments are usually in excess of £100,000.

Courses and literature

Provision for courses to help business start-ups will vary from area to area, so check with your local Business Link. Many courses are run in partnership with Business Link and are likely to cover topics such as:

- assessing your business idea
- writing a business plan
- management and supervision of staff
- finance/book-keeping
- health and safety
- export/import
- computers
- sales and marketing
- communications.

A vast range of published material useful to the small-business person is available. In addition to those mentioned in this chapter, a selection appears at the back of this book.

This chapter has shown that although the rewards of self-employment are many, it also involves risks. If you decide to opt for self-employment, it will be important to replace – or replicate – the business environment, support and infrastructure that you are familiar with from your previous organisation. You will need to be completely sure that you are committed and determined to work hard for success, to choose your business wisely, and to be as well prepared as you possibly can.

Chapter 7

Early retirers seeking new careers

- Pre-retirement planning can help minimise the negative effects of early retirement and can be done over a period of time.
- Many options are open to those taking early retirement, whether in employment (paid or unpaid), self-employment, leisure or further education.
- Your choices will be influenced by your financial situation, which you will need to assess carefully.

Few of the generalisations about retirement – it happens at a fixed age; it marks the time when one stops work; it signals either a decline into poverty and decrepitude or a comfortable, leisured existence with plenty of money to spend – reflect the wide range of experiences which different people go through at this stage of their lives. This is particularly true of early retirement. Some people may find themselves pushed into it, perhaps through redundancy or ill health before retirement age, or the offer of voluntary redundancy. Many then find that the opportunities open to them in terms of work, leisure and further education are numerous and exciting, and that they can lead fulfilling, productive and busy lives if they so desire.

This chapter is aimed mainly at those who want a second career after early retirement. It first examines the financial and emotional consequences of early retirement, then explores the avenues open to those who plan to carry on working – in paid employment or for themselves – or to pursue leisure/education interests. It also looks at pre-retirement planning and financial issues such as state pensions and benefits, personal and employers' pensions, investments and savings, and tax.

Early retirement through redundancy

If the organisation you work for is going through a bad time and has to shed staff you may find that your job is under threat. You may be made compulsorily redundant or have the option to volunteer for early retirement. In either case you will find that you have to deal with four major issues:

- the emotional impact on you
- the emotional impact on other people close to you
- the financial consequences
- how to occupy yourself and whether you should work or not.

The emotional impact on you

You may have worked in your job and/or industry for some years, so the prospect of taking early retirement could seem very attractive. You may see it as allowing you to escape from some aspect of your work with which you are dissatisfied – for example, the commuting, a changed work climate, or doing work with which you are bored or over-familiar. However, do not underestimate the emotional impact that taking early retirement could have on you.

- The way we view ourselves tends to be determined by what we do. Irrespective of whether you retire because of voluntary or compulsory redundancy, you may feel some loss of identity: you will no longer be, say, 'a supermarket manager, married with two children'. Do you need or want something with which to replace this defining role? If so, what will that be?
- If you are in employment, you are likely to be busy and working hard. Unless you can gradually reduce your hours of work, you will find it very hard to go from this situation to one in which your day is unstructured. You will need to get used to this change in your daily rhythm. Again, think about whether you want to replace it with another label such as, for example, 'part-time lecturer', 'charity worker' or 'school volunteer'.
- The loss of status (to say nothing of the loss of regular income) can be hard to bear. This will be especially true if you are

accustomed to being in a senior post, with staff reporting to you, and having a place in the hierarchy which ensures a respectful audience for your views. Perhaps you like to be in a position of authority. How will you replace this?

- Working with others is a great way of having companions who share the same ups and downs as you do. If you retire early, and this sort of close companionship is important to you, you need to plan how you will manage this change. Perhaps the best thing for you, rather than going into self-employment, for example, would be to seek paid or unpaid work so you have colleagues around you.

- Being employed entails having to make decisions on how to manage crises, plan resources, and manage people, your own time and projects. Many people feel a buzz of achievement when they are doing this, and it is an important part of their job satisfaction. When you leave, will you miss this? If so, how will you accommodate this change?

- Taking early retirement will enable you to spend more time with your family, and to balance up your life so you spend less time working for others and more time focusing on yourself. If you have family and/or a spouse, early retirement may alter some of the long-held assumptions about who does what in the household and family unit. For example, if you retire early and your partner carries on working, it will make sense for you to do the shopping and the lion's share of the cooking and other household basics. If this is a change from the normal pattern of family life, it could cause friction. You need to be aware of this and to make allowances for it.

The emotional impact on others

If you are made redundant or take early retirement, it is more than likely that your family and close friends will be affected emotionally too. It is not an easy time, and you may want to seek professional guidance and support. The British Association for Counselling and Psychotherapy★ and Relate★ are useful points of contact. The emotional effects of redundancy, both on yourself and on those close to you, is also addressed in Chapter 3.

Your family's reactions may vary depending on whether your redundancy was forced or voluntary. You may have very valid reasons for taking voluntary early retirement, such as wanting to start a small business or spending more time on leisure interests or with your family. However, people close to you may not feel the same – indeed, they may feel resentful that you willingly chose to make the changes which will have so great an impact on their lives too. When you have actually stopped work, and perhaps feel down or at a loose end, you may get a reaction along the lines of, 'Well, you brought it on yourself, didn't you?' So take the time beforehand to discuss your reasons with your family and close friends, and to talk over what the consequences will be for everyone.

On the other hand, if you were made compulsorily redundant you will probably be treated with more sympathy, as people will see you as a victim. Take care in these circumstances that their sympathy, although well-meaning, does not overwhelm you. As was explained in Chapter 3, when dealing with loss you must move through the 'grief cycle', and not get stuck in a particular phase. So make sure that others do not impede your recovery.

The financial consequences

The practical and financial implications of early retirement and redundancy are looked at in detail in Chapter 2. The complex issue of pensions and early retirement is discussed later in this chapter.

If redundancy is forcing you to leave work earlier than you expected to, you will be entitled to redundancy pay. If you are under state pension age and are capable of, and are actively seeking, work, you may be eligible for Jobseeker's Allowance (JSA), which can be contribution-based or income-based. Get in touch with your Jobcentre as soon as you become (or know that you are going to be) unemployed, even if you think you will not qualify for JSA: this will ensure that you get National Insurance (NI) credits to protect your rights to benefits or pensions in the future. You do not need to do this if you are aged 60 or over, as you will get credits automatically.

Occupying your time

If you have worked full-time for a long time, stopping work will herald a big and perhaps not entirely welcome change. You may find it hard to structure your time and to muster up the enthusiasm to start on a new venture. Chapter 3 offered tips on how to cope with an unfamiliar state of inactivity, in the context of looking for work (see 'Sanity savers'). In the case of early retirement, some amount of pre-retirement planning (see below) can help you prepare for it.

Early retirement through ill health

If you retire because your health is no longer good enough to allow you to do your job, there may be emotional and financial repercussions.

The emotional impact on you and other people

The emotional impact of taking early retirement will be greatly increased if the condition which forced your retirement is severe enough to compel you to make major changes to your lifestyle, and particularly so if it was unexpected. If either situation is true for you, you will need time to adjust to the new situation and to come to terms with the change in your circumstances and expectations of what retirement will now be like. Do seek help if you feel you are not coping with the emotional impact of your ill health. It is also important for you to discuss with your family and close friends what effect any changes are having on them.

The financial implications

If you are forced into retiring early because of poor health, although you cannot receive a state retirement pension early, you may get other state benefits – for example, incapacity benefit, or disability living allowance if you need help with personal care and getting about. For guidance on the state benefits available if you are sick or disabled call the Benefits Enquiry Line.★

The Inland Revenue does not set a limit on the age at which you can draw an occupational pension from an employers scheme on ill-health grounds, and it relaxes the limits on the tax-free amounts the scheme can pay out if you are terminally ill. Each employer's pension scheme usually sets its own conditions, which may be more rigorous and less generous than the Inland Revenue rules.

If you have to retire because of ill health, you can draw a pension from a personal pension or stakeholder scheme at any age, although the amount is likely to be smaller than it would have been had you contributed to the plan until your planned retirement date. Again, see later in this chapter for a detailed discussion of pensions and early retirement.

You may also have some relevant insurance. Permanent health insurance, whether a personal purchase or a perk from your employer, will pay out an income if you are unable to work because of ill health or disability, but it usually stops at retirement age. Credit insurance covers loan payments for you if you cannot make them yourself because of sickness, accident or redundancy, but often for only one or two years.

Do remember that with all these options, definitions of 'ill health' will vary, and medical evidence is likely to be required.

Pre-retirement planning

Retirement is a big change for anyone to make, whether it is taken early or not. You can minimise the effects of it on you if you take positive action as early as possible in preparation for this new part of your life – your so-called third age.

Pre-retirement planning has many aspects – financial, emotional and physical – and can be done over a period of time. It may consist of any or all of the following:

- keeping records of your spending in the years running up to your retirement so you can see where the money is going. In this way you can gradually reduce your expenditure to match your after-tax pension
- if you have an employer pension, discussing the options with the pensions department in your organisation
- if you have a personal pension or stakeholder scheme, consulting your pensions adviser to discuss, for example, whether to take part of your pension fund as a tax-free lump sum, whether to use some or all of the rest to buy an annuity, and if so, what type of annuity, or whether you should consider taking an income direct from your pension fund (called 'income drawdown'). The decisions you make will depend, among other things, on the size of your pension fund, your attitude towards risk and your tax position

- re-thinking your insurance cover in a number of different areas: car, health and household insurance (which is available at preferential rates for older people through organisations such as Saga★ and Age Concern★), hospital insurance, life insurance, investment-type insurance, credit insurance and mortgage protection. Help the Aged★ now runs a special Care Fees Advisory Service★ to help older people plan for their long-term care, which includes advice on investing to meet the cost
- considering how you will keep fit and healthy and making any lifestyle changes now so they are simply part of your life rather than part of retirement
- doing a pre-retirement course (see below)
- taking advantage of secondments, one-off project assignments, or mentoring opportunities offered by your employer (see 'Help from your employer' below)
- continuing to work for your organisation but in a different capacity: for example, perhaps you could take redundancy, but continue to work part-time as a consultant for your former employer. This is particularly common for people who have been in a reasonably senior, and perhaps a technical, role and their organisation needs to tap into that technical or managerial expertise
- looking at interim management, both paid and unpaid. This is an increasingly common option for middle and senior level staff. Contact the Association of Temporary and Interim Executive Services★
- becoming the minority partner in an 'informal' small business as a way of testing whether it would suit you or not
- doing vocational courses in the evenings and at weekends so that as one career finishes you can launch yourself into a new one
- developing a hobby into a small business
- taking business courses
- taking computer courses
- thinking about travelling abroad
- finding out which of your hobbies and leisure interests can be pursued during the day or in the evenings and weekends so you can think about structuring your time
- becoming involved in community volunteer work, organised either by yourself because you are aware of local needs, or by

your employer as a one-off project or secondment (see 'Business in the Community',* below)

- involving your partner in all these ideas, so that he or she does not feel excluded from your plans
- gradually easing off the hours you work so that stopping work completely does not come as a big shock. This will also free up more time for you to investigate other possibilities for the future.

Pre-retirement courses

Pre-retirement courses are run by some organisations for their employees, and by some insurance companies, voluntary organisations and local authorities. They can be free or cost several hundreds of pounds, and are aimed at preparing those retiring – early or otherwise – for the new phase in their lives.

The Pre-Retirement Association* publishes an annual guide to pre-retirement courses offered by a number of organisations throughout the UK. It also runs its own courses conducted by trained and qualified tutors; contact it to find out what is on offer in your local area. The courses generally cover topics such as financial issues (tax, pensions, balancing income/expenditure), leisure, relationships, health, working, etc. Most courses are open to anyone who wishes to attend them; some are held for specific organisations.

Before signing up for a pre-retirement planning course, consider the following questions.

- What do you want from the course? Is it hard factual information or an opportunity to think more generally about retirement? Can you influence the course content?
- Who will be running the course? What qualifications and experience do they have? If course tutors are giving financial information, are they authorised to provide independent financial advice?
- What will be expected of you? Can you take your partner?
- What background materials will be provided?
- How will the course be designed – as a workshop, lectures or small discussion groups?
- How many participants will there be, and what is their background likely to be?
- How much does it cost and what does this include?

Other possible sources of information about pre-retirement planning, including courses, are your local Careers Service, local library, Age Concern, Help the Aged, your local Citizens Advice Bureau, Business Link (or regional equivalent – see Chapter 6) and Learn Direct.* Contacting Learn Direct will give you access to training course information in your local area as well as nationwide.

Help from your employer

If you are taking early retirement, it is likely that your employer will be able to provide some practical assistance to help you adjust to retired life. The form this takes will vary: it could include a golden handshake, enhanced pension arrangements, pre-retirement planning, an opportunity to reduce the number of hours worked, the offer of secondment, project work, part-time or consultancy work, or the provision of continued access to social facilities and networks.

Business in the Community

Many leading British employers have found that one way of using the skills of employees taking early retirement and preparing the individuals for life after retirement is to get them involved with community projects such as wildlife trusts, centres for the homeless, women's refuges, hospitals, drug dependence units, children's charities and inner-city schools. Employees – who continue to be paid a salary by their employers – can take on specific tasks in these projects or act as mentors for those in the centres, for varying lengths of time from a few hours a month to full-time for one or two years. All three parties – the employer, the individual and the community project in question – benefit from such arrangements. Business in the Community offers a service matching up companies and charities, though it does not deal with individuals.

Options open to early retirers

If you are taking early retirement, especially on a voluntary basis and not because of ill health, you will have a choice as to how you spend your time in the future: you could find employment (paid or unpaid), be self-employed, or not work at all.

Each of these choices will be driven by different motivations, such as wanting to turn a hobby into a business, wanting the status and lifestyle associated with full-time work, or wanting time to devote to other interests, and will in turn have different consequences for your retirement. Indeed, if you decide to work, say, on a voluntary (and unpaid) basis or set up your own business for the first time in your life after having been employed throughout your career, you are not really retiring but starting a new career.

Whether or not to carry on working following early retirement is a decision you have to make based on your personal priorities and circumstances. It may be that you have chosen to take early retirement to pursue something specific, in which case there will be no dilemma. Otherwise, you need to think first of what you would like to do with your life and then investigate whether you can afford to financially. 'The financial aspects of early retirement', below, should help you answer the second question.

Working as a volunteer

If your primary reason for wanting to continue to work is not financial – or you are finding it hard to get a paid job but want to keep your hand in – voluntary work may be the answer.

There is always someone somewhere who needs a volunteer to help with something. The list of tasks to be done is endless, from helping in classrooms to organising community events. You will be able to find something which uses your talents, whether they are:

- practical (e.g. painting, cooking, knitting, dress-making, DIY, decorating, gardening, carpentry or building)
- concerned with people (e.g. helping families, delivering Meals on Wheels, working with Victim Support, reading to a blind person, providing practical help to a young family under stress, working in your local CAB, working with Relate or the Samaritans, visiting people in hospital, helping in your local school, being a prison visitor, working in a hospice, being a school governor, being a classroom volunteer, helping with Cubs, Brownies, Scouts or Guides, or helping at day centres and old people's homes)
- business skills (e.g. doing administrative work for voluntary organisations, managing and organising staff rotas, stock and

window displays in a charity shop, designing an extension/new facilities, raising money, applying for grants, or auditing the accounts of small local charities)

- sporting (e.g. helping disabled children to ride or blind people to swim, raising money for your favourite charity by running a marathon, teaching fitness classes, or doing music and movement in old people's homes).

To do some of these voluntary jobs you may need extra training, which may be classroom-based, on the job (coaching, shadowing) or a mixture of the two. All will introduce you to new people, networks and skills, or reactivate skills you had forgotten you had.

Getting voluntary work

In the same way as for searching for paid work, think about what interests you and apply all the principles of job search detailed in previous chapters. Respond to advertisements, look out for cards in shop windows, get in touch with local groups, ask around your friends and neighbours and read the local papers. The following organisations will have lists of voluntary agencies in your area:

- your local library
- CAB
- Council for Voluntary Service (in England. In Scotland, contact the Council for Social Service, in Wales the County Voluntary Council, and in Northern Ireland the Council for Voluntary Action in Northern Ireland or the Rural Community Council)
- Community Service Volunteers (CSV).★ Their scheme for retired people is called the Retired and Senior Volunteer Programme (RSVP)
- National Association of Volunteer Bureaux★ (in England. In Scotland, contact Volunteer Development Scotland★, in Wales the Wales Council for Voluntary Action (WCVA),★ and in Northern Ireland the Northern Ireland Volunteer Development Agency★)
- National Centre for Volunteering★
- British Trust for Conservation Volunteers (BTCV)★ in England. Also BTCV Scotland,★ Conservation Volunteers Northern Ireland (CVNI),★ and Wales Conservation Centre★
- Council for the Protection of Rural England (CPRE).★

Once you have found a charity or other organisation to which you wish to volunteer your services, visit it, and before committing yourself check on how many hours you will be expected to work and how often, whether expenses are paid, and so on.

If you wish to apply for Jobseeker's Allowance, and want to do voluntary work, you should discuss this with your adviser at the Jobcentre (see Chapter 2).

The opportunity to do voluntary work overseas on a short-term basis may appeal to you. The British Executive Service Overseas (BESO)* places volunteers who are professionaly trained experts in certain fields to carry out specific tasks in the developing world and eastern Europe, for periods of between two weeks and six months. BESO promotes sustainable economic and social development through providing professional, technical and specialist skills and training. The organisations the volunteers assist may be from the private, public or voluntary sector – what they have in common is the fact that they are unable to afford the services of commercial consultants. The assignments are varied, and include experimental zoology, retail management, accountancy, agriculture, health, water supply, manufacturing, teacher training, human resources, textiles and many others.

Voluntary Service Overseas (VSO)* recruits volunteers with professional skills aged up to 70 for placements in developing countries, for projects generally lasting two years. It too has a very broad range of assignments. VSO has reported that the number of people over 50 volunteering to work overseas has quadrupled from 4 per cent in 1992 to 16 per cent in 2000.

Both the above organisations have thorough recruitment procedures to check that you could cope (in every sense) with what you may face during your placement(s). They have informative web sites which provide a good picture of the sorts of assignments they recruit people into, the professional skills required, and the recruitment procedures.

John, for example, became a volunteer with BESO after retiring as general manager of a large department store in the south Midlands. He visited Omsk in Russia (four times), the Seychelles and Fiji for the organisation. In Omsk he advised grocery stores on issues such as profitability, productivity, motivation and incentives, shop layouts, merchandising, profit-related pay and bonuses. John saw big changes following his first visit to Omsk, with the stores he advised having increased their sales by over 40 per cent, begun acting as wholesaler and distributor for other retailers, and moved to larger premises.

Paid work

You may not feel ready to leave the world of work, even after you retire from your main career. However, it may not be easy to find paid work if you are near retirement age, partly because long-term unemployment among the young remains fairly high in the UK and some employers still specify age restrictions when advertising new posts, although this practice is now less common. There are some good indications that these discriminatory practices may die out. In July 2000 the government published its voluntary Code of Practice on Age Diversity for employers. At the time of writing, the EU has a draft directive on discrimination in employment, including age, which may become law during 2001. See Chapters 1 and 4 for more on employment trends and overcoming the potential disadvantage of age in the job market.

An ageing population and changes in the working environment – especially the growing number of people employed in service industries and the shift towards more part-time and casual work – could work in favour of older jobseekers. According to the Industrial Society, during 2000 the over-50s returned to work faster than the rest of the population as demand for their skills increased – the employment rate for women aged 50 or over has increased at almost three times the rate for the workforce as a whole – and by 2020, one in four of the workforce will be aged 50 or over. At present, overall, one-third of people aged between 50 and the state retirement age do not work, for various reasons: difficulty in finding suitable work, age discrimination, not wishing to work, preferring to do voluntary work, or disability or long-term sickness.

You can boost your chances of employment by improving your existing skills or learning new ones. It is worth bearing in mind that networking becomes even more important as you get older, so make sure you keep up your contacts and develop new ones in areas of work that attract you. Research the fields of employment in which you are interested, thinking about what you have to offer and how this corresponds to employers' needs. Chapters 4 and 5 give advice on how to look for and apply for jobs.

Changing motivations and circumstances

If you are seeking paid work after taking early retirement from an organisation, your motivation for working and your personal circumstances may change or have already changed for a number of reasons:

- if you decide to work part-time but have to commute a long way, your travel costs will take a larger proportion of your income than before, so you may choose to work nearer home
- you may want to spend more time with a partner who has already retired, or with young grandchildren
- you may wish to combine work with an existing leisure activity
- your pre-retirement planning course may have suggested new directions which you have never explored before
- if you are drawing a pension, your tax position may mean you need to earn below a certain amount to avoid falling into a higher tax bracket (see 'Financial aspects of early retirement', below)
- you may want to work part-time rather than full-time, so you have more freedom to pursue caring responsibilities, further education or leisure interests.

Make sure when you apply for jobs that your 'thought bubbles' (see Chapter 4) change to reflect these new priorities and situations. This will have an impact on your networking strategies and tactics, how you write your CV and letters of application, how you fill in application forms, and your interview technique. Of course, the factors listed above may not apply to you at all, and you may decide you want to continue to work full-time, and in a similar position (in terms of seniority, responsibilities, pay and perks) to the one you have just left. If so, you can regard yourself as retired from one profession, industry or company, and starting afresh with another.

Maureen, for example, retired as head teacher of a state nursery school on the grounds of ill health at the age of 51. She then took a part-time administrative job with her local FE college working with adult learners four days a week. She regards herself as retired from teaching, but not as a retired person, and works hard at her new career. Although Maureen can draw her teacher's pension, she has joined the pension scheme with her new employer, and will build up a new pension with it.

Many of the job-search techniques covered elsewhere in this book apply no matter what age you are. As discussed, however, being older you may face particular difficulties, and it may help to use the additional sources of information and help listed below.

Employment agencies

Using an employment agency (see Chapters 4 and 5 on choosing and dealing with agencies) is a good way of finding a job that suits you. Some agencies specialise in helping older people, and you may find that they dovetail with your interests, experience and location:

- Charity Recruitment and Charity and Fundraising Appointments★ recruit middle and senior managers for charities
- Charity People★ recruits all grades of staff for UK charities, mostly London-based
- some agencies – including members of the Association of Temporary and Interim Executive Services and the Board Appointments department of the Institute of Directors★ – specialise in short-term (temporary or interim) work for business executives
- the Corps of Commissionaires★ finds part-time work for ex-service personnel, police and fire officers
- Execucare★ recruits short-term contract staff, and part-time and full-time workers for charities and other not-for-profit organisations, but not voluntary or temporary workers
- the Over-50s Employment Bureau,★ a service of the National Association of CABx, operates in the London area in a wide variety of sectors. It does not charge a fee, even to employers for finding staff. Because it is part of the CAB network, it can offer a broad CAB service, advising on tax, benefits, pre-retirement issues and other sources of information
- the Third Age Network★ recruits for voluntary and paid work in the south-east of England
- The Third Age Employment Network (TAEN)★ campaigns for better opportunities for older people to learn, work and earn. You can register with your local group. It is in regular contact

with employment agencies, and is a useful point of contact for information about local opportunities.

- Third Age Challenge Ltd★ provides free mentoring, guidance and help with job search for people in their 'third age'. Its Back-on-Track project is a national programme for adults of any age who are trying to get a job
- your local Jobcentre can arrange for you to meet a Disability Adviser if you have special needs or suffer from ill health. The Disability Alliance★ and the Royal Association for Disability and Rehabilitation (RADAR)★ have useful publications.

Becoming self-employed

If, after a lifetime of working for other people, working for yourself remains a long-held ambition, it can be realised if you retire early. Many people plan for this by starting an informal business sometime before they intend to retire, and running it on a small scale, perhaps with help from their family. When they are made redundant or retire early they can develop the business, giving it more of their time and energy.

Adrian, for example, had worked for a large IT company for 30 years. He started a contract cleaning company with his wife, doing domestic and small industrial cleaning contracts. While he worked full-time, his wife did the lion's share of the work on the business. Together, they built the business up over about four years. When he was made redundant at the age of 54, he took a sizeable amount of his redundancy money and expanded the business. He was ready for the change and relished the new challenge.

The statistics are encouraging. Businesses set up by entrepreneurs in their early 50s are twice as likely to survive as businesses started by those in their early 20s (Industrial Society, 2000). This implies that the skills and knowledge gained from years of experience – such as strategic know-how, experience of previous economic cycles, deep market and technical knowledge – are an invaluable resource to bring to a new venture. See Chapter 6 for more details on self-employment.

Pursuing leisure interests or further education

Leisure education (i.e. learning that is not work-related) is becoming increasingly important for people of all ages, but particularly for many older people who are retired or semi-retired. People are motivated by various reasons: the desire to acquire or augment skills, knowledge or continued good health is a primary one. Opportunities for leisure activities and further education abound, but will vary according to where you live, so what follows are guidelines only on where you can go to find out what is available.

Sometimes doing a short course can help you decide whether to carry on working, or what new direction to take, even if it does not lead you back into paid employment. Classes run by your local authority can provide a good opportunity to try out a particular subject; they sometimes offer cheaper fees for retired people. You could also ask at your local reference library, or contact Learn Direct. Both can give you information about local and national training opportunities.

Your local area

Many services are available through your local authority and other organisations in your neighbourhood. A useful starting point for information is your library. Libraries welcome leaflets and posters from local groups, so they are usually good places to browse. There will be plenty of reference material available as well as the latest periodicals. Many libraries are happy to help you with your research, and also have photocopying facilities. They may have 'open learning' centres where you can use computers and surf the Internet. The larger libraries can be busy and confusing places, but there is almost always a reference librarian whom you can ask for help.

- Many leisure centres and swimming pools have special programmes, such as reserved sessions during the day, for older people, or have facilities for groups who want to organise their own activities. They often have rooms available for hire at competitive rates, and your group may qualify for a discount.
- Local schools often welcome older people as regular volunteers, or on a one-off basis to talk about their childhood memories, local history, and so on.
- Many universities and colleges are very welcoming to older students, because they realise how helpful it is to have people with different and broader experience in the student body. Increasingly, they will accept you on the basis of your past experi-

ence rather than the exams you have passed. Some encourage this through a pre-study course called Access to Learning. This may lead to a degree or diploma, but does not have to. Because funding has changed, many universities and colleges make additional income by having an External Studies Department (the name may vary) which offers courses of varying length on a broad range of subjects, some vocational and others for general or academic interest. Some of the courses may be free or available at a low cost, especially for people who are considered to be in special need (for example, the long-term unemployed, the disabled, or those over the age of 50). Some offer free places to local retired people.

- Your local education office will offer adult education classes, both during the day and in the evening, usually at a discount to pensioners. Many councils have educational guidance services for adults – you will be able to ask for advice from trained staff on the educational opportunities in your area.

- Community Education Centres offer day, evening and weekend courses on a broad range of subjects, usually in community halls, neighbourhood centres and local secondary schools. Some courses lead to qualifications, others are for your leisure, health or personal development. Most offer discounts to pensioners.

- Local church groups are usually very active, and often provide opportunities for leisure education.

- Museums and galleries tend to hold special classes or activities, often over a period of weeks. Ask at your local library.

National groups and resources
A number of national bodies provide options for people who wish to pursue leisure interests and further education.

- Age Concern has an Education and Leisure Officer to promote education and leisure opportunities for older adults through an exchange of information. Age Concern publishes the *Age Concern Education & Leisure Newsletter* three times a year, and also a series of free *Education & Leisure Guides*. It also supports Age Resource, which promotes education and volunteering. Ageing Well is a national programme to promote healthy living in later life.

- The Health Development Agency⋆ provides information on aspects of health education. Ask for information on its Active for Life campaign.

- Help the Aged has material on fitness and volunteering in retirement.
- Learning Link is a local service which covers all aspects of adult education.
- The National Association for Educational Guidance for Adults (NAEGA)★ can provide addresses of local services.
- National Extension College (NEC)★ is an educational trust offering home study courses, covering general education, languages, counselling, IT for beginners and improvers, and professional and vocational subjects (such as marketing, management, accounting and book-keeping). Its main market is the 17–35 age group, but people of any age are welcome, and fees are reduced for those on a state pension. In addition to GCSE and A-levels courses, the college has 'starter' courses designed to ease the way for people who feel unsure of their academic skills. A free *Guide to Courses* is available.
- The National Federation of Women's Institutes★ runs courses for members at Denham College in Oxfordshire.
- The National Institute for Adult Continuing Education (NIACE)★ organises Adult Learner's Week in May each year. Its Older and Bolder initiative, on which there is a free newsletter, runs regional seminars and a national conference. There is an (email) information exchange and discussion group, where you can post information about events in your area, and take part in debates on a variety of topics. You can join the group via the NIACE web site★
- FT Knowledge★ offers short practical courses, usually at local colleges.
- The Open College of Arts★ is an educational charity which offers home study courses in art and design, painting, sculpture, textiles, photography, writing, garden design, art history and music. Completing a course may give you credits towards a degree. With their UK network of tutors you can have a personal tutorial as well as postal tuition.
- The Open and Distance Learning Quality Council★ can send you a list of accredited colleges which offer distance learning.
- The Open University (OU)★ offers a wide range of long and short courses which can be used as credits towards a degree. It also has a Leisure Series of short, self-contained special-interest courses.

- Sport England★ is the first point of contact for addresses of Regional Sports Councils which will have more local information. It produces a booklet called *50+ and All to Play For*.
- The Third Age Trust★ has over 430 local University of the Third Age (U3A) groups in the UK with about 100,000 members who are studying a broad range of courses, not all of which are academic or educational. It does not award qualifications or diplomas. The fees are modest and all the activities are arranged by members of the local group. It publishes *U3A News* and also has a travel club which organises special-interest holidays, and a subject network which links up members around the UK who have similar interests. For a list of local groups contact the trust.
- The Workers Educational Association (WEA)★ operates all over the UK, offering a wide range of courses. You do not need qualifications to enrol and your fellow students will come from a variety of ages and backgrounds. The study courses usually last for a term, and can include visits to the theatre (for modern drama courses) or field study trips (for wildlife, history, or local landscapes courses). Residential courses are also available. Course fees vary, so enquire about reductions for retired people. Ask your library for the address of your local branch or contact the WEA.

Residential courses

The range of residential study courses is vast and growing all the time. Courses are held virtually anywhere: at a local college or university, a school, a field study centre or country mansion in beautiful grounds. Residential courses are an ideal way of combining a holiday with your study, and if you go on your own you will find plenty of single companions. The best starting point for researching such courses is *Time to Learn*, a guide published twice yearly by the City & Guilds of London Institute★ – probably best known as one of the UK's leading providers of vocational qualifications. Other useful publications are the *Spring/Summer Schools Supplement*, available from the Independent Schools Information Service (ISIS),★ and the *Summer Academy Brochure*, available free from the Summer Academy.★

Moving abroad

Moving permanently abroad to live needs careful consideration. Quite apart from the issue of being separated from family and friends, you should also be aware that:

- selling up and moving abroad, and then finding you do not settle, can be an expensive mistake. A trial period of residence at different times of the year would be a good idea; if there are British people already living there permanently, ask their opinions and try to discover the reality as opposed to the dream.
- you can miscalculate living costs. These can include food, heating, accommodation, insurance, travel/running a car, local taxes, etc. You will also need to research the local health facilities. Will they be sufficient for your needs? If you have private health insurance in the UK, will it cover you in your chosen country?
- check what the pension arrangements are. Ask your local Benefits Agency Office for leaflets NI38 (*Social Security Abroad*), and NI106 (*Pensioners or widows going abroad*), which give information on receiving your UK pension while living abroad. For advice on conditions of residence, local tax regulations, your legal position as a foreign resident and whether you will need a work permit if you plan to take on any sort of job, enquire first at the embassy or consulate of the relevant country.
- even if you regard your move abroad as permanent, you will still count as a UK resident for tax purposes if you make visits back to the UK which average 91 days or more a year. And even non-residents may have to pay some UK tax, for example, on investment income arising in the UK, or inheritance tax on gifts made (e.g. on death). For details, consult Inland Revenue booklets IR20 (*Residents' and Non-residents' Liability to Tax in the United Kingdom*) and IHT18 (*Inheritance Tax - Foreign Aspects*), available from tax enquiry centres and tax offices.

The financial aspects of early retirement

If you retire early, your main source of income is likely to be the pension you receive, whether from an employer's pension scheme or a personal pension plan. This will usually be smaller than it would have been if you had worked on until normal retirement age. You will not be eligible yet for your state pension. If your employer is seeking to shed staff and offering a voluntary redundancy package, you will probably get a better pension deal than if the decision to retire is yours alone. You may also have income from savings and investments, or you may be eligible for some state benefits.

Whatever the circumstances of your early retirement, it is extremely important to make sure that you can afford it. Do a personal budget (see Chapter 2) to see how much you need to live on. If you find that you do not need to earn an income after taking early retirement, and that you can live off your pension(s) and/or savings, you could choose to do unpaid work in the voluntary sector or, of course, retire from work completely. This section is aimed at those changing careers after retiring early, so if you fall into this category, you need to be aware of the implications of your decision on your financial situation.

The four main sources of income, then, on which you may be able to rely in retirement are:

- state pensions (payable only on reaching state pensionable age) and state benefits
- private pensions you built up while working, for example, through an occupational pension scheme, personal pension or stakeholder scheme
- interest and other income from investments and savings
- pay or profits from work you continue to do after retirement.

Each of these sources of income will be considered in separate sections below. If you receive redundancy pay (see Chapter 2 for details), you can choose to spend it, invest it, or use it to start a business – which may become a source of income in itself.

One consideration, if you continue working, is that you will have to carry on paying National Insurance (NI) contributions, unless you are over state pension age (at present, 60 for women, 65 for men) or your earnings are small. Even if you stop work, if you are under 60, you might want to consider paying voluntary NI contributions to increase your eventual pension. Get a retirement pension forecast from the DSS (see 'Checking your state pension', below) to check whether this would be worthwhile.

State pensions and benefits

It is likely that you will eventually qualify for some pension from the state. You cannot start to receive state retirement pension before you reach state pension age. So if you retire before then, you may need to make up that part of your retirement income from other sources. Some employer pensions do this for you automatically, paying a sum which is higher for younger retirees and reducing it by the amount of the state pension once the pension holder reaches state pension age.

The main advantage of state pensions is that they are inflation-proofed, in line with the Retail Prices Index, both during the time you are building up an entitlement to them and while they are being paid out. The drawback is that state pensions are low, and therefore insufficient on their own to support a comfortable lifestyle. In recent years, the government has introduced a minimum income guarantee (MIG), which means that pensioners can claim Income Support to bring their total income from all sources up to a minimum level which is higher than the state basic pension alone. The MIG is increased each year in line with earnings (which generally rise faster than prices). And, from 2003, the government plans a pension credit which will reward people who have built up private pensions. However, if your retirement is some way off, be wary of relying too much on state benefits and credits – a consistent feature of the state pension system since 1975 has been constant change, so there is no guarantee that these top-ups will still be in place when you retire.

State pensions, then, can be a useful backbone for your retirement income which you should supplement through other sources. To work out how much extra pension income you will have to plan for, you will first need to know roughly how much income you can expect from the state. What follows is a summary of how the state pension works, as a basis for your calculations. The state pension scheme has two main components: the basic pension and an additional pension.

Basic pension

A person builds up his or her entitlement to basic pension (up to £72.50 per week in 2001–2) by paying NI contributions throughout his or her working life. If both husband and wife qualify for a basic pension in their own right, they can get a maximum of two single persons' pensions (up to £145 per week in 2001–2). Otherwise, they may be able to claim up to £115.90 based on the husband's NI alone. If the wife is aged under 60, the whole of this is paid to the husband; if the wife is 60 or over, up to £43.40 a week is paid directly to her.

Additional pension

Additional pension is paid on top of any basic pension you get. At the time of writing, the additional pension is provided through the State Earnings Related Pension Scheme (SERPS). From April 2002, this is being replaced by the State Second Pension (S2P). The changeover will not affect any SERPS pension rights you built up before April 2002. If you retire between 2003–4 and 2051–52, your additional pension may include both SERPS and S2P elements.

You can build up a SERPS pension only if you are paying full-rate Class 1 NI, so if you are self-employed, unemployed or on low earnings you are not building up SERPS. The amount of pension you eventually get is linked to your earnings.

Even if you are eligible for SERPS, you may have 'contracted out' of the scheme. This means that instead of building up a SERPS pension you build up one that will be paid from an employer's scheme or from a personal pension plan.

Initially, S2P will also be an earnings-related pension scheme, but it is designed to give more generous pensions to:

- people on low-to-moderate earnings. Using 1999–2000 values, for someone earning between £3,500 and £9,500 a year, their S2P entitlement will be worked out as if they were earning £9,500
- carers with low or no earnings because they are looking after children under six or an elderly or disabled person. Carers' S2P entitlement will also be worked out as if they were earning £9,500 a year
- long-term disabled people who have a broken work record.

The scheme will encourage higher earners to contract out of S2P, relying instead on occupational schemes and stakeholder schemes (see below). Non-stakeholder personal pensions can also be used for contracting out. Once stakeholder schemes are well established, the government plans to remove the earnings link from S2P and convert it to a flat-rate pension.

Checking your state pension

Before you take early retirement you may wish to check how much basic SERPS pension and S2P you qualify for to date, based on your record of NI contributions. You can do this by getting Form BR19 from your local Benefits Agency or the DSS web site.* Complete the form and send it to the Retirement Pension Forecasting and Advice (RPFA) Unit* at the address given on the form. Contact the RPFA Unit if you need help filling in the form.

If you have any other queries or problems relating to your state pension or NI position, contact your local Benefits Agency office, preferably in writing. Do not forget to put your NI number on all correspondence.

Other state benefits

Taking voluntary redundancy does not count as making yourself unemployed, so provided you are under state pension age and are actively seeking work, you may qualify for JSA (see Chapter 2).

If you are not able to work, but your income is low, you might qualify for Income Support and other means-tested benefits, such as Housing Benefit and Council Tax Benefit. If, despite working, your income is still very low and you have children to support, you could be eligible for Family Credit.

Your local Benefits Agency can help you to sort out which, if any, state benefits you are entitled to.

Pensions from employer schemes

From October 2002, all employers with five or more employees must offer you access to a pension scheme at work. This could be:

- an occupational scheme (which can be either 'money purchase' or 'salary-related' – see below)
- a group personal pension scheme to which your employer makes contributions equal to at least 3 per cent of your basic pay
- a stakeholder scheme.

Stakeholder schemes

The name 'stakeholder' is given to pension schemes which meet certain conditions, such as flexibility and low charges, and have been registered with the Occupational Pensions Regulatory Authority

(OPRA).* Stakeholder schemes can be either personal pensions or occupational money purchase schemes. Broadly speaking, anyone can have a stakeholder personal scheme, but a stakeholder occupational scheme is run by an employer for his or her employees.

Occupational schemes

Group personal pension schemes and stakeholder schemes (other than occupational stakeholder schemes) are types of personal pension and are covered in the next section. For simplicity, the term 'stakeholder scheme' in this section refers to a stakeholder personal pension, unless stated otherwise.

Occupational schemes are usually the best way to save for retirement because your employer must pay a substantial part of the cost of providing your pension. In a non-contributory scheme, the employer pays the whole cost. Most schemes, however, are contributory, which means you pay in something as well – for example, 3 or 5 per cent of your pay. You get tax relief on the amount you pay in and the contributions are deducted directly from your pay before tax is worked out. Whatever your employer pays does not count as salary or fringe benefits, so you don't pay any tax on this perk.

There are two main types of occupational pension scheme: salary-related schemes and money purchase schemes. Whichever scheme you are in, you can expect a lower pension if you decide to retire early. Special rules apply if you have to retire early because of ill health, which allow a scheme to pay out higher than normal pensions (see below).

If you are made redundant or leave your job before retirement you need to find out how your pension rights will or may be affected. Not all employer schemes will pay a pension if you leave before your normal retirement date. In the first instance, consult the pensions department in your organisation for advice. You may want to take extra advice from an independent pension consultant. The Society of Pension Consultants* will be able to find one in your area. If you have a problem with your employer scheme pension, try to resolve it through the scheme's complaints mechanism (it must by law have one). If this fails, contact the Pensions Advisory Service (OPAS).*

Be careful if you take early retirement within two years or so of your pension scheme's 'normal retirement age' (most commonly

65 for both sexes) because your employer may be entitled to offset part of your pension payment against your redundancy payment. The 1996 Employment Rights Act states that 'an employer who intends to dismiss an employee to whom a payment is due under an occupational pension scheme not more than 90 weeks after the dismissal may offset part of the pension payment against the redundancy payment'. The whole of the redundancy payment can be offset if the annual value of the pension and/or lump sum is equal to one-third or more of the employee's pay. The redundancy payment is reduced by one-twelfth for each complete month between the 64th birthday and the termination date.

If you are unsure of your position, see the employment legislation leaflets available from your local Jobcentre or phone the Redundancy Payments Helpline.*

Salary-related schemes

In a salary-related scheme, you are promised a given level of pension and other benefits. Your contributions, if any, go part-way towards the cost of meeting this promise and your employer contributes whatever is required to meet the balance. The contributions are invested in a fund from which the benefits are paid. The retirement pension is worked out according to a formula based on your pay at or near the point of either retirement or when you leave the scheme, if this is earlier, and the number of years for which you have been a member of the scheme. The great advantage of final pay schemes is that you have a good idea in advance of roughly how much pension you will get at retirement in today's money. Retiring early means accepting a lower pension, because:

- you will have been in the scheme for fewer years. However, if you are retiring because of ill health, the tax rules allow schemes to base the pension on the full number of years you would have worked had you been able to stay on until normal retirement age. Your own scheme might have less generous rules
- the starting pension will be based on your pay at the time you leave – this may be a lot less than you would have been earning by normal retirement age
- the scheme may make an 'actuarial reduction' to reflect the fact that your pension will have to be paid out for more years than if you had stayed on to normal retirement age. Different schemes

have different rules, but a common deduction is 5 per cent of your pension for each year of early retirement (see example below). The reduction might be waived if your firm is looking for redundancies.

If you have time to plan ahead for early retirement, consider saving extra to compensate for the above factors. You can do this through an in-house additional voluntary contribution (AVC) scheme, a free-standing additional voluntary contribution (FSAVC) scheme or, from April 2001, using stakeholder schemes and personal pensions (see below).

Diana's retirement age would normally be 65, but she has decided to retire early at age 60. Her present salary is £36,000 and she has been in the pension scheme for 28 years. The scheme pays 1/80th of leaving salary for each year of membership, so her basic pension calculation is: 1/80th × £36,000 × 28 = £12,600 a year. But the scheme then applies an actuarial reduction of 5 per cent for each year of early retirement. Because Diana is retiring five years early, the total reduction is: 5 × 5% = 25%. So her pension is reduced by a quarter to: (100% – 25%) × £12,600 = £9,450 a year.

Money purchase schemes

With a money purchase scheme your employer – and you too if it is a contributory scheme – pay in contributions which are usually a set percentage of your pay. These contributions are used to build up a fund, which is used at retirement to buy a pension. How much pension you get depends on annuity rates at the time you retire. The annuity rate is the rate at which an insurance company will convert the lump sum in your fund into a regular income for life. The amount of pension you get from a money purchase scheme depends on five factors:

- how much is invested
- how long the money is invested for
- how well the invested money grows
- how much is deducted in charges
- annuity rates at the time you retire.

It is therefore much more difficult to predict how much pension you can expect from a money purchase scheme. If annuity rates are low when you retire you may end up with a smaller pension than you expected. If your pension fund is into six figures, you could consider 'income drawdown' instead (see below), either direct from the employer's scheme, if the rules allow it, or by transferring first to a personal pension.

As with the salary-related scheme, if you retire early from a money purchase scheme, your pension will be reduced. This will be because you will have paid in contributions for fewer years, the invested contributions will not have had as long to grow, and your fund will have to buy a pension which you expect to last for longer.

Again, if you have time to plan ahead for early retirement, consider saving extra to compensate for these factors. You can do this through an in-house AVC scheme, an FSAVC scheme, or using personal pensions and stakeholder schemes (see below).

When you reach retirement

No later than three months before you reach the normal retirement age for your job, or before the date on which you have decided to retire early, you should contact the administrators of your pension scheme – if they have not already been in touch with you – to find out how much pension you can expect, and what options you have. If you have lost touch with the administrators of your employer pension schemes, contact the OPRA Pension Schemes Registry,★ which runs a free tracing service.

You may like to maintain or establish contact with other retired members of the scheme, so see if there is a pensioners' association. These associations will have a number of purposes: to be a social network, or to provide advice or even financial support.

Personal pensions and stakeholder schemes

Through your workplace, you may have joined a group personal pension scheme or a stakeholder scheme. If in the past there has been no scheme at work, or if you work for yourself, you may have a stakeholder scheme, personal pension or a retirement annuity contract. From April 2001 onwards, even if you do not work at all, you may have a stakeholder pension scheme.

What these schemes and plans have in common is that they all work on a money purchase basis. So, like the occupational money purchase scheme discussed above, your eventual pension depends on five factors:

- how much is invested
- how long the money is invested for
- how well the invested money grows
- how much is deducted in charges
- annuity rates at the time you start drawing a pension.

The earliest you can normally take a pension from a personal pension (including one you have under a group scheme or one that qualifies as a stakeholder scheme) is age 50. With a retirement annuity contract, the minimum is 60, though by transferring to a personal pension first you could start your pension up to ten years earlier. (There is no minimum age if you are retiring due to ill health.) Note that transferring may be costly and could affect the size of your pension and other benefits, so get advice before you do this. Financial advisers need extra qualifications before they can give advice about pension transfers. You can check whether an adviser has the appropriate qualification by contacting the Financial Services Authority (FSA) Central Register.★

The earlier you retire, the smaller your pension will be because less will have been paid in, the money will have been invested for less time, and annuity rates will be lower reflecting the fact that the pension will have to be paid out for longer. If you are able to plan ahead for early retirement, you should pay extra into your pension arrangement to compensate for these factors.

When you reach retirement

About three months before you intend to start taking a pension from a personal pension, you should contact the provider for information about the options you have and an estimate of the pension and other benefits you can expect. The OPRA Pension Schemes Registry, which runs a free tracing service for employer pension schemes, may also be able to help with some personal pension queries.

You do not have to take an annuity from the same pension provider with whom you built up your pension fund. You can instead switch to another provider. This is called exercising your 'open market option', and is usually worth doing, because some companies specialise in annuities and others do not. So get quotes from a range of other companies as well to see who offers the best deal.

For more guidance, see 'Buying an annuity', below. Instead of buying an annuity, you could take a pension direct from your pension fund – see 'Income drawdown', below.

Tax-free cash

Occupational pension schemes, stakeholder schemes, personal pensions and retirement annuity contracts all allow you to give up some of your pension and instead receive a tax-free lump sum. The rules are complicated, but very broadly: in occupational schemes, the maximum cannot be more than 1½ times your salary; with personal pensions and stakeholder schemes, the maximum is often a quarter of the pension fund you have built up.

The more cash you take, the lower the pension you will get from the scheme. But, even if you need the maximum possible retirement income, it can still be worth taking the biggest lump sum you can. This is because the pension counts as taxable income, but the lump sum is tax-free. You could use the tax-free sum to buy a 'purchased life annuity' – these are similar to the annuities you buy with a pension fund in that you hand over a lump sum and in return get an income for life. But only part of the income from a purchased life annuity is taxable – the other part counts as a gradual return of your original capital and is tax-free. Therefore, the after-tax income you can buy by taking the tax-free cash may be greater than the after-tax pension you have given up.

Buying an annuity

If you have saved through any money purchase arrangements – such as an occupational money purchase scheme, stakeholder scheme, personal pension, retirement annuity contract or AVC scheme – you need to turn the pension fund you have built up into income when you want to start drawing a pension. You can do this by buying an annuity. There are different types of annuity; the main ones are briefly described below.

You do not have to use all of your pension fund in one go; you can use part to buy an annuity now, another part later on, and so on. But if your pension fund is relatively small, you may get a better deal by using the whole lot to buy just one annuity now. Get advice from an independent financial adviser.

Level annuities

A level annuity provides the same income every year for the rest of your life. Annuity rates at the time you buy the annuity determine the income you will get. Rates vary according to:

- **your age**. The older you are, the higher the income – because on average, older people have less time left to live than younger people
- **your sex**. Men usually get a higher income than women of the same age, because on average, women live longer. With some pension schemes, you must buy a unisex annuity which offers the same income to both men and women
- **your state of health**. Most annuities assume you enjoy average health, but if you know your health is poor or your lifestyle endangers your health (for example, you smoke heavily) you might qualify for an 'impaired life annuity'. This pays a higher-than-normal income because your life expectancy is shorter than for an average person of your age.

The main problem with a level annuity is that your income stays the same even though prices tend to rise from year to year. So, as your retirement progresses, the buying power of your income falls. To counter this, you could save part of the income in the early retirement years to supplement your income later on.

Increasing annuities

Another way to combat the effects of inflation is to choose an annuity which increases each year. There are three main types:

- **fixed increase**. The annuity income increases by, say, 3 per cent or 5 per cent every year. If prices rise by more than this, the buying power of your pension will still fall
- **RPI-linked**. The income increases in line with inflation as measured by the Retail Prices Index, so the buying power of your pension stays the same. (If price levels fell, your income would also fall, but periods of falling prices have historically been rare and short and, in any case, the buying power of the income would still be unchanged)
- **LPI annuities**. With Limited Price Indexation, the income increases in line with inflation but only to a maximum of 5 per cent a year. The rules of some pension schemes and plans require

you to buy this type of annuity. The buying power of your pension is maintained, provided inflation does not exceed 5 per cent a year.

The snag with increasing annuities is that the starting income is a lot lower than you would get from a level annuity. In general, it would take many years before the income caught up and even longer before you had received as much in total from the increasing annuity as you would have done from the level annuity.

Investment-linked annuities

A further way to tackle the problem of inflation is to choose an annuity whose income is linked to an underlying fund of investments. Provided the investments grow by a certain amount, so too does your income. But if investment growth is poorer than expected, your income falls, so these are more risky than either level or increasing annuities.

There are two types of investment-linked annuities: with-profits and unit-linked. With-profits annuities are the less risky of the two and the more popular choice. If this option appeals to you, get advice from an independent financial adviser.

Joint-life last survivor annuities

These pay out an income during the lifetimes of two people until they both die. If anyone (say, your husband, wife or an unmarried partner) is dependent on you financially, you should choose this type of annuity. It can be combined with any of the other annuity options described above.

Income drawdown

Instead of buying annuities, you can draw a pension direct from your pension fund, leaving the rest of the fund still invested. Under current rules, you can carry on doing this until age 75, at which time the remaining pension fund must be used to buy an annuity.

There are rules about how much income you can take each year from the fund. These are designed to prevent you running out of money before the end of retirement. The maximum income is broadly the same as a level annuity for someone of your age and sex. The minimum is 35 per cent (just over a third) of the maximum.

There are costs involved in leaving your pension fund invested. Also, to get a better deal than you would have done from buying an annuity, you will generally need to invest in share-based investments, which involve risk. As a result, income drawdown is generally suitable only if you have at least a six-figure pension fund. Get advice from an independent financial adviser before taking this course.

Retiring gradually

If you are changing career, you might want to start drawing just part of your pension now to supplement the earnings from your new job. Later on, you could increase your pension as you gradually decrease your work. Money purchase schemes and plans are very flexible and there are several ways you can use them to gradually phase in your pension:

- use just part of your pension fund to buy an annuity now and convert more to annuities later on
- buy an investment-linked annuity, choosing the options which let you have a low pension at the start and a good chance of increases later on – an adviser can explain to you how this works
- go for income drawdown, choosing a low pension now which you can increase later on.

All these options have complications, so discuss them with an independent financial adviser before making your choice.

Deferring your pension

Despite taking early retirement, you might decide not to take a pension from some or all of your pension arrangements immediately. This will be sensible, particularly if you are planning to start a new career, because you probably will not need your full retirement income yet.

This raises the question of whether to leave your pensions invested as they are now or whether to switch from the old arrangements to new ones. This is discussed in Chapter 2.

Investments and savings

You will need to think carefully, when planning to take early retirement, about the investments and savings you have already built up.

This section does not offer advice on what investments to make, but highlights some issues to take into account when reviewing your investments. Consider the following questions.

- Do you have something put aside for emergencies which you can get at quickly?
- Have you organised all the insurance you need – for example, life insurance to protect your dependants, permanent health insurance to protect your income, and so on?
- Do you know or anticipate when you are likely to need lump sums, for example, to replace your car, or take an expensive and/ or long holiday?
- Have you thought about how much risk you can afford to take in search of higher growth? Although you cannot lose any capital with deposit-type investments, historically they have given returns far lower than equity-based investments, such as shares and unit trusts, and in some periods the return from deposits has not even kept pace with inflation so the buying power of your investment would have actually fallen. To strike a balance between risk and returns, you probably need a mix of investments.
- Do you have any special circumstances which are likely to be a drain on your resources, such as dependant children in private or higher education?
- Have you considered whether you eventually want to pass your wealth on to your heirs? If so, consider what impact paying for help in the home or the cost of living in a residential or nursing home, if your health fails in later life, would have on your wealth. Taking out long-term care insurance could help you to protect your heirs' inheritance.
- Once you have retired, you will need to consider investments which give you income both now and in the short term, and income for the longer term.
- Do you know the tax consequences of your investments, and have you minimised any adverse ones?

Tax

Retired people are liable to tax on their income in the same way as anyone else, with one notable exception: the benefits of advancing years can mean a lower tax bill because of higher personal allowances given to people of 65 and over (see 'Working out your tax bill', below, for 2000–1 allowances).

Another difference between the retired and those in employment is that retired people – who have pensions and other income from various sources – often fall into the category, in the view of the Inland Revenue, of basic-rate taxpayers whose tax affairs are not entirely straightforward. This means that they will receive a tax return each year. Only a minority of taxpayers are sent a tax return – other groups who automatically receive them include the self-employed and higher-rate taxpayers.

For the majority of taxpayers – who are employees without any tax complications and who do not pay higher-rate tax – tax is deducted each week or month through the Pay-As-You-Earn (PAYE) system, and other tax owing, such as tax on savings interest, is usually deducted at source. If you will be receiving a pension from a former employer or a personal pension, it is likely that you will pay your tax through the PAYE system. The tax office will therefore send the pension provider a tax code and send you a PAYE *Coding Notice* so you can check the code is correct. However, the onus is on you as a taxpayer to tell the Inland Revenue if you have income or gains on which tax is due, even if you are not sent a tax return.

The tax year runs from 6 April to 5 April. Tax returns are sent out at this time of year to collect all the information needed to work out your tax bill for the tax year just ended. If you receive a tax return you are legally obliged to fill it in. You can either work out your own tax bill (see below) or ask your tax office to work it out.

Several key dates in the year are worth remembering:

- **31 July and 31 January**. These are the last dates to pay tax for those who pay some or all of their tax and NI in one or two instalments. This includes the self-employed, those who have freelance earnings outside their main job, those who have income from a job that is not taxed at source, those who owe tax (including higher-rate tax) on investments or from renting property, and those who have made taxable capital gains. 31 January is also the date by which you should send back your tax return if you want to avoid a fine

- **30 September**. Send back your tax return by this date if you want your tax office to work out your tax bill in time to meet the 31 January payment deadline or if you owe less than £1,000 in tax and want it collected under PAYE (see 'Paying tax', below)
- **5 October**. If you have not already been sent a tax return for the previous tax year, tell your tax office by this date that you had taxable income or capital gains in the previous tax year on which tax is due.

You are legally obliged to keep all records and documents – such as bank statements, interest statements, tax credits for share dividends, business invoices and receipts – that support the information given on your tax return or the information you would need to give should you be sent a tax return. The self-employed should keep records for just under six years after the end of the tax year to which they relate; others need to keep records for just under two years from the end of the tax year to which they relate. Failure to keep adequate records could incur a fine of up to £3,000.

Working out your tax bill

Endless complications in the tax rules can make it difficult to work out your own tax bill or check a tax bill worked out by your tax office. What follows is a very rough guide to working out what you owe. For particular points, the Inland Revenue publishes a range of leaflets and helpsheets. *Which? Way to Save Tax*, updated and published each year by Which? Books, is also useful, as is *TaxCalc 2000* – a PC CD-ROM program that can do the hard work for you – available from Which? Software.

Step 1 Add up all the money you received during the tax year plus any tax on that money that has already been deducted at source or paid under PAYE. You may need to include some income you were owed but did not receive, such as rental income.

Step 2 Deduct capital gains such as gains from selling investments, property and other assets. Deduct money that is tax-free. This might include a gift of money (though inheritance tax sometimes affects gifts and is explained in Inland Revenue leaflets), betting and lottery winnings and premium bond prizes, tax-free investment income and gains such as those on investments held in a tax-free ISA (Individual Savings Account), maintenance payments, some grants and some social security benefits. This list is not exhaustive. If in doubt, contact your tax office.

Step 3 Deduct outgoings or expenses that qualify for tax relief. For example, you can deduct business expenses from your business income. You can deduct payments towards a pension scheme from earned income and payments to charity under a payroll-giving scheme from the income out of which the payments are made. Do not deduct payments where basic-rate tax relief is deducted at source. This includes payments made by employees to personal pensions where the scheme provider reclaims the basic-rate tax relief and pays it into the scheme. It also includes gift aid donations to charity where the charity reclaims your basic-rate tax relief.

Step 4 Deduct your personal allowance and blind person's allowance (see below) if applicable. You can use these allowances in the way that is the most beneficial to you. For example, a basic-rate taxpayer would probably want to deduct them from employment or pension income which is taxed at 22 per cent, rather than savings income, which is taxed at 20 per cent.

In the 2000–1 tax year, the personal allowance is £4,385 and the blind person's allowance £1,400. People who reach 65 or over at some point in the tax year can claim a higher personal allowance of £5,790 for the whole of the tax year. This goes up to £6,050 if you reach 75 or over during the tax year.

However, in 2000–1 you lose £1 of the extra allowance for every £2 your income goes over £17,000. The £17,000 figure relates only to your taxable income plus what would be taxable if you were not able to claim allowances such as the personal allowance, the blind person's allowance and the married couple's allowance (see below). So you can exclude tax-free income and amounts on which you can claim tax relief (including gross payments to personal pensions).

Step 5 You are left with what is taxable. List it in the following order:

- non-savings income (excluding taxable redundancy and lump-sum compensation payments and life insurance pay-outs)
- savings income, i.e. interest
- dividend income, i.e. from shares and share-based investments
- taxable redundancy and lump-sum compensation payments

- taxable life insurance pay-outs
- taxable capital gains – for how capital gains tax works and what might be taxable, see Inland Revenue leaflets and helpsheets.

Then allocate it to the following tax bands and rates in the same order:

- £1,520, the starting-rate band – 10 per cent
- £1,501 to 28,400, the basic-rate band – 22 per cent on non-savings income, 20 per cent on savings income, 10 per cent on dividend income, 22 per cent on taxable redundancy payments and the taxable part of life insurance proceeds, and 20 per cent on capital gains
- £28,401 and over – 40 per cent on everything except dividends, which are taxed at 32.5 per cent.

Step 6 Deduct from your tax bill (excluding tax on capital gains and 10 per cent tax on dividend income) the tax saving available from the married couple's allowance, if applicable. Married couple's allowance has now been abolished for people who have not reached 65 by 5 April 2000 – so you can claim it only if you or your spouse was born before 6 April 1935. This date is fixed and does not change each tax year. Broadly speaking, the married couple's allowance can be used to reduce either the husband's or the wife's tax bill. Get the appropriate Inland Revenue leaflets or helpsheets for details of how this works.

The allowance is worth 10 per cent of £5,185, or £5,255 if either partner reaches 75 during the tax year. In 2000–1, it is reduced by £1 for every £2 the husband's income exceeds £17,000 (see step 4) but it is never reduced to below £2,000. If the husband's income does exceed £17,000, his higher personal allowance is reduced first until it is down to £4,385. If he is still over the £17,000 limit, the married couple's allowance is then reduced.

Step 7 Higher-rate taxpayers can deduct higher-rate tax relief for payments on which basic-rate tax relief has been given at source. For example, gross payments (i.e. including the basic-rate tax relief) made by an employee to a personal pension or FSAVC plan can be deducted from earnings that fall into the higher-rate band. Gift-aid donations to charity can be deducted from any income or gains that fall into the higher-rate tax band.

Paying tax

A lot of income tax is deducted at source, but at the end of a tax year you may still owe some tax. For example, you may owe higher-rate tax on investment income, or basic rate tax on taxable investment income paid without deduction of basic-rate tax, or tax on freelance earnings. You can ask for the tax to be collected through an adjustment to your PAYE code if it comes to less than £1,000. Otherwise, you normally have to pay it in two instalments by 31 January and 31 July. Capital gains tax has to be paid in one go, by 31 January for the tax year ending the previous April.

You may find at the end of a tax year that you have overpaid tax. In this case you can claim a refund – though you cannot reclaim the 10 per cent tax credit that accompanies dividends even if you are a non-taxpayer. You can also claim a refund during the tax year if the refund comes to more than £50.

This chapter has aimed to provide practical advice about the different options that are open to you if you retire early. Work, whether paid or unpaid, can bring benefits of all kinds, be they financial or social. Opportunities for learning abound. Many people today are leaving work earlier than their parents and grandparents did, and often living for longer. There *is* a lot of life left after retirement, and we hope we have given you some food for thought about making the most of that time.

Bibliography

Chapter 1

References

Department for Education and Employment. 2000. *Labour Market and Skill Trends 2000*

Department for Education and Employment. November 2000. *Labour Market Quarterly Report*

Department for Education and Employment. Spring 1997. *Labour Force Survey*

Equal Opportunities Commission. 1997. *Briefings on Men and Women in Britain: Management and the Professions*

Institute of Employment Research. 2000. *Projections of Occupations and Qualifications*

Reading material

Bridges, W. 1996. *Jobshift: How to Prosper in a Workplace Without Jobs*. Nicholas Brealey Publishing

Comfort, M. 1997. *Portfolio People: How to Create a Workstyle as Individual as You Are*

Connor, D. 1993. *Managing at the Speed of Change: How Resilient Managers Succeed and Prosper Where Others Fail*. Villard Books

Handy, C. 1994. *The Empty Raincoat: Making Sense of the Future*. Arrow Business Books

Chapter 2

References

Department for Education and Employment. 2000. *Education & Training Development Agenda, 2000–01*

Department for Education and Employment. 2000. *Second Chances, a National Guide to Adult Education and Training Opportunities*

Department for Education and Employment. 1999. *Learning to Succeed, Post-16 Education*. DfEE White Paper, Cm 4392

Department of Social Security. 2000. *Opportunity for All, One Year On: Making a Difference*. DSS Second Annual Report, Cm 4865

Chartered Institute of Personnel & Development. 2000. *Code of Conduct and Directory of Career and Outplacement Consultants 1999/2000*

Reading material

Chartered Institute of Personnel & Development. 1996. *IPD Guide on Redundancy*

Jay, L., Patchett, B. 1995. *Croner's Guide to Managing Redundancy*. Croner Publications

Chapter 3

References

Dearlove, D., Clutterbuck, D. 2000. *The Interim Manager: a New Career Model for the Experienced Manager*. FT Professional

Reading material

Bolles, R.N. 1997. *What Color is Your Parachute?* Ten Speed Press

Clark, R. 1993. *How to Change Your Career*. University of London Careers Advisory Service

Francis, D. 1994. *Managing Your Own Career*. HarperCollins

Jackson, T. 2000. *Career development*. Chartered Institute of Personnel & Development

Schein, E.H. 1990. *Career Anchors: Discovering Your Real Values*. Pfeiffer & Company

Ward, S. 1996. *Changing Direction*. ACE Books

Chapter 4

References

Cranfield School of Management. Autumn 2000. *Recruitment Confidence Index* (quarterly report)

PriceWaterhouseCoopers. 2000. *HR Benchmarking Report 2000*

Reed Business Information. 2000. *Job Seeker Strategies Among Recent Recruits*

Reading material

Bridges, W. 1997. *Creating You and Co: Be the Boss of Your Own Career*. Nicholas Brealey Publishing

Carlton Careers. 2000. *The Career Steps Guide*. Carlton Publishing

Eggert, M. 1994. *The Perfect Career*. Arrow Business Books

Hopson, B., Scally, M. 1997. *Build Your Own Rainbow*. Management Books 2000

Chapter 5

Reading Material

Eggert, M. 1992. *The Perfect CV*. Arrow Business Books

Eggert, M. 1992. *The Perfect Interview*. Arrow Business Books

Jackson, T. 1993. *How to Find the Perfect Job*. Piatkus Books

Jackson, T. 1996. *How to Write the Perfect CV*. Piatkus Books

Johnstone, J. 1996. *How to Pass that Interview*. How To Books

Leigh, A., Maynard, M. 1993. *The Perfect Presentation*. Arrow Business Books

Perkins, G. 1995. *Killer CVs and Hidden Approaches*. Pitman Publishing

Segall, A., Grierson, W. 1994. *Finding the Right Job*. BBC Books

Chapter 6

References

Barclays Bank. 2000. *Economic Review* (published quarterly)

Barclays Bank. 2000. *Small Business Bulletins, 1999 & 2000* (published quarterly)

Department for Education and Employment. November 1999. *Labour Market Quarterly Report*

Department for Education and Employment. August 2000. *Labour Market Quarterly Report*

Department of Trade & Industry. August 1999. *DTI Statistical Bulletin*

Reading Material

Barrow, C., Colzen, G. 1992. *Taking up a Franchise*. Kogan Page

Marriot, S., Jacobs, P. 1995. *Perfect Freelancing*, Arrow Business Books

Wallis, V. 1998. *The Which? Guide to Insurance*. Which? Books

The Which? Guide to Starting Your Own Business. 1999. Which? Books
Which? Way to Save Tax 2000–1 (Updated each year.) Which? Books

Chapter 7

References
City & Guilds. 2000. *Time to Learn.* City & Guilds of London Institute
Thorne, C. 2000. *Experience Necessary, the Business Case for Wisdom.* Industrial Society

Reading Material
Lowe, J. 1999. *The Which? Guide to Pensions.* Which? Books
TaxCalc 2000. 2000. Which? Ltd
Vass, J. (ed) 2000. *The Which Guide to an Active Retirement.* Which? Books

Booklets and leaflets to send off for, by source

British Venture Capital Association*
A Guide to Venture Capital

Benefits Agencies and post offices
Self-employed? A Guide to your National Insurance Contributions and Social Security Benefits (Benefits Agency leaflet FB30)

Contributions Agencies
Employed or Self-employed? A Guide for Tax and National Insurance (Contributions Agency Business Series IR56/N139)
National Insurance Contributions for Self-employed People, Class 2 and Class 4 (CA 03)
Starting Your Own Business (CWL1), issued jointly with HM Customs and Excise, and Inland Revenue

DTI publications* for small firms
Better Payment Practice (URN 98/965)
Employing Staff: a Guide to Regulatory Requirements (URN 00/736)
Financing Your Business (URN 98/805)
A Guide to Help for Small Firms (URN 99/1112)
An Introduction to Franchising: Buying a Franchise (URN 98/940)

An Introduction to Franchising: Franchising your Business (URN 98/941)
Setting Up in Business: a Guide to Regulatory Requirements (URN 97/524)
Small Firms Loan Guarantee Scheme (URN 94/1189)
Tendering for Government Contracts (URN 98/1055)

State benefits and help

Are You Entitled to Help with Health Costs?	HC11	Benefits Agencies, post offices
Back to Work Benefits	WWB11	Jobcentes, Benefits Agencies, post offices
Be Better Off Working	JSAL10	Jobcentres, Benefits Agencies
Help with the Council Tax	CTB1	Benefits Agencies, local councils
Homeowners – Help with Housing Costs	IS8	Benefits Agencies
Income Tax and the Unemployed	IR41	Jobcentres, Inland Revenue Offices
Jobseeker's Allowance, Helping you Back to Work	JSAL5	Jobcentres
Jobseeker's Allowance, the Rules on Part-time Education and Training	JSALS4	Jobcentres
Just the Job	JTJ1	Jobcentres
Social Security Benefit Rates	NI 196	Jobcentres, Benefits Agencies
Work for Yourself	WFYL1	Jobcentres

Addresses and web sites

Addresses

ACAS Publications
Tel: (01455) 852225

Age Concern Cymru
4th Floor
1 Cathedral Road
Cardiff CF11 9SD
Tel: (02920) 371566
Fax: (02920) 399562
Email: enquiries@accymru.org.uk
Web site: www.accymru.org.uk

Age Concern England
Astral House
1268 London Road
London SW16 4ER
Tel: 020-8765 7200
Fax: 020-8765 7211
Email: infodep@ace.org.uk
Web site: www.ace.org.uk

Age Concern Northern Ireland
3 Lower Crescent
Belfast BT7 1NR
Tel: (028) 9024 5729
Fax: (028) 9023 4597

Age Concern Scotland
113 Rose Street
Edinburgh EH2 3DT
Tel: 0131-220 3345
Fax: 0131-220 2779
Email:
enquiries@acsinfo3.freeserve.co.uk

Association of British Insurers
51 Gresham Street
London EC2V 7HQ
Tel: 020-7600 3333
Fax: 020-7696 8996
Email: info@abi.org.uk
Web site: www.abi.org.uk

Association of Investment Trust Companies
Durrant House
8–13 Chiswell Street
London EC1Y 4YY
Tel: 020-7431 5222
Fax: 020-7282 5556
Web site: www.aitc.co.uk

Association of Temporary and Interim Executive Services
see *Recruitment and Employment Confederation*

Benefits Enquiry Line
(0800) 882200

British Association for Counselling and Psychotherapy
1 Regent Place
Rugby CV21 2PJ
Tel: (01788) 550899
Fax: (01788) 562189
Email: bac@bac.co.uk
Web site: www.counselling.co.uk

British Chambers of Commerce
Manning House
22 Carlisle Place
London SW1P 1JA
Tel: 020-7565 2000
Fax: 020-7565 2049
Web site: www.britishchambers.org.uk

**British Executive Services Overseas
(BESO)**
164 Vauxhall Bridge Road
London SW1V 2RB
Tel: 020-7630 0644
Fax: 020-7630 0624
Web site: www.beso.org

British Franchise Association (BFA)
Thames View
Newtown Road
Henley-on-Thames RG9 1HG
Tel: (01491) 578049
Fax: (01491) 573517
Email: mailroom@british-
franchise.org.uk
Web site: www.british-
franchise.org.uk

**British Trust for Conservation
Volunteers (BTCV)**
36 St Mary's Street
Wallingford OX10 0EU
Tel: (01491) 839766
Fax: (01491) 839646
Email: natural-break@btcv.org.uk
Web site: www.btcv.org

**British Venture Capital Association
(BVCA)**
Essex House
12–13 Essex Street
London WC2R 3AA
Tel: 020-7240 3846
Fax: 020-7240 3849
Email: bvca@bvca.co.uk
Web site: www.bvca.co.uk

BTCV Scotland
Balallan House
24 Allan Park
Stirling FK8 2QG
Tel: (01786) 479697
Fax: (01786) 465359
Email: scotland@btcv.org.uk
Web site: www.btcv.org

BTG plc
10 Fleet Place
Limeburner Lane
London EC4M 7SB
Tel: 020-7575 0000
Fax: 020-7575 0010
Email: info@btgplc.com
Web site: www.btgplc.com

Business in the Community
137 Shepherdess Walk
London N1 7RQ
Tel: (0870) 6002482
Web site: www.bitc.org.uk

Business Connect (Wales)
Tel: (0845) 7969798

Business Information Source
20 Bridge Street
Inverness IV1 1QR
Tel: (01463) 715400
Email: bis@hient.co.uk
Web site: www.bis.uk.com

Business Link
Signpost number: (0845) 7567765
Web site:
www.businessadviceonline.org

**Charity and Fundraising
Appointments**
Longcroft House
Victoria Avenue
Bishopsgate
London EC2M 4NS
Tel: 020-7623 9292
Fax: 020-7623 9494
Email: enquiries@charity-
executives.co.uk
Web site: www.charity-
executives.co.uk

Charity People
38 Bedford Place
London WC1B 5JH
Tel: 020-7636 3900
Fax: 020-7636 3331
Email:
registrations@charitypeople.co.uk
Web site: www.charitypeople.co.uk

Charity Recruitment
40 Rosebery Avenue
London EC1R 4RX
Tel: 020-7833 0770
Fax: 020-7833 0188
Email: enquiries@charityrecruit.com
Web site: www.charec.com

**Chartered Institute of Personnel &
Development (CIPD)**
CIPD House
35 Camp Road
London SW19 4UX
Tel: 020-8971 9000
Fax: 020-8263 3333
Email: cipd@cipd.co.uk
Web site: www.cipd.co.uk

City & Guilds of London Institute
1 Giltspur Street
London EC1A 9DD
Tel: 020-7294 2468
Fax: 020-7294 2400
Email: enquiry@city-and-guilds.co.uk
Web site: www.city-and-guilds.co.uk

**Commission for Racial Equality
(CRE)**
Elliot House
10–12 Allington Street
London SW1E 5EH
Tel: 020-7828 7022
Fax: 020-7630 7605
Web site: www.cre.gov.uk

Community Service Volunteers (CSV)
237 Pentonville Road
London N1 9NJ
Tel: 020-7278 6601
Fax: 020-7833 0149
Email: information@csv.org.uk
Web sites: (general) www.csv.org.uk
(RSVP) www.rsvpuk.freeserve.co.uk

**Companies House (England and
Wales)**
Crown Way
Cardiff CF14 3UZ
Tel: (02920) 380801
Fax: (02920) 380900
Web site:
www.companieshouse.gov.uk

Companies House (Scotland)
37 Castle Terrace
Edinburgh EH1 2EB
Tel: 0131-535 5800
Fax: 0131-535 5820
Web site:
www.companieshouse.gov.uk

**Companies Registry (Northern
Ireland)**
IDB House
64 Chichester Street
Belfast BT1 4JX
Tel: (028) 9023 4488
Fax: (028) 9054 4888
Web site: www.detini.gov.uk

**Conservation Volunteers Northern
Ireland (CVNI)**
Beech House
159 Ravenhill Road
Belfast BT6 0BP
Tel: (028) 9064 5169
Fax: (028) 9064 4409
Information line: (0845) 6030472
Email: CVNI@btcv.org.uk
Web site: www.btcv.org/cv1.html

Corps of Commissionaires
Market House
85 Cowcross Street
London EC1M 6PF
Tel: 020-7490 1125
Fax: 020-7566 0650
Email: information@the-corps.co.uk
Web site: www.the-corps.co.uk

**Council for the Protection of Rural
England (CPRE)**
25 Buckingham Palace Road
London SW1W 0PP
Tel: 020-7976 6433
Fax: 020-7976 6373
Email: info@cpre.org.uk
Web site: www.cpre.org.uk

Data Protection Commissioner
Wycliffe House
Water Lane
Wilmslow SK9 5AF
Tel: (01625) 545740

Department of Enterprise, Trade and Investment
Companies Registry
IDB House
64 Chichester Street
Belfast BT1 4JX
Tel: (028) 9023 4488
Fax: (028) 9054 4888

Department for Education and Employment (DfEE)
Sanctuary Buildings
Great Smith Street
London SW1P 3BT
Tel: (0870) 000 2288
Fax: (01928) 794248
Email: info@dfee.gov.uk
Web sites: (general)
www.dfee.gov.uk
(Code of Practice on age diversity)
www.dfee.gov.uk/agediversity
(Learning Partnerships)
www.lifelonglearning.co.uk/llp

Department of Education Northern Ireland
Rathgael House
Balloo Road
Bangor
County Down BT19 7PR
Tel: (028) 9127 9279
Fax: (028) 9127 9100
Web site:
www.irlgov.ie/educ/default.htm

Department of the Environment, Transport and the Regions (DETR)
Eland House
Bressenden Place
London SW1E 5DU
Tel: 020-7944 3000
Web site: www.detr.gov.uk

Department of Social Security (DSS)
(For general enquiries contact your local office)
Public Enquiry Office
Tel: 020-7712 2171
Fax: 020-7712 2386
Web site: www.dss.gov.uk
New Deal
Information line (24-hour):
(0845) 6062626
Web site: www.newdeal.gov.uk

Department of Trade and Industry (DTI)
Enterprise Zone web site:
www.enterprisezone.org.uk

DETR Free Literature
P.O. Box 236
Wetherby LS23 7NB
Tel: (0870) 1226236

DETR Traffic Area Office
Scotland: 0131-529 8500
North-east and North-west
England: (0113) 283 3533
West Midlands: 0121-608 1000
West Country: (0117) 975 5000
South-east and London:
(01323) 451400

DIAL UK
St Catherine's
Tickhill Road
Doncaster DN4 8QN
Tel: (01302) 310123
Fax: (01302) 310404
Email: dialuk@aol.com
Web site:
http://members.aol.com/dialuk

Disability Alliance
Universal House
88–94 Wentworth Street
London E1 7SA
Tel: 020-7247 8776
Fax: 020-7247 8765
Email: office.da@dial.pipex.com
Web site: www.disabilityalliance.org

Disability Information Trust
Mary Marlborough Centre
Nuffield Orthopaedic Centre
Headington
Oxford OX3 7LD
Tel: (01865) 741155
Fax: (01865) 227596
Email: ditrust@btconnect.com
Web site: http://home.btconnect.
com/ditrust/home.htm

Disabled Living Foundation
380–384 Harrow Road
London W9 2HU
Tel: 020-7289 6111
Fax: 020-7266 2922
Helpline: (0845) 1309177
Email: info@dlf.org.uk
Web site: www.dlf.org.uk

DTI Publications Orderline
Admail 528
London SW1W 8YT
Tel: (0870) 1502500
Fax: (0870) 1502333
Web site: www.dti.gov.uk/pip

Employee Ownership Scotland (EOS)
Robert Owen House
87 Bath Street
Glasgow G2 2EE
Tel/Fax: 0141-304 5465
Email: eos@sol.co.uk
Web site: www.eos-online.co.uk

Employers Forum on Age (EFA)
Astral House
1268 London Road
London SW16 4ER
Tel: 020-8765 7597
Fax: 020-8765 7293
Web site: www.efa.org.uk

Employment Agency Standards Office
Department of Trade and Industry
Room UG65
1 Victoria Street
London SW1H 0ET
Helpline: (0645) 555105
Fax: 020-7215 2636
Email: eas@dti.gsi.gov.uk
Web site: www.dti.gov.uk/er

Environment and Energy Helpline
Tel: (0800) 585794

Equal Opportunities Commission
Arndale House
Arndale Centre
Manchester M4 3EQ
Tel: 0161-833 9244
Fax: 0161-838 8312
Email: info@eoc.org.uk
Web site: www.eoc.org.uk

Execucare
34 Ebury Street
London SW1W 0LU
Tel: 020-7761 0700
Fax: 020-7761 0707
Email: info@execucare.com
Web site: www.execucare.com

Federation of Small Businesses
Whittle Way
Blackpool Business Park
Blackpool FY4 2FE
Tel: (01253) 336000
Fax: (01253) 348046
Email: HO@fsb.org.uk
Web site: www.fsb.org.uk

Financial Services Authority (FSA)
25 The Colonnade
Canary Wharf
London E14 5HS
Tel: 020-7676 1000
Fax: 020-7676 1099
Web site: www.fsa.gov.uk

FSA Central Register
Enquiry line: (0845) 6061234
Web site:
www.thecentralregister.co.uk

FT Knowledge
16th Floor
Portland Tower
Portland Street
Manchester M1 3LD
Tel: 0161-245 3300
Fax: 0161-245 3301
Web site: www.ftknowledge.com

Health Development Agency
Trevelyan House
30 Great Peter Street
London SW1P 2HW
Tel: 020-7222 5300
Fax: 020-7413 8900
Email: hda.enquirydesk@hda-online.org.uk
Web site: www.hda-online.org.uk

Health and Safety Executive
Information line: (0541) 545500

Help the Aged
16–18 St James's Walk
London EC1R 0BE
Tel: 020-7253 0253
Fax: 020-7251 0747
Email: info@helptheaged.org.uk
Web site: www.helptheaged.org.uk
Care Fees Advisory Service
Tel: (0500) 767476

Highlands & Islands Enterprise (HIE)
Bridge House
20 Bridge Street
Inverness IV1 1QR
Tel: (01463) 234171
Fax: (01463) 244469
Email: hie.general@hient.co.uk
Web site: www.hie.co.uk

Independent Schools Information Service (ISIS)
Grosvenor Gardens House
35–37 Grosvenor Gardens
London SW1W 0BS
Tel: 020-7798 1500
Fax: 020-7798 1501
Email: national@isis.org.uk
Web site: www.isis.org.uk

Industrial Common Ownership Finance Ltd (ICOF)
227C City Road
London EC1V 1JT
Tel: 020-7251 6181
Fax: 020-7336 7407
Email: icof@icof.co.uk
Web site: www.icof.co.uk

Industrial Common Ownership Movement (ICOM)
74 Kirkgate
Leeds LS2 7DJ
Tel: (0113) 246 1737
Fax: (0113) 244 0002
Email: icom@icom.org.uk

Instant Muscle
Springside House
84 North End Road
London W14 9ES
Tel: 020-7603 2604
Fax: 020-7603 7346
Email: head-office@instant-muscle.org.uk

Institute of Careers Guidance
27A Lower High Street
Stourbridge DY8 1TA
Tel: (01384) 376464
Fax: (01384) 440830
Web site: www.icg-uk.org

Institute of Directors
116 Pall Mall
London SW1Y 5ED
Tel: 020-7839 1233
Fax: 020-7930 1949
Web site: www.iod.co.uk

Institute of Patentees and Inventors
Suite 505A
Triumph House
189 Regent Street
London W1B 4JY
Tel: 020-7434 1818
Fax: 020-7434 1727
Email: enquiries@invent.org.uk
Web site: www.invent.org.uk

Learn Direct
(0800) 100900

Local Enterprise Development Unit (LEDU)
LEDU House
Upper Galwally
Belfast BT8 6TB
Tel: (028) 9049 1031
Freephone: (0800) 0925529
Fax: (028) 9069 1432
Email: ledu@ledu-ni.gov
Web site: www.ledu-ni.gov

National Assembly for Wales Education Department
Further and Higher Education Division
4th Floor
Cathays Park
Cardiff CF10 3NQ
Tel: (02920) 826116
Fax: (02920) 825823
Web site: www.wales.gov.uk

National Association for Educational Guidance for Adults (NAEGA)
P.O. Box 1106
Kettering NN16 0YX
Enquiry line: (01536) 516244
Fax: (01536) 414274
Email: naega.admin@virgin.net
Web site: www.naega.org.uk

National Association of Pension Funds
NIOC House
4 Victoria Street
London SW1H 0NX
Tel: 020-7808 1300
Fax: 020-7222 7585
Web site: www.napf.co.uk

National Association of Volunteer Bureaux (NAVB)
New Oxford House
16 Waterloo Street
Birmingham B2 5UG
Tel: 0121-633 4555
Fax: 0121-633 4043
Email: info@navb.org.uk
Web site: www.navb.org.uk

National Business Angels Network (NBAN)
40–42 Cannon Street
London EC4N 6JJ
Tel: 020-7329 2929
Information line: 020-7329 4141
Fax: 020-7329 2626
Email: info@bestmatch.co.uk
Web site: www.bestmatch.co.uk

National Centre for Voluntary Organisations (NCVO)
Regents Wharf
8 All Saints Street
London N1 9RL
Tel: 020-7713 6161
Freephone: (0800) 2798798
Fax: 020-7713 6300
Email: ncvo@ncvo-vol.org.uk
Web site: www.ncvo-vol.org.uk

National Centre for Volunteering
8 All Saints Street
London N1 9RL
Tel: 020-7520 8900
Fax: 020-7520 8910
Email: volunteering@thecentre.org.uk
Web site: www.volunteering.org.uk

National Debtline
0121-359 8501

National Endowment for Science, Technology and the Arts (NESTA)
Fishmonger's Chambers
110 Upper Thames Street
London EC4R 3TW
Tel: 020-7645 9500
Fax: 020-7645 9501
Email: nesta@nesta.org.uk
Web site: www.nesta.org.uk

National Extension College (NEC)
The Michael Young Centre
Purbeck Road
Cambridge CB2 2HN
Tel: (01223) 450200
Fax: (01223) 450505
Email: info@nec.ac.uk
Web site: www.nec.ac.uk

National Federation of Enterprise Agencies
Trinity Gardens
9–11 Bromham Road
Bedford MK40 2UQ
Tel/Fax: (01234) 354055
Email: alan.bretherton@nfea.com
Web site: www.nfea.com

National Federation of Women's Institutes
104 New Kings Road
London SW6 4LY
Tel: 020-7371 9300
Fax: 020-7736 3652
Email: hq@nfwi.org.uk
Web site: www.womens-institute.org.uk

National Institute for Adult
Continuing Education (NIACE)
21 De Montfort Street
Leicester LE1 7GE
Tel: (0116) 255 1451
Fax: (0116) 285 4514
Email: enquiries@niace.org.uk
Web site: www.niace.org.uk

Employers Enquiry Line
(0345) 143143

New Ways to Work
22 Northumberland Avenue
London WC2N 5AP
Tel: 020-7930 0093
Fax: 020-7930 3366
Email: info@new-ways.co.uk
Web site: www.new-ways.co.uk

Northern Ireland Volunteer
Development Agency
70–74 Ann Street
Belfast BT1 4EH
Tel: (028) 9023 6100
Fax: (028) 9023 7570
Email: info@volunteering-ni.org
Web site: www.volunteering-ni.org

Occupational Pensions Regulatory
Authority (OPRA)
Invicta House
Trafalgar Place
Brighton BN1 4DW
Tel: (01273) 627600
Fax: (01273) 627688
Email: helpdesk@opra.gov.uk
Web site: www.opra.gov.uk

Office of Fair Trading (Consumer
Credit Licensing Bureau)
Craven House
40 Uxbridge Road
Ealing
London W5 2BS
Tel: 020-7211 8608
Fax: 020-7211 8605
Email: enquiries@oft.gov.uk
Web site: www.oft.gov.uk

Open College of Arts
Unit 1B
Redbrook Business Park
Wilthorpe Road
Barnsley S75 1JN
Tel: (01226) 730495
Freephone: (0800) 7312116
Fax: (01226) 730838
Email: open.arts@ukonline.co.uk
Web site: www.oca-uk.com

Open and Distance Learning Quality
Council
16 Park Crescent
London W1B 1AH
Tel: 020-7612 7090
Fax: 020-7612 7092
Email: odlqc@dial.pipex.com
Web site: www.odlqc.org.uk

Open University (OU)
Walton Hall
Milton Keynes MK7 6AA
Tel: (01908) 274066
Brochure request line:
(01908) 653231
Fax: (01908) 653744
Email: enquiries@open.ac.uk
Web site: www.open.ac.uk

OPRA Pension Schemes Registry
Occupational Pensions Regulatory
Authority
P.O. Box 1NN
Newcastle upon Tyne NE99 1NN
Tel: 0191-225 6393
Fax: 0191-225 6390 (A–JE by scheme
name), 0191-225 6391 (JF–Z by
scheme name)
Email: helpdesk@opra.gov.uk
Web site: www.opra.gov.uk

Over-50s Employment Bureau
90 Central Street
London EC1V 8AQ
Tel: 020-7608 1395
Fax: 020-7251 8738
Email:
over50semploymentbureau@ukgate
way.net

Patent Office
Concept House
Cardiff Road
Newport NP10 8QQ
Tel: (01633) 814000
Central Enquiry Unit:
(0845) 9500505
Fax: (01633) 814444
Email: enquiries@patent.gov.uk
Web site: www.patent.gov.uk

Pensions Advisory Service (OPAS)
11 Belgrave Road
London SW1V 1RB
Tel: 020-7233 8080
Fax: 020-7233 8016
Email: opas@iclwebkit.co.uk
Web site: www.opas.org.uk

Pre-retirement Association
9 Chesham Road
Guildford GU1 3LS
Tel: (01483) 301170
Fax: (01483) 300981
Email: info@pra.uk.com
Web site: www.pra.uk.com

The Prince's Trust
18 Park Square East
London NW1 4LH
Tel: 020-7543 1234
Fax: 020-7543 1200
Web site: www.princes-trust.co.uk

Project North East
Hawthorn House
Forth Banks
Newcastle upon Tyne NE1 3SG
Tel: 0191-261 7856
Fax: 0191-261 1910
Web sites: (general) www.pne.org
(Cobweb) www.cobwebinfo.com

*Recruitment and Employment
Confederation*
36–38 Mortimer Street
London W1N 7RB
Tel: 020-7462 3260
Fax: 020-7255 2878
Email: info@rec.uk.com
Web site: www.rec.uk.com

Redundancy Payments Helpline
(0500) 848489

*Registry of Friendly Societies
(England and Wales)*
see *Financial Services Authority*

*Registry of Friendly Societies
(Scotland)*
58 Frederick Street
Edinburgh EH2 1NB
Tel: 0131-226 3224
Fax: 0131-200 1300

Relate (National Headquarters)
Herbert Gray College
Little Church Street
Rugby CV21 3AP
Tel: (01788) 573241
Web site: www.relate.org.uk

*Retirement Pension Forecasting and
Advice (RPFA) Unit*
Pensions & Overseas Benefits
Directorate
Newcastle upon Tyne NE98 1BA
Tel: 0191-218 7585
Fax: 0191-218 7006
Web site:
www.dss.gov.uk/lifeevent/benefits/
retirement_pension_forecast.htm

*Royal Association for Disability and
Rehabilitation (RADAR)*
12 City Forum
250 City Road
London EC1V 8AF
Tel: 020-7250 3222
Fax: 020-7250 0212
Email: radar@radar.org.uk
Web site: www.radar.org.uk

Saga
Saga Building
Middleburg Square
Folkestone
Kent CT20 1AZ
Tel: (Household insurance)
(0800) 414525, (Private medical
insurance) (0800) 857857
Web site: www.saga.co.uk

Scottish Business in the Community
P.O. Box 408
Bankhead Avenue
Edinburgh EH11 4HE
Tel: 0131-442 2020
Fax: 0131-442 3555
Email: info@sbcscot.com
Web site: www.sbcscot.com

Scottish Environment Protection Agency (SEPA)
Erskine Court
The Castle Business Park
Stirling SK9 4TR
Tel: (01786) 457700
Fax: (01786) 446885
Email: info@sepa.org.uk
Web site: www.sepa.org.uk

Scottish Executive Enterprise and Lifelong Learning Department
The Scottish Executive
6th Floor
Meridian Court
Cadogan Street
Glasgow G2 6AT
Tel: 0141-248 4774
Fax: 0141-242 5665
Email: ceu@scotland.gov.uk
Web site: www.scotland.gov.uk/who/dept_enterprise.asp

Shell LiveWIRE
Hawthorn House
Forth Banks
Newcastle upon Tyne NE1 3SG
Tel: 0191-261 5584
Enquiry line: (0845) 7573252
Fax: 0191-261 1910
Email: livewire@projectne.co.uk
Web site: www.shell-livewire.org

Small Business Gateway
Tel: (0845) 6078787 (if outside Scotland), (0845) 6096611 (if within Scotland)
Web site: www.sbgateway.com

Small Business Service (SBS)
1 Victoria Street
London SW1H 0ET
and
St Mary's House
c/o Moorfoot
Sheffield S1 4PQ
Tel: (0114) 259 7788
Fax: (0114) 259 7330
Email: gatewayenquiries@sbs.gsi.gov.uk
Web site: www.businessadviceonline.org

Social Economy Agency
2 Bay Road
Derry BT48 7SH
Tel: (028) 7137 1733
Fax: (028) 7137 0114
Email: info@socialeconomyagency.org
Web site: www.socialeconomyagency.org

Society of Pension Consultants
St Bartholomew House
92 Fleet Street
London EC4Y 1DG
Tel: 020-7353 1688
Fax: 020-7353 9296
Email: john.mortimer@spc.uk.com
Web site: www.spc.uk.com

Sport England
16 Upper Woburn Place
London WC1H 0QP
Tel: 020-7273 1500
Fax: 020-7383 5740
Web site: www.english.sports.gov.uk

Stationery Office
Tel: (0870) 600 5522

Summer Academy
Keynes College
The University
Canterbury CT2 7NP
Tel: (01227) 470402/823473
Fax: (01227) 784338
Email: summeracademy@ukc.ac.uk
Web site: www.ukc.ac.uk/sa/index.html

Third Age Challenge Ltd
39 Hawkins Street
Redbourne
Swindon SN2 2AQ
Tel: (01793) 533370
Fax: (01793) 533390
Email: office@thirdagers.net
Web site: www.thirdagers.net

Third Age Employment Network (TAEN)
York House
207–221 Pentonville Road
London N1 9UZ
Tel: 020-7843 1590
Fax: 020-7843 1599
Email: taen@helptheaged.org.uk
Web site: www.taen.org.uk

Third Age Network
Friary Mews
28 Commercial Road
Guildford GU1 4SX
Tel: (01483) 440582

Third Age Trust
University of Third Age (U3A)
26 Harrison Street
London WC1H 8JG
Tel: 020-7837 8838
Fax: 020-7837 8845
Email: national.office@u3a.org.uk
Web site: http://3a.org.uk

3i plc
91 Waterloo Road
London SE1 8XP
Tel: 020-7928 3131
Fax: 020-7928 0058
Web site: www.3i.com

UK Business Incubation (UKBI)
Aston Science Park
Love Lane
Birmingham B7 4BJ
Tel: 0121-250 3538
Fax: 0121-250 3542
Email: info@ukbi.co.uk
Web site: www.ukbi.co.uk

UK Science Park Association (UKSPA)
Aston Science Park
Love Lane
Birmingham B7 4BJ
Tel: 0121-359 0981
Fax: 0121-333 5852
Email: info@ukspa.org.uk
Web site: www.ukspa.org.uk

University for Industry (UfI)
Dearing House
1 Young Street
Sheffield S1 4UP
Tel: (0114) 291 5000
Fax: (0114) 291 5492
Web site: www.ufiltd.co.uk

Voluntary Service Overseas (VSO)
317 Putney Bridge Road
London SW15 2PN
Tel: 020-8780 2266
Fax: 020-8780 7300
Email: enquiry@vso.org.uk
Web site: www.vso.org.uk

Volunteer Development Scotland
72 Murray Place
Stirling FK8 2BX
Tel: (01786) 479593
Fax: (01786) 449285
Email: vds@vds.org.uk
Web site: www.vds.org.uk

Wales Conservation Centre
Forest Farm Road
Whitchurch
Cardiff CF14 7JJ
Tel: (02920) 520990
Fax: (02920) 522181
Email: wales@btcv.org.uk
Web site: www.btcv.org

Wales Council for Voluntary Action (WCVA)
Baltic House
Mount Stuart Square
Cardiff Bay
Cardiff CF10 5FH
Tel: (02920) 431700
Fax: (02920) 431701
Email: enquiries@wcva.org.uk
Web site: www.wcva.org.uk

Welsh Development Agency
Principality House
The Friary
Cardiff CF10 3FE
Tel: (0845) 7775577
Fax: (02920) 828912
Email: enquiries@wda.co.uk
Web site: www.wda.co.uk

Workers Educational Association
(WEA)
17 Victoria Park Square
London E2 9PB
Tel: 020-8983 1515
Fax: 020-8983 4840
Email: info@wea.org.uk
Web site: www.wea.org.uk

Recruitment web sites

Recruitment web sites are subject to rapid change and many will appear or disappear too quickly for a printed book to keep pace. Despite this problem, however, because searching for jobs on the Internet is such a growing area, a number of those available at the time of writing are listed below.

Some of the sites simply post advertisements for jobs. With others, you can also post your career details and job criteria so that automatic searches can identify potential matches. Some offer extra services such as careers advice, questionnaires and so on. The majority of sites present a wide variety of jobs, although some specialise in certain industries, such as, for example, IT/new media.

Note that the sites given here are only suggestions, not recommended. By using a search engine – such as Altavista (*www.altavista.com*), Lycos (*www.lycos.co.uk*), Ask Jeeves (*www.ask.com*) or Yahoo (*www.yahoo.co.uk*) – you can do your own research for job sites, as well as identifying the web sites of any particular organisations you are interested in. *www.agencycentral.co.uk* can help you find job sites for the kind of work you are looking for.

Recruitment web sites and on-line agencies

www.appointments-plus.co.uk
www.best-people.co.uk
www.bigbluedog.com
www.businessfile-online.com
www.careermosaic-uk.co.uk
www.computerweekly.co.uk
www.dotjobs.co.uk
www.execnet.co.uk
www.fish4jobs.co.uk
www.futurestep.co.uk
www.gisajob.co.uk
www.jobhunter.co.uk
www.jobmall.co.uk

www.jobs.ac.uk
www.jobsearch-online.co.uk
www.jobserve.com
www.stepstone.co.uk
www.jobsite.co.uk
www.jobsunlimited.co.uk
www.jobworld.co.uk
www.monster.co.uk
www.netjobs.co.uk
www.peoplebank.com
www.reed.co.uk
www.topjobs.net
www.totaljobs.com

Index

The Which? Guide to Working from Home

Have you taken early retirement but would like to continue earning some money? Do you need to boost the family income but are tied to the home by young children or a disability? Are you sick of commuting and office life, or facing mid-life redundancy, but cannot afford to retire just yet?

The Which? Guide to Working from Home explores the practical, legal and financial aspects of working from home. From running a bed and breakfast or a children's adventure playground to skin piercing, hairdressing and complementary therapies, the range of possibilities is vast.

The guide covers everything you need to make a success of working from home: assessing what you can do and researching the market before you start; raising the money and keeping control of your finances; costing your work appropriately; taking on a franchise; dealing with suppliers effectively; wading through the red tape - the regulations and bylaws; getting involved with mail order; tax and how to cope with self-assessment; insurance cover and liabilities; and taking on staff as your business expands.

In addition, the book explores how to make the most of technologies such as the Internet and how to capitalise on both your home and your land.

Paperback   216 x 135mm   256 pages   £9.99

Available from bookshops, and by post from
Which?, Dept TAZM, Castlemead,
Gascoyne Way, Hertford X, SG14 1LH
or phone FREE on (0800) 252100
quoting Dept TAZM and your credit card details

The Which? Guide to Pensions

State pensions are a foundation for your retirement income but will not, on their own, provide enough to fund a comfortable old age. But do the savings you've made so far through company pension schemes or other arrangements put you on track for the retirement you want? *The Which? Guide to Pensions* shows you how to assess the value of your retirement savings and fill the gaps in your retirement planning. It covers, in simple language, all the important issues, such as:

- how much you should save
- what the state will provide
- getting the best from an employer's scheme
- what new stakeholder plans will offer
- choosing the best personal plans
- alternatives to formal pension plans, such as ISAs
- boosting your pension
- pension choices when you change jobs
- aspects relevant to those facing redundancy or divorce
- pension planning in a family context
- tracing old pensions and claiming your pensions once you retire
- how retirement savings and pensions are treated for tax.

Clear explanations, charts, an extensive glossary and numerous examples unravel the mysteries to put you firmly in control of your future.

Paperback   216 x 135mm   336 pages   £9.99

Available from bookshops, and by post from
Which?, Dept TAZM, Castlemead,
Gascoyne Way, Hertford X, SG14 1LH
or phone FREE on (0800) 252100
quoting Dept TAZM and your credit card details

The Which? Guide to Starting Your Own Business

'The comprehensive guide.' *Daily Mail*

The Which? Guide to Starting Your Own Business explains the best way to tackle each stage of building a business and how to avoid the pitfalls. It provides all the information you need to give your enterprise the best chance of success, including how to decide on the best product or service to offer; how to raise the necessary finance; whether to set up as a sole trader, partnership, limited company and so on, or buy an established business; how to deal with tax, including VAT and self-assessment, and accounts; the potential of advertising and selling on the Internet; and the impact of the euro.

This handbook also points you in the right direction for planning an effective marketing strategy, buying insurance, finding the right premises, employing staff, equipping an office, setting up a computer system, and selling abroad. Legislation, including the minimum wage, which might affect owners of small businesses, is also covered, along with details of some of the most popular small-business products.

Paperback   216 x 135mm   288 pages   £10.99

Available from bookshops, and by post from
Which?, Dept TAZM, Castlemead,
Gascoyne Way, Hertford X, SG14 1LH
or phone FREE on (0800) 252100
quoting Dept TAZM and your credit card details

The Which? Guide to Computers for Small Businesses

How do you use your computer to produce professional-looking documents, make VAT and income tax calculations, create promotions and advertising, connect with other computers to share information, keep track of sales and client records, and exploit the Internet's potential for increasing business? *The Which? Guide to Computers for Small Businesses* answers all these questions and many more in simple, non-technical language. The handbook also includes a hardware and software reference section, guidance for buying portable computers, and a glossary of technical and advertising terms.

Written by Richard Wentk, author of *The Which? Guide to Computers* and *The Which? Guide to the Internet*, this guide offers practical advice on choosing the best hardware and software for small businesses; finding training and support; getting free help before buying; and how to avoid common computer problems. Whether you run a small company or simply work at home, this guide will show you how to make the most of your computer system.

Paperback   216 x 135mm   352 pages   £10.99

Available from bookshops, and by post from
Which?, Dept TAZM, Castlemead,
Gascoyne Way, Hertford X, SG14 1LH
or phone FREE on (0800) 252100
quoting Dept TAZM and your credit card details